Liz Magic Laser
Public Relations / Öffentlichkeitsarbeit

Liz Magic Laser
Public Relations / Öffentlichkeitsarbeit

Westfälischer Kunstverein
Sternberg Press

This publication was supported as Catalog No. 129 by the Alfried Krupp von Bohlen und Halbach-Stiftung under its support prize Catalogs for Young Artists / Diese Publikation wurde als 129. Katalog von der Alfried Krupp von Bohlen und Halbach-Stiftung im Rahmen des Förderpreises Kataloge für junge Künstler gefördert.

Contents / Inhalt

[25, Monitor]

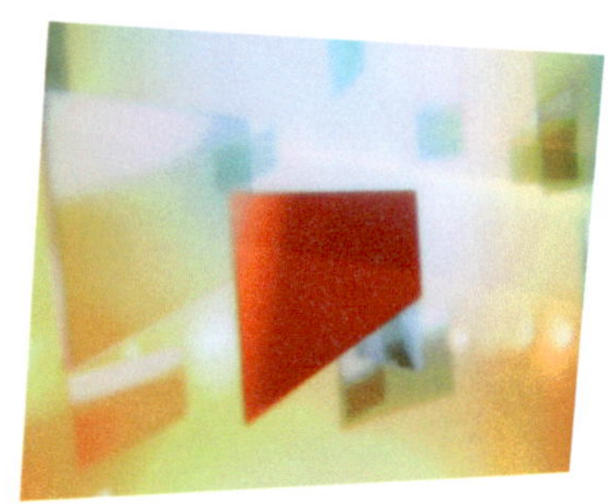

[51, Projection / Projektion]

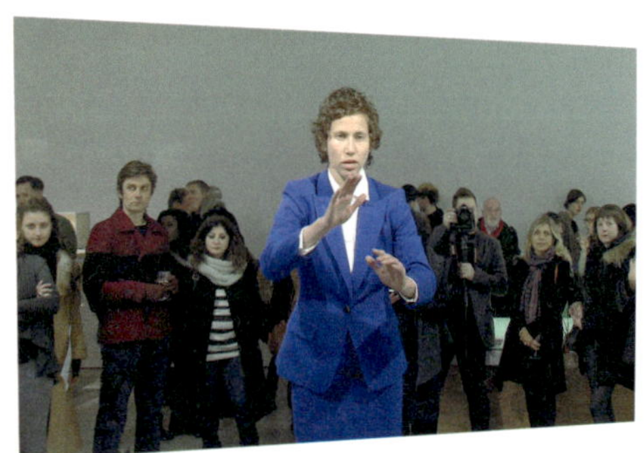

[95, Monitor]

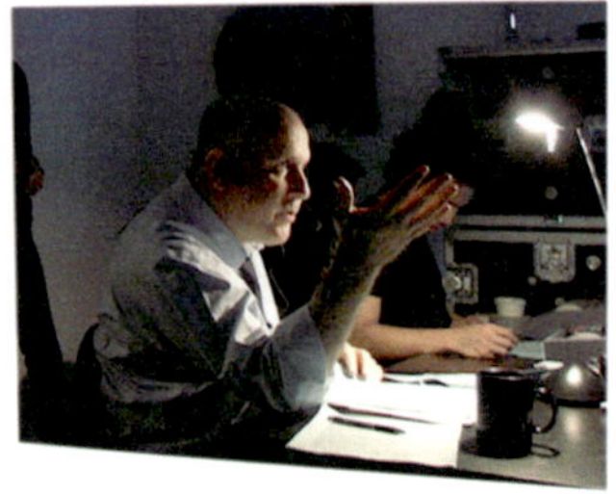

[47, Projection / Projektion]

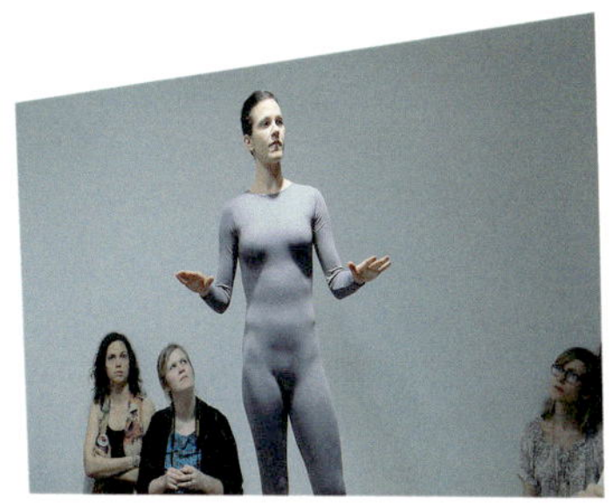

[77, Monitor] [84, Projection / Projektion]

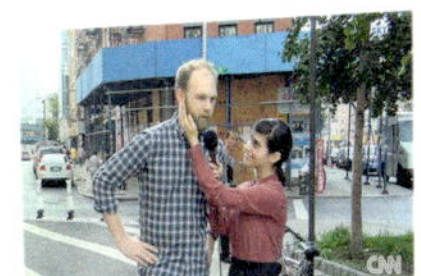 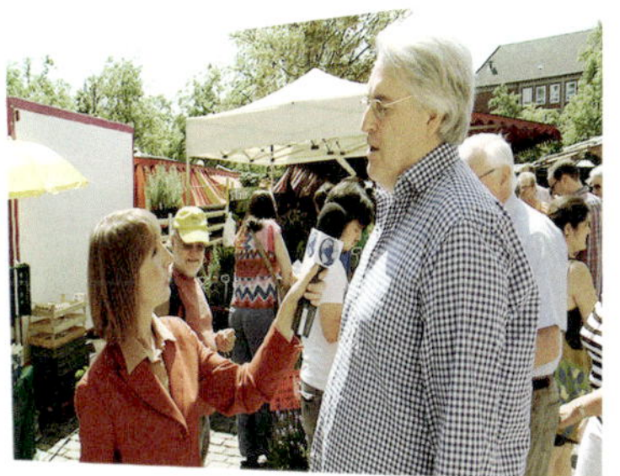

[5, Projection / Projektion]

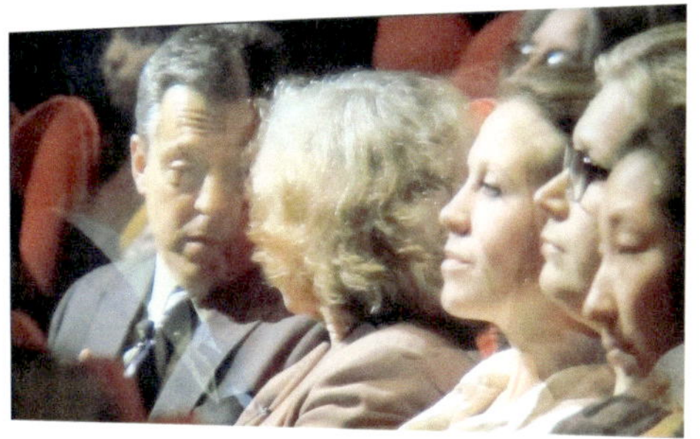

Works Illustrated / Abgebildete Arbeiten

I Feel Your Pain, 2011

    A Performa Commission / Im Auftrag von Performa, performed and filmed / Performance und Aufnahme:
    –Performa 11, SVA Silas Theatre, New York, USA, 13, 14 Nov 2011
    Performance and single-channel video / Performance und Video, 80 min
    With actors / Mit den SchauspielerInnen Lynn Berg, Audrey Crabtree, Ray Field, Annie Fox, Kathryn Grody, Rafael Jordan,
Liz Micek, Ryan Shams
    Produced by / Eine Produktion von Performa, Producer / Produzent: David Guinan
    Cinematographers / Kamera: Matthew Nauser, Collin Kornfeind, Alex Hadjiloukas (Polemic Media)
    Costume Stylist / Kostümdesign: Felicia Garcia-Rivera
    Still Photographer / Fotografie: Yola Monakhov
    Technical Crew / technische Crew: Will Chu, Brandon Polanco, Irwin Seow, Tristan Shepherd
    Production Assistants / Produktionsassistenz: Jamie Kelly, Lucia Hinojosa
    The script includes editorial contributions from / Das Skript enthält redaktionelle Beiträge von Scott Indrisek, Wendy Osserman,
Jess Wilcox, Tom Williams
    Co-presented by / in Kooperation mit der School of Visual Arts' Visual and Critical Studies and / und BFA Fine Arts Departments
    Supported by Performa Curators Circle member / Mit Unterstützung des Mitglieds des Performa Curators Circle Joanne Cassullo
(Dorothea Leonhardt Fund), Esther Kim Varet, Joseph Varet, Communities Foundation of Texas, The Andy Warhol Foundation for
the Visual Arts, National Endowment for the Arts, The Dedalus Foundation

The Digital Face, 2012

    Performed and filmed / Performance und Aufnahme:
    –Derek Eller Gallery, New York, USA, 23 Mar / März 2012
    –MoMA PS1, New York, USA, 1 Apr 2012
    –Calder Foundation Exhibition, New York, USA, 5 May / Mai 2012
    Performance and two-channel video / Performance und Zweikanalvideo, 10 min
    With dancers / Mit den TänzerInnen Alan Good, Cori Kresge
    Movement adapted from / Nach den Bewegungen von President George H.W. Bush, State of the Union Address, 31 Jan 1990,
and / und Barack Obama, State of the Union Address, 24 Jan 2012

In Camera, 2012

    Exhibition / Ausstellung Malmö Konsthall, Malmö, Sweden / Schweden, 4–28 Oct / Okt 2012
    Five-channel video / Fünfkanalvideo, 121 min, Malmö Konsthall
    Script adapted from / Adaption von Jean Paul Sartre, H u i s c l o s (No Exit / Geschlossene Gesellschaft; 1944), by / durch
Liz Magic Laser and / und Sofia Pontén
    With actors / Mit den SchauspielerInnen Anders E Larsson, Karin Hallén, Maria Lindh
    Produced by / Eine Produktion der Malmö Konsthall in collaboration with / in Zusammenarbeit mit dem SVT
    Assistant Director / Assistentin: Sofia Pontén
    Curator / Kurator: Jacob Fabricius
    Production Coordinator / Produktionskoordination: Mats Fastrup
    Technical Director at / Technischer Leiter beim SVT: Olof Tilly
    Broadcasting Producer / Sendeproduzent: Nader Hammoud
    Still Photographers / Fotografie: Kasper Akhøj, Amanda Nordgren, Sebastian Peña
    Production Assistants / Produktionsassistenz: Anna Johansson, Cindy Lee, Karin Rydberg
    Director of Photography at / Bildregisseur im Finn Juhls hus: Martin Top Jacobsen
    Director of Photography at / Bildregie auf dem Gustav Adolfs torg: Lars-Gunnar Bengtsson
    Special thanks to / Besonderer Dank gilt Finn Juhls hus, Ordrupgaard, Denmark / Dänemark
    Video features a painting by / Das Video zeigt ein Gemälde von Vilhelm Lundstrøm of / von Hanne Wilhelm Hansen

Stand Behind Me, 2013

    Performed and filmed / Performance und Aufnahme:
    –The Magic of the State, Lisson Gallery, London, UK, 26 Mar 2013
    –Experienz, Wiels, Brussels, Belgium / Brüssel, Belgien, 18, 19, 20 Apr 2013
    –Sofia Contemporary, National Palace of Culture / Nationaler Kulturpalast Sofia, Bulgaria / Bulgarien, 23, 24 Apr 2013
    Performance and two-channel video / Performance und Zweikanalvideo, 10 min
    With dancer / Mit der Tänzerin Ariel Freedman
    Costume Stylist / Kostümdesign: Felicia Garcia-Rivera

Public Relations / Öffentlichkeitsarbeit, 2013
Exhibition / Ausstellung Westfälischer Kunstverein, Münster, Germany / Deutschland, 13 July / Juli – 22 Sept 2013
Two-channel video installation / Zweikanalvideoinstallation, 17 min, Westfälischer Kunstverein
With actors / Mit den SchauspielerInnen Florian Kleine, Elisabeth Weydt
Script written by / Skript entwickelt von Liz Magic Laser and / und Sofia Pontén in collaboration with / in Zusammenarbeit
mit Kristina Scepanski, Jenni Henke, Elisabeth Weydt, Florian Kleine
Curated by / Kuratiert von Kristina Scepanski
Curatorial Assisting / Kuratorische Assistenz: Anna Sabrina Schmid
Set Design in collaboration with / Bühnendesign in Zusammenarbeit mit Christian Kiehl
Costume Design in collaboration with / Kostümdesign in Zusammenarbeit mit Nils von Berg
Painting by / Gemälde von Sanya Kantarovsky
Videography / Kamera: Jan Enste, Gunar Peters
Audio Engineering / Tontechnik: Jan Enste, Sven Stratmann
Production Assisting / Produktionsassistenz: Malte Rommel, Clara Napp
Installation photography / Fotodokumentation: Thorsten Arendt
Project Coordination / Projektkoordination: Anna Sabrina Schmid
Set building / Kulissenbau: Alfred Boguszynski, Johann Crne, Thomas Erdmann, Richard Schulte, Beate Sikora
Installation / Aufbau: Clara Napp, Inga Krüger, Tobias Bohn
Special thanks to the Extras / Besonderer Dank an die StatistInnen Cornelia Baumgart-Göder, Regina und Hermann Dörner,
Silvia Fassel, Ulrike Fink, Brigitte Groll, Jenni Henke, Richard Hoene, Albert Schnieders, Peter Schott, Carola Uehlken

Absolute Event, 2013
Exhibition / Ausstellung Paula Cooper Gallery (197, 10th Avenue), New York, USA, 16–30 Nov 2013
Performed and filmed / Performance und Aufnahme:
–Paula Cooper Gallery (197, 10th Avenue), New York, USA, 14, 16 Nov 2013
Performance and eight-channel video installation / Performance und Achtkanalvideoinstallation, 45 min, Paula Cooper Gallery
With actors and former congressional staffers / Mit den Schauspielern und ehemaligen Kongress-Mitarbeitern Daniel Abse,
Gary Lee Mahmoud
Script written by / Skript von Liz Magic Laser in collaboration with / in Zusammenarbeit mit Sofia Pontén, based on /
auf der Grundlage von Cyrano de Bergerac by / von Edmund Rostand
Script Advisor / Beratung Skripterstellung: Political Strategist / politischer Strategieberater Mustafa Tameez
Set Design in collaboration with / Bühnenbild in Zusammenarbeit mit Andrea Huelse
Costume Stylist / Kostümdesign: Felicia Garcia-Rivera
Technical Director / Technische Leitung: Irwin Seow
Director of Photography / Bildregie: Laura Cooper
Audio Engineer / Toningenieur: Tristan Shepherd
Research Assistant / Rechercheassistenz: Rachel Zaretsky
Production Managers / Produktionsleitung: Lucia Hinojosa and Brian Mcelroy
Special thanks / Besonderer Dank an: Paula Cooper, Anthony Allen, Jake Ewert, Kristoffer Haynes, Alexis Johnson,
Margaret Kross, Steven Probert, David Guinan, Sanya Kantarovsky, Ken Laser, Hanna Novak, Wendy Osserman, Romy Scheroder,
Esther Kim Varet, Joseph Varet, Plum TV and / und The School of Visual Arts MFA Photo, Video and Related Media Department
Produced with support from / entstand mit Unterstützung von Paula Cooper Gallery, New York

Image Captions / Bildunterschriften

[1]
I Feel Your Pain, 2011
Act 1 Scene 1 – First Date / Akt 1, Szene 1 – Das erste Date
Dialogue adapted from / Adaption von
– Sarah Palin interview with / im Interview mit Glenn Beck
about the future of the Republican Party / über die Zukunft der
Republikaner, Glenn Beck, Fox News, 14 Jan 2010
Production still / Produktionsfoto
With actors / Mit den SchauspielerInnen Annie Fox,
Rafael Jordan
Photo / Foto: Paula Court
Courtesy Performa

[2] [3]
I Feel Your Pain, 2011
Act 1 Scene 1 – First Date / Akt 1, Szene 1 – Das erste Date
Dialogue adapted from / Adaption von
– Sarah Palin interview with / im Interview mit Glenn Beck
about the future of the Republican Party / über die Zukunft der
Republikaner, Glenn Beck, Fox News, 14 Jan 2010
Production still / Produktionsfoto
With actors / Mit den SchauspielerInnen Annie Fox,
Rafael Jordan
Photo / Foto: Yola Monakhov
Courtesy Performa

[4]
Sarah Palin interview with / im Interview mit Glenn Beck
about the future of the Republican Party / über die Zukunft der
Republikaner, Glenn Beck, Fox News, 14 Jan 2010

[5]
I Feel Your Pain, 2011
Act 3 Scene 1 – Infidelity / Akt 3, Szene 1 – Untreue
Dialogue adapted from / Adaption von
– Bill and / und Hillary Clinton interview with / im Interview
mit Steve Kroft, 60 Minutes, CBS, 26 Jan 1992
– George W. Bush, Final Presidential Press Conference /
letzte Pressekonferenz als Präsident, 12 Jan 2009
Production still / Produktionsfoto
With actors / Mit den SchauspielerInnen Ray Field,
Kathryn Grody
Photo / Foto: Kasper Akhøj

[6]
John Boehner interview with / im Interview mit Lesley Stahl,
60 Minutes, CBS, 12 Dec / Dez 2010

[7]
I Feel Your Pain, 2011
Act 3 Scene 1 – Infidelity / Akt 3, Szene 1 – Untreue
Dialogue adapted from / Adaption von
– Bill and Hillary Clinton interview with / im Interview mit
Steve Kroft, 60 Minutes, CBS, 26 Jan 1992
– George W. Bush, Final Presidential Press Conference, /
letzte Pressekonferenz als Präsident, 12 Jan 2009
Video still
With actors / Mit den SchauspielerInnen Ray Field, Kathryn Grody
Courtesy Performa

[8]
I Feel Your Pain, 2011
Act 1 Scene 3 – Insecurity / Akt 1, Szene 3 – Unsicherheit
Dialogue adapted from / Adaption von
– Hillary Clinton interview with / im Interview mit Katie
Couric, 60 Minutes, CBS, 10 Feb 2008
– Barack Obama, Victory speech after winning Democratic
Primary / Siegesrede nach dem Gewinn der Vorwahlen der
Demokraten, Columbia, South Carolina, 26 Jan 2008
– Hillary Clinton, Trail of Tears speech at campaign stop /
Pfad der Tränen-Rede zum Abbruch ihres Wahlkampfs,
Portsmouth, New Hampshire, 7 Jan 2008
Production still / Produktionsfoto
With actor / Mit der Schauspielerin Liz Micek
Photo / Foto: Yola Monakhov
Courtesy Performa

[9]
I Feel Your Pain, 2011
Act 1 Scene 2 – Gratification / Akt 1, Szene 2 – Genugtuung
Dialogue adapted from / Adaption von
– Barack Obama interview with / im Interview mit Steve
Kroft about Osama Bin Laden's death / über den Tod Osama
bin Ladens, 60 Minutes, CBS, 4 May / Mai 2011
Production still / Produktionsfoto
With actors / Mit den Schauspielern Ray Field, Ryan Shams
Photo / Foto: Paula Court
Courtesy Performa

[10]
Barack Obama interview with / im Interview mit Steve Kroft
about Osama Bin Laden's death / über den Tod Osama bin
Ladens, 60 Minutes, CBS, 4 May / Mai 2011

[11]
I Feel Your Pain, 2011
Act 3 Scene 2 – Politics of Emotion / Akt 3, Szene 2 – Politik
der Emotionen
Dialogue adapted from / Adaption von
– The Cultural Politics of Emotion by / von Sara
Ahmed (New York: Routledge, 2004)
– Crying: A Natural and Cultural History of Tears
by / von Tom Lutz (W.W. Norton & Company, 2001)
Production still / Produktionsfoto
With actors / Mit den Schauspielerinnen Liz Micek,
Audrey Crabtree
Photo / Foto: Yola Monakhov
Courtesy Performa

[12]
I Feel Your Pain, 2011
Act 4 Scene 2 – Coming to Blows / Akt 4, Szene 2 –
Aneinandergeraten
Dialogue adapted from / Adaption von
– George W. Bush interview with / im Interview mit Candy
Crowley, State of the Union, CNN, 14 Nov 2010
– Gubernatorial candidate Carl Paladino's altercation
with / Der Kandidat für die Gouverneurswahl im Wortwechsel
mit Reporter Frederic Dicker in Bolton Landing, 28 Sept 2010

–Injunction Granted, Federal Theatre Project Living
Newspaper production / Aufführung, staged by / Inszenierung
von Joseph Losey, New York, USA, 1936
    Production still / Produktionsfoto
    With actors / Mit den SchauspielerInnen Audrey Crabtree,
Ray Field, Ryan Shams
    Photo / Foto: Yola Monakhov
    Courtesy Performa

[13]
I Feel Your Pain, 2011
    Act 4 Scene 4 – Coming to Blows / Akt 4, Szene 4 –
Aneinandergeraten
Dialogue adapted from / Adaption von
    –Anthony Weiner press conference / Pressekonferenz, 6 Jun 2011
    –Congressman / Der Kongressabgeordnete Joe Wilson
heckling Barack Obama / attackiert Barack Obama mit
Zwischenfragen, 9 Sept 2009
    –Barack Obama speaking about / spricht über Michelle Obama
during 1996 interview / in einem 1996 gegebenen Interview,
Le Monde, 11 Jan 2009
    –Barack Obama speaking to Hearst Magazine publishers /
im Gespräch mit den Herausgebern des Hearst Magazine,
FoxNews.com, 4 April 2011
    –Arnold Schwarzenegger interview with / im Interview mit
Michael Lewis, California and Bust, Vanity Fair, Nov 2011
    –George W. Bush, Speech to the Nation on the Economic
Crisis / Rede an die Nation zur Wirtschaftskrise, 24 Sept 2008
    Production still / Produktionsfoto
    With actor / Mit dem Schauspieler Ryan Shams
    Photo / Foto: Yola Monakhov
    Courtesy Performa

[14]
Arnold Schwarzenegger interview with / im Interview mit
Jay Leno, The Tonight Show with Jay Leno, 6 Aug 2003

[15] [16] [17] [18] [19] [20] [21] [22] [23] [24] [25]
In Camera, 2012
    Video still
    With actors / Mit den SchauspielerInnen Anders E Larsson,
Karin Hallén, Maria Lindh

[26]
In Camera, 2012
    Video still
    With actor / Mit der Schauspielerin Maria Lindh
    Painting by / Gemälde von Vilhelm Lundstrøm Portrait of /
Porträt der Hanne Wilhelm Hansen, Finn Juhls hus, Ordrupgaard,
Denmark / Dänemark

[27]
In Camera, 2012
    Production still / Produktionsfoto
    Photo / Foto: Amanda Nordgren

[28]
In Camera, 2012
    Video still

[29]
In Camera, 2012
    Production still / Produktionsfoto
    Photo / Foto: Kasper Akhøj

[30]
    Liz Magic Laser, In Camera, Malmö Konsthall, Malmö,
Sweden / Schweden, 2012
    Installation view / Installationsansicht
    Photo / Foto: Liz Magic Laser

[31] [32] [33] [34] [35] [36] [37]
The Digital Face, 2012
Movement adapted from / Adaption der Bewegungen von
    –George H. W. Bush, State of the Union Address / Rede zur
Lage der Nation, 31 Jan 1990
    Production still / Produktionsfoto
    With dancer / Mit dem Tänzer Alan Good
    Photo / Foto: Liz Magic Laser

[38] [39] [40] [41] [42] [43] [44] [45]
The Digital Face, 2012
Movement adapted from / Adaption der Bewegungen von
    –Barack Obama, State of the Union Address / Rede zur Lage
der Nation, 24 Jan 2012
    Production still / Produktionsfoto
    With dancer / Mit der Tänzerin Cori Kresge
    Photo / Foto: Liz Magic Laser

[46]
The Digital Face, 2012
    Production still / Produktionsfoto, MoMA PS1, New York
    With dancers / Mit der Tänzerin Cori Kresge
    Photo / Foto: Loren Wohl

[47]
The Digital Face, 2012
    Installation view / Installationsansicht, Derek Eller
Gallery, New York, USA
    With dancers / Mit den TänzerInnen Alan Good,
Cori Kresge
    Photo / Foto: Liz Magic Laser

[48]
The Digital Face, 2012
    Production still / Produktionsfoto, MoMA PS1, New York
    With dancers / Mit den TänzerInnen Alan Good,
Cori Kresge
    Photo / Foto: Loren Wohl

[49]
Stand Behind Me, 2013
Movement adapted from / Adaption der Bewegungen von
    –Barack Obama, Plan to Reduce Gun Violence,
White House / Plan zur Bekämpfung von Waffengewalt,
Weißes Haus, Washington DC, 16 Jan 2013
    Production still / Produktionsfoto
    With dancer / Mit der Tänzerin Ariel Freedman
    Photo / Foto: Liz Magic Laser

[50]

Stand Behind Me, 2013
Movement adapted from / Adaption der Bewegungen von
 – Chancellor / Bundeskanzlerin Angela Merkel, 18th
Political Ash Wednesday Speech, Mecklenburg-West
Pomerania / Rede zum 18. Politischen Aschermittwoch,
Mecklenburg-Vorpommern, Germany / Deutschland, 13 Feb 2013
 Production still / Produktionsfoto
 Photo / Foto: Liz Magic Laser

[51]

Stand Behind Me, 2013
Movement adapted from / Adaption der Bewegungen von
 – Prime Minister / Premierminister David Cameron,
House of Commons, London, United Kingdom, 13 Feb 2013
 Production still / Produktionsfoto
 Courtesy Lisson Gallery, London

[52] [53]

Stand Behind Me, 2013
Movement adapted from / Adaption der Bewegungen von
 – President / Präsident Mohamed Morsi, Declaration of
State of Emergency in Port Said and Suez / Ausrufung des
Notstands in Port Said und Suez, Cairo, Egypt / Kairo, Ägypten,
27 Jan 2013
 Video still

[54]

Stand Behind Me, 2013
Movement adapted from / Adaption der Bewegungen von
 – Prime Minister / Ministerpräsident Benjamin Netanyahu,
Conference of Presidents Speech / Rede auf der Gipfelkonferenz,
New York, USA, 11 Feb 2013
 Video still

[55]

Stand Behind Me, 2013
Movement adapted from / Adaption der Bewegungen von
 – International Monetary Fund Chief / Direktorin
des Internationalen Währungsfonds Christine Lagarde,
World Economic Forum / Weltwirtschaftsforum, Davos,
Switzerland / Schweiz, 24 Jan 2013
 Video still

[56]

Stand Behind Me, 2013
Movement adapted from / Adaption der Bewegungen von
 – Leader of the Opposition Labour Party / Oppositionsführer
der Labour Party Ed Miliband, Questions to the Prime Minister /
Fragen an den Premierminister David Cameron, House of
Commons, London, United Kingdom, 13 Feb 2013
 Video still

[57]

Stand Behind Me, 2013
Movement adapted from / Adaption der Bewegungen von
 – Prime Minister / Premierminister David Cameron, House
of Commons, London, United Kingdom, 13 Feb 2013
 Video still

[58] [59]

Stand Behind Me, 2013
Movement adapted from / Adaption der Bewegungen von
 – International Monetary Fund Chief / Direktorin
des Internationalen Währungsfonds Christine Lagarde,
World Economic Forum / Weltwirtschaftsforum, Davos,
Switzerland / Schweiz, 24 Jan 2013
 Video still

[60] [61]

Stand Behind Me, 2013
Movement adapted from / Adaption der Bewegungen von
 – Movement for Rights and Freedoms Chairman / Vorsitzender
der Bewegung für Rechte und Freiheiten Ahmed Dogan,
Annual Party Conference / Jahresparteitag, National Palace of
Culture / Nationaler Kulturpalast, Sofia, Bulgaria / Bulgarien,
19 Jan 2013
 Video still

[62]

Stand Behind Me, 2013
Movement adapted from / Adaption der Bewegungen von
 – Prime Minister / Premierminister David Cameron,
House of Commons, London, United Kingdom, 13 Feb 2013
 Video still

[63] [64]

Public Relations / Öffentlichkeitsarbeit, 2013
 Set Model / Bühnenbildmodell (Wood, paper, foamcore,
wire, paint and glue / Holz, Papier, Hartschaumplatte, Draht,
Farbe, Kleber, 60cm × 15cm × 40cm)
 Installation view / Installationsansicht
 Set Design in collaboration with / Bühnendesign in
Zusammenarbeit mit Christian Kiehl
 Photo / Foto: Thorsten Arendt

[65]

Public Relations / Öffentlichkeitsarbeit, 2013
 TV Set / TV-Kulisse (Wood, scrim, PVC, video projection,
flat screen monitor, scripts, office chairs, bar stools, liquor
bottles, glasses, drink shakers, ice buckets, fruit bowls,
plastic fruit, and sand bags / Holz, Projektionsfolie, PVC,
Videoprojektion, Flachbildschirm, Manuskripte, Bürostühle,
Barhocker, Spirituosenflaschen, Gläser, Cocktailshaker,
Eiskübel, Obstschalen, Plastikobst, Sandsäcke, 8m × 3m × 4m)
 Installation view / Installationsansicht
 Set Design in collaboration with / Bühnendesign in
Zusammenarbeit mit Christian Kiehl
 Photo / Foto: Thorsten Arendt

[66]

Public Relations / Öffentlichkeitsarbeit, 2013
 Café Set / Café-Kulisse (Wood, plexiglass, PVC, vinyl lettering,
flat screen monitor, café tables, café chairs, office chairs,
bulletin board, paper, clocks, menus, coffee, sugar, sugar containers,
ceramic cups and saucers, plastic cups, paper cups, stirrers,
newspapers, newspaper holders, metal bar, acrylic paint, sand
bags / Holz, Plexiglas, PVC, Plastikbuchstaben, Flachbildschirm,
Kaffeehaustische und -stühle, Bürostühle, Schwarzes Brett,

Papier, Uhren, Speisekarten, Kaffee, Zucker, Zuckerstreuer,
Keramiktassen und -untertassen, Plastikbecher, Papierbecher, Rühr-
stäbchen, Zeitungen, Zeitungshalter, Metallleiste, Acrylfarbe,
Sandsäcke, 8m×3m×4m; Disco Ball Globe / Discokugel-Globus,
51cm×51cm×51cm; painting by / Gemälde von Sanya
Kantarovsky, acrylic and watercolor on canvas / Acrylfarbe und
Tempera auf Leinwand, 90cm×120cm)
Installation view / Installationsansicht
Set Design in collaboration with / Bühnendesign in
Zusammenarbeit mit Christian Kiehl
Photo / Foto: Thorsten Arendt

[67] [68]
Public Relations / Öffentlichkeitsarbeit, 2013
Production still / Produktionsfoto
With Reporter / Mit der Reporterin Elisabeth Weydt
Photos/ Foto: Liz Magic Laser

[69]
Public Relations / Öffentlichkeitsarbeit, 2013
TV Set / TV-Kulisse
Installation view / Installationsansicht
Photo / Foto: Thorsten Arendt

[70]
Public Relations / Öffentlichkeitsarbeit, 2013
Production still / Produktionsfoto
With Reporter / Mit der Reporterin Elisabeth Weydt
Photo / Foto: Liz Magic Laser

[71]
Public Relations / Öffentlichkeitsarbeit, 2013
Video still
With Reporter / Mit der Reporterin Elisabeth Weydt

[72]
Public Relations / Öffentlichkeitsarbeit, 2013
Disco Ball Globe / Discokugel-Globus (Mirrored glass, black
glass, plastic core, chain, rotary engine / Spiegelglas, schwarzes
Glas, Kunststoffkern, Kette, Drehmotor, 51cm×51cm×51cm)
Installation view / Installationsansicht
Photo / Foto: Thorsten Arendt

[73]
Public Relations / Öffentlichkeitsarbeit, 2013
Video still
With actor / Mit dem Schauspieler Florian Kleine

[74]
Public Relations / Öffentlichkeitsarbeit, 2013
TV Set / TV-Kulisse
Installation view / Installationsansicht
Photo / Foto: Thorsten Arendt

[75]
Public Relations / Öffentlichkeitsarbeit, 2013
Production still / Produktionsfoto
With Reporter / Mit der Reporterin Elisabeth Weydt
Photo / Foto: Liz Magic Laser

[76]
Public Relations / Öffentlichkeitsarbeit, 2013
Production still / Produktionsfoto
With actor / Mit dem Schauspieler Florian Kleine
Photo / Foto: Thorsten Arendt

[77]
Public Relations / Öffentlichkeitsarbeit, 2013
Installation view / Installationsansicht with painting by /
mit einem Gemälde von Sanya Kantarovsky and Video Installation
of / und Videoinstallation von Push Poll (Liz Magic Laser,
commissioned by / im Auftrag von CNN, 2012)
Photo / Foto: Thorsten Arendt

[78]
Public Relations / Öffentlichkeitsarbeit, 2013
Production still / Produktionsfoto
With actor / Mit dem Schauspieler Florian Kleine
Photo / Foto: Thorsten Arendt

[79]
Public Relations / Öffentlichkeitsarbeit, 2013
Café Set / Café-Kulisse
Installation view / Installationsansicht
Set Design in collaboration with / Bühnendesign in
Zusammenarbeit mit Christian Kiehl
Photo / Foto: Thorsten Arendt

[80]
Public Relations / Öffentlichkeitsarbeit, 2013
Production still / Produktionsfoto
With actor / Mit dem Schauspieler Florian Kleine
Photo / Foto: Thorsten Arendt

[81]
Public Relations / Öffentlichkeitsarbeit, 2013
Costumes / Kostüme
Installation view / Installationsansicht
Costume Design / Kostümdesign Liz Magic Laser in
collaboration with / in Zusammenarbeit mit Nils von Berg
Photo / Foto: Thorsten Arendt

[82] [83] [84]
Public Relations / Öffentlichkeitsarbeit, 2013
TV Set / TV-Kulisse
Installation view / Installationsansicht
Photo / Foto: Thorsten Arendt

[85]
Public Relations / Öffentlichkeitsarbeit, 2013
Production still / Produktionsfoto
With Reporter / Mit der Reporterin Elisabeth Weydt
Photo / Foto: Liz Magic Laser

[86]
Absolute Event, 2013
Installation view / Installationsansicht
Photo / Foto: Steven Probert
Courtesy Paula Cooper Gallery, New York

[87] [88] [89] [90] [91] [92] [93]

Absolute Event, 2013
Production still / Produktionsfoto
With actors and former congressional staffers / Mit den
Schauspielern und ehemaligen Kongress-Mitarbeitern
Daniel Abse, Gary Lee Mahmoud
Photo / Foto: Steven Probert
Courtesy Paula Cooper Gallery, New York

[94]

Absolute Event, 2013
Video still

[95]

Absolute Event, 2013
Installation view / Installationsansicht
Photo / Foto: Steven Probert
Courtesy Paula Cooper Gallery, New York

[96] [97]

Absolute Event, 2013
Video still

[98] [99] [100]

Absolute Event, 2013
Production still / Produktionsfoto
Photo / Foto: Steven Probert
Courtesy Paula Cooper Gallery, New York

[101]

Absolute Event, 2013
Video still

[102] [103] [104]

Absolute Event, 2013
Production still / Produktionsfoto
Photo / Foto: Steven Probert
Courtesy Paula Cooper Gallery, New York

[105] [106] [107] [108]

Absolute Event, 2013
Video still

Images / Abbildungen

[1]

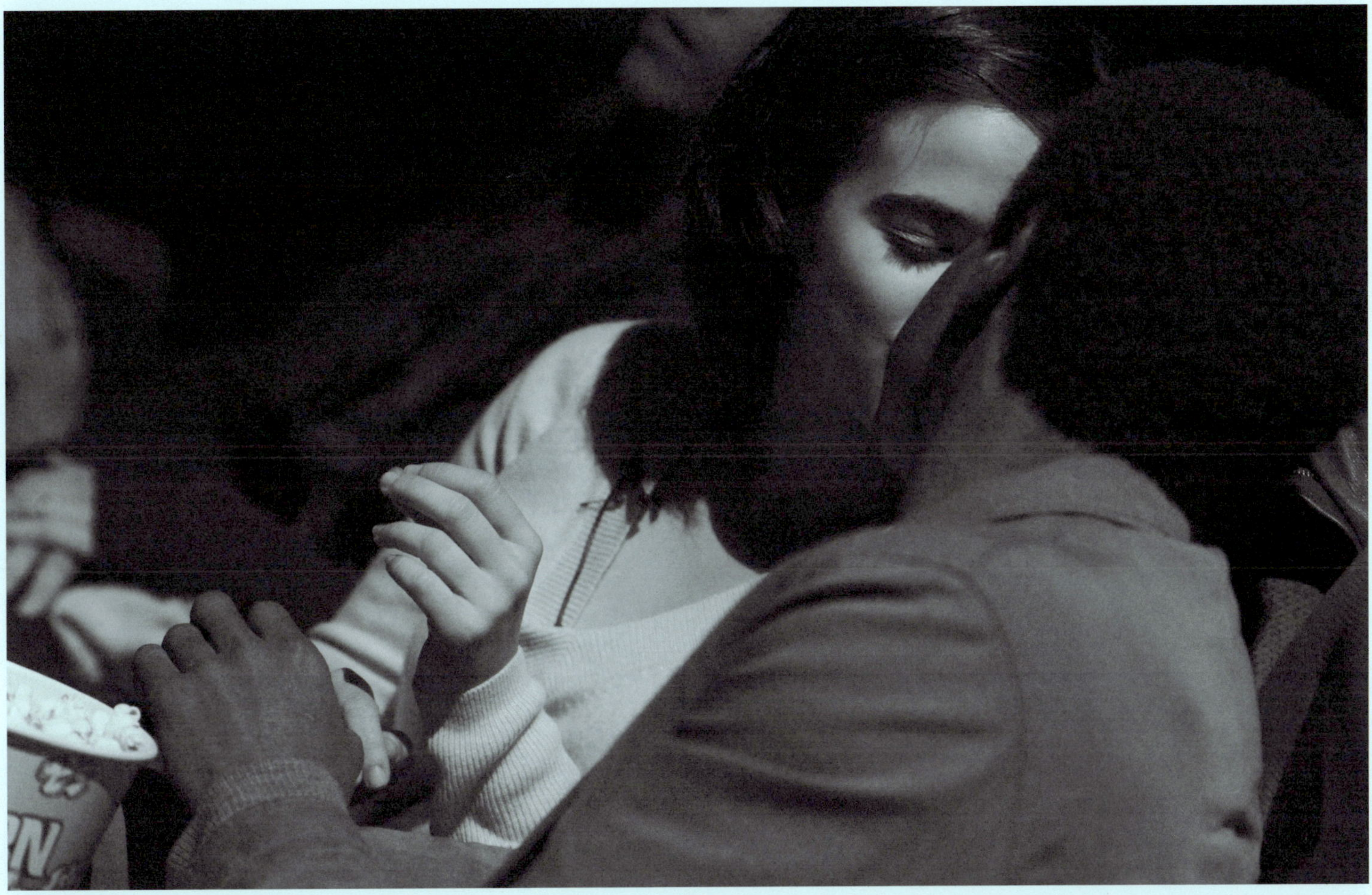

[2]

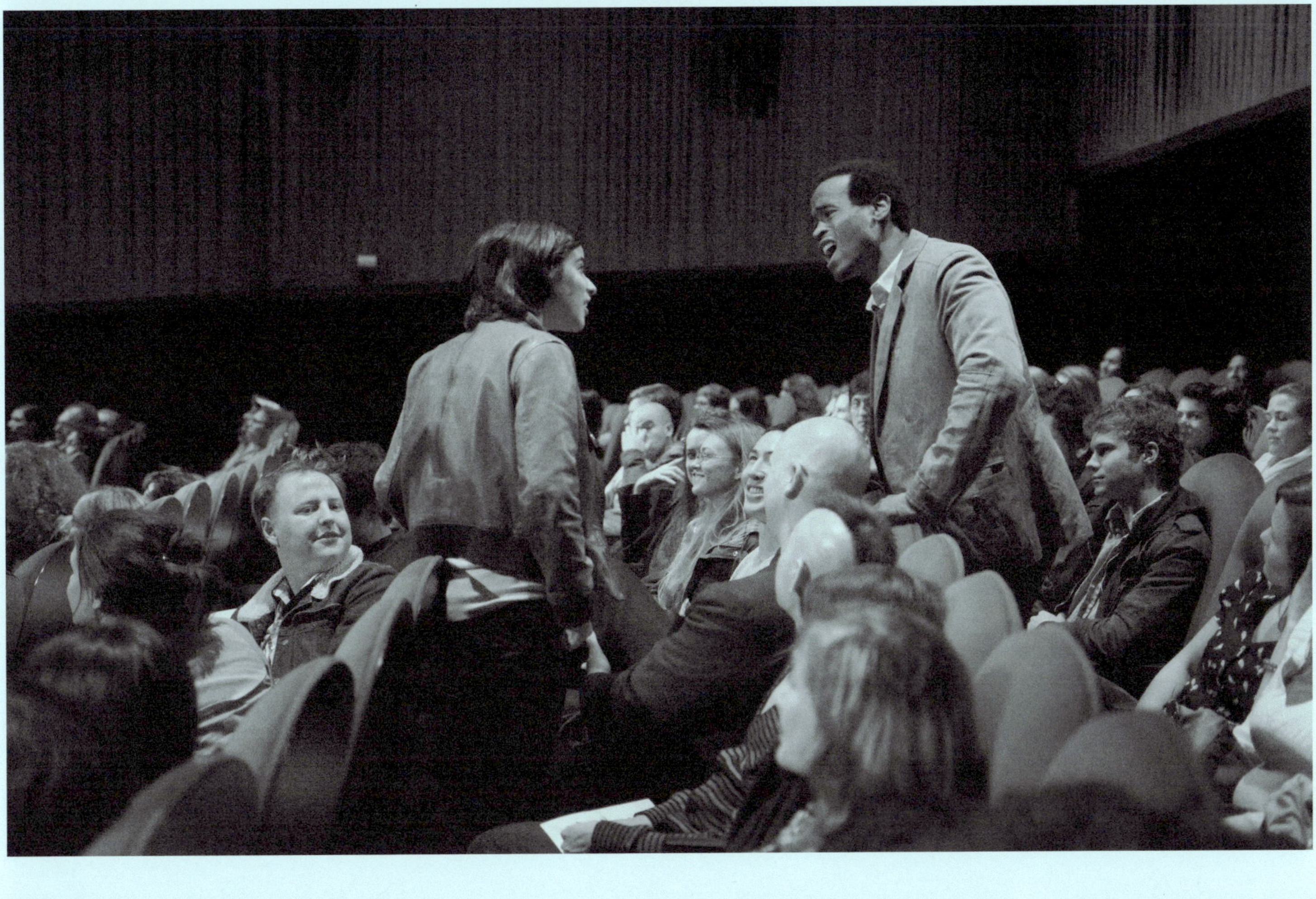

[3]

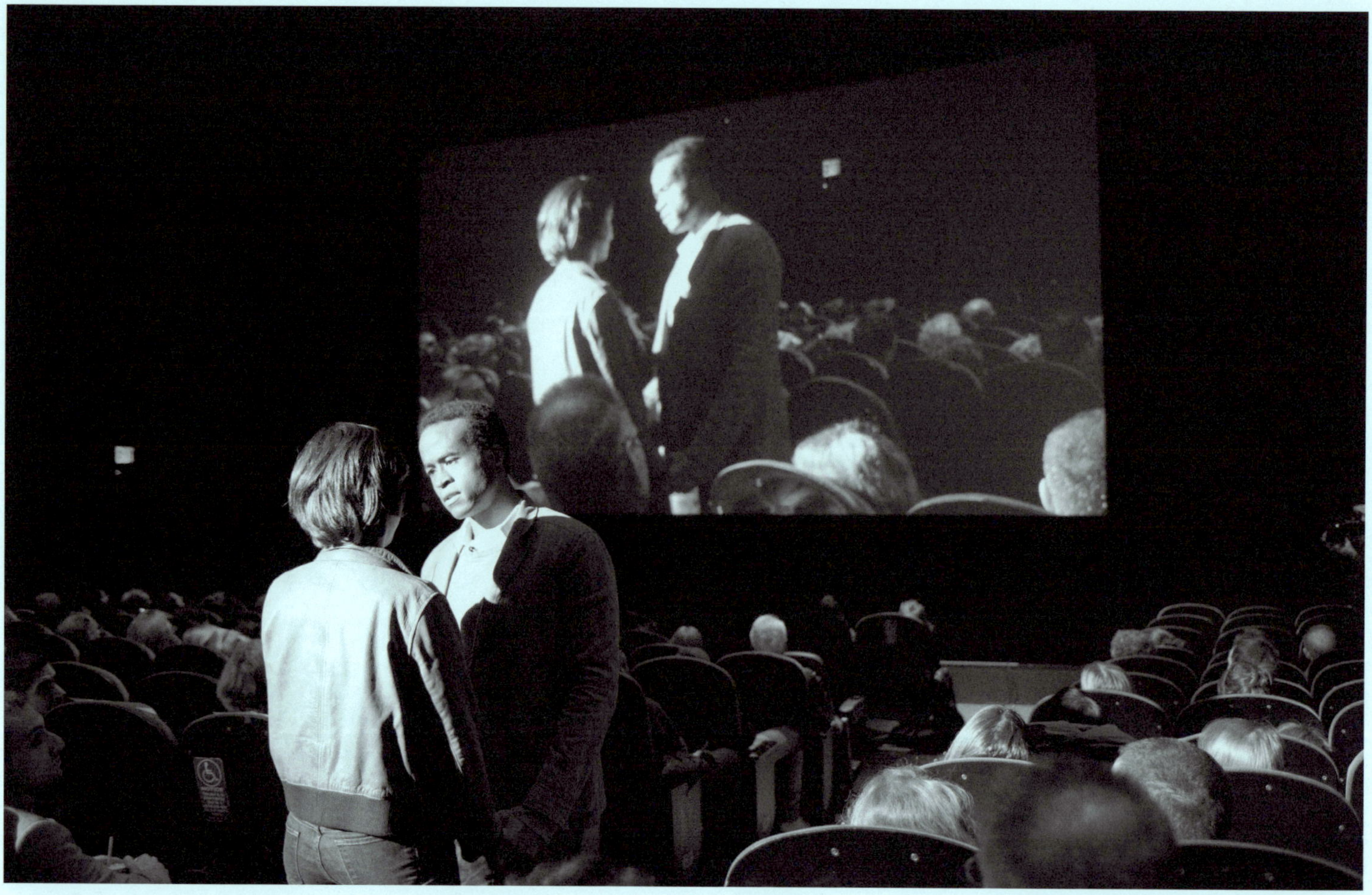

[4]

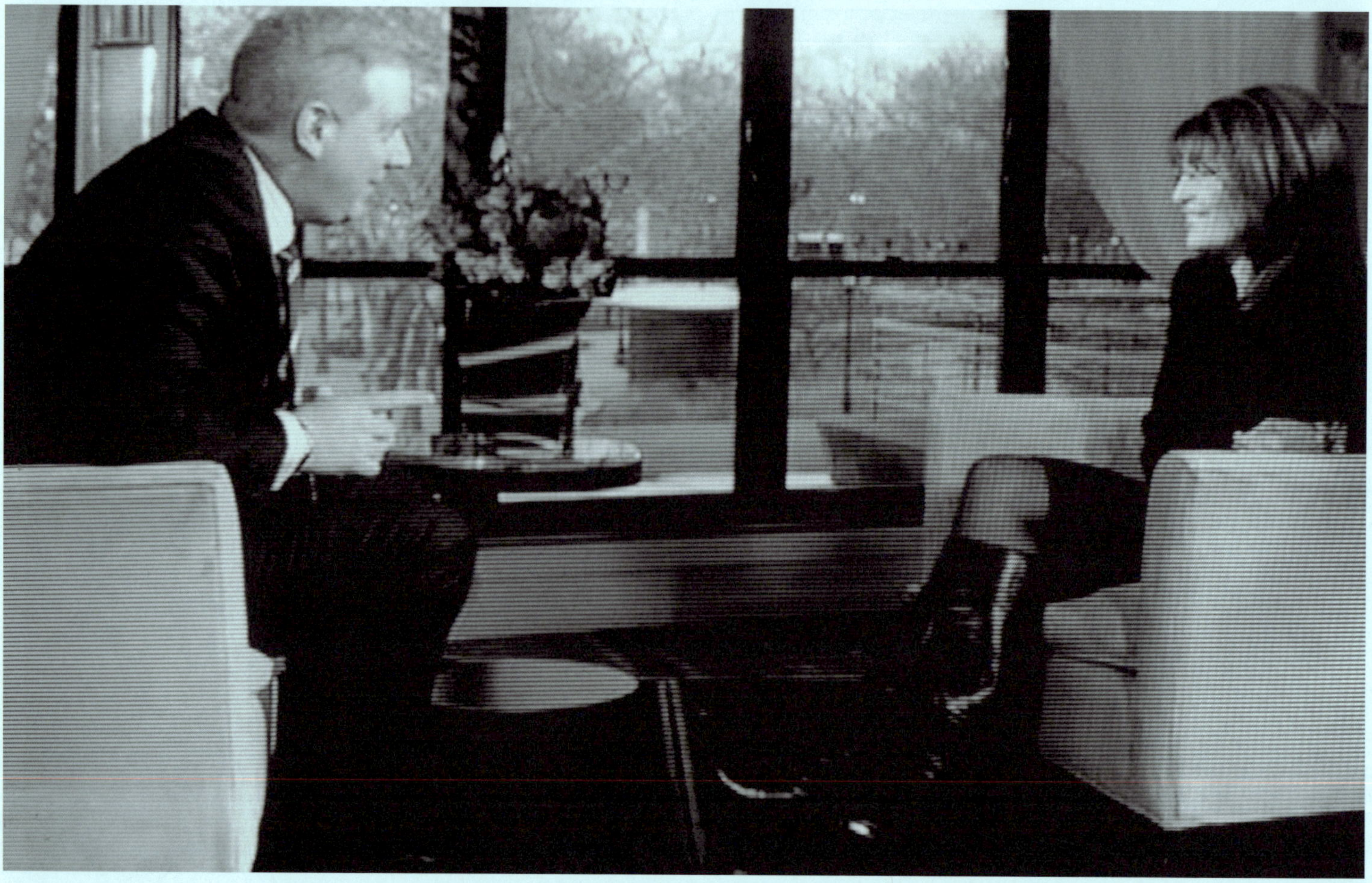

[5]

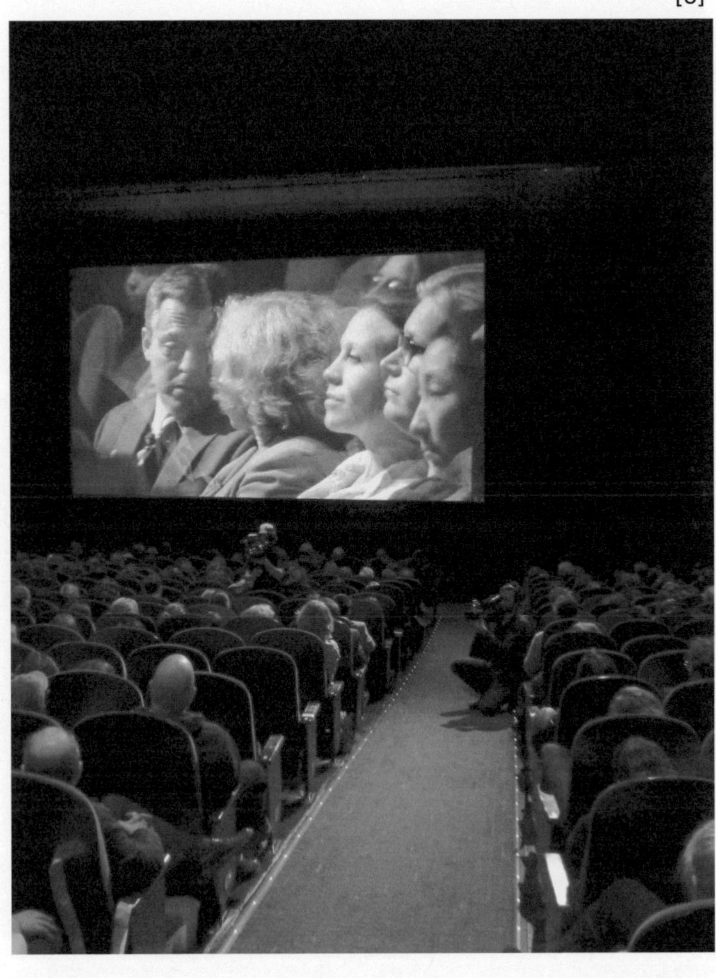

[6] [7]

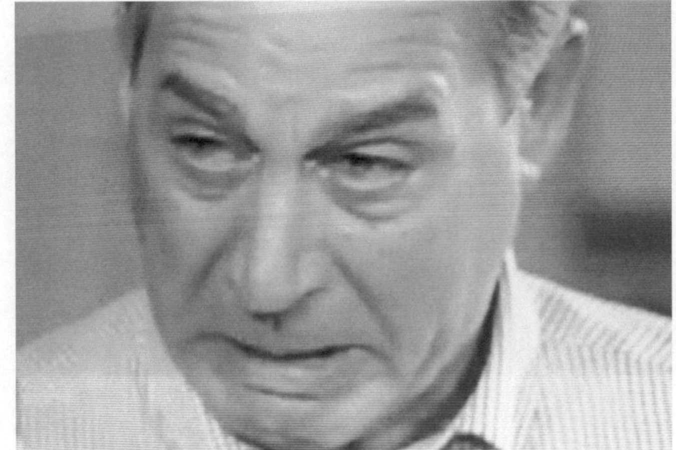

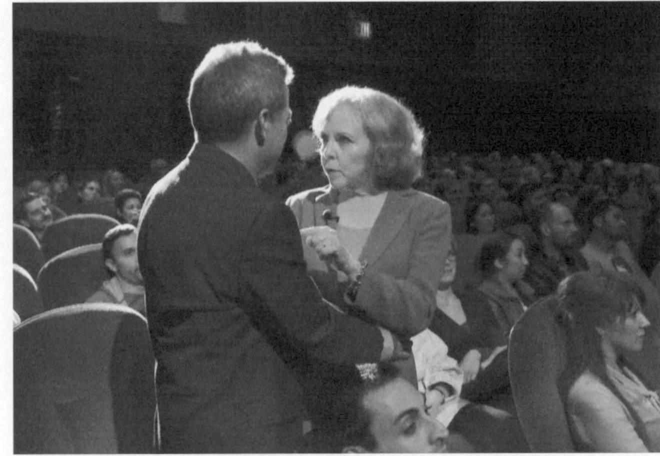

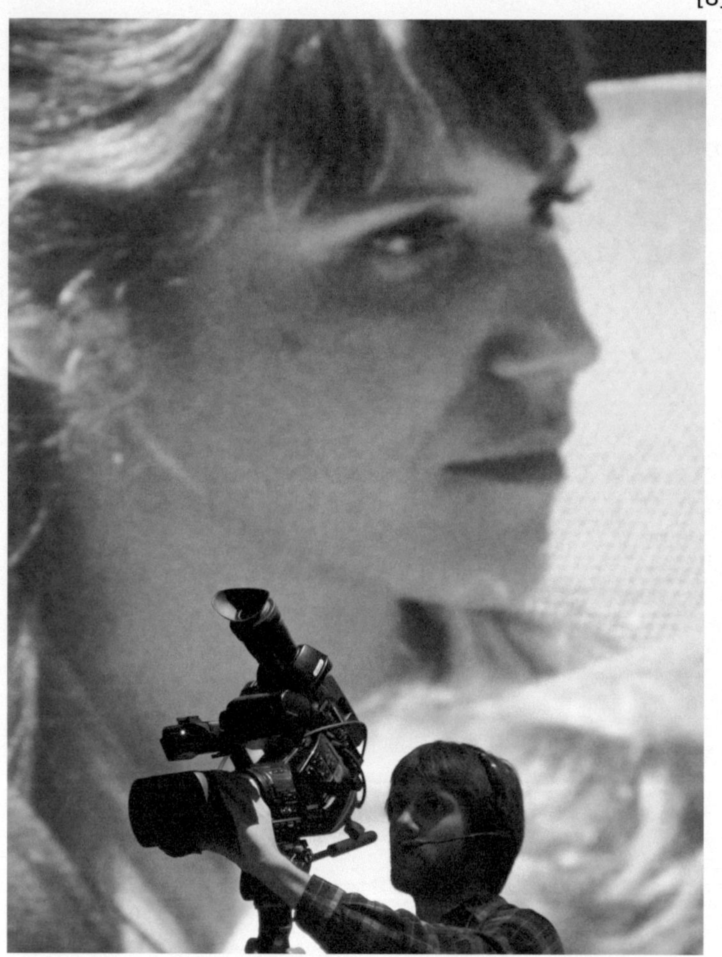
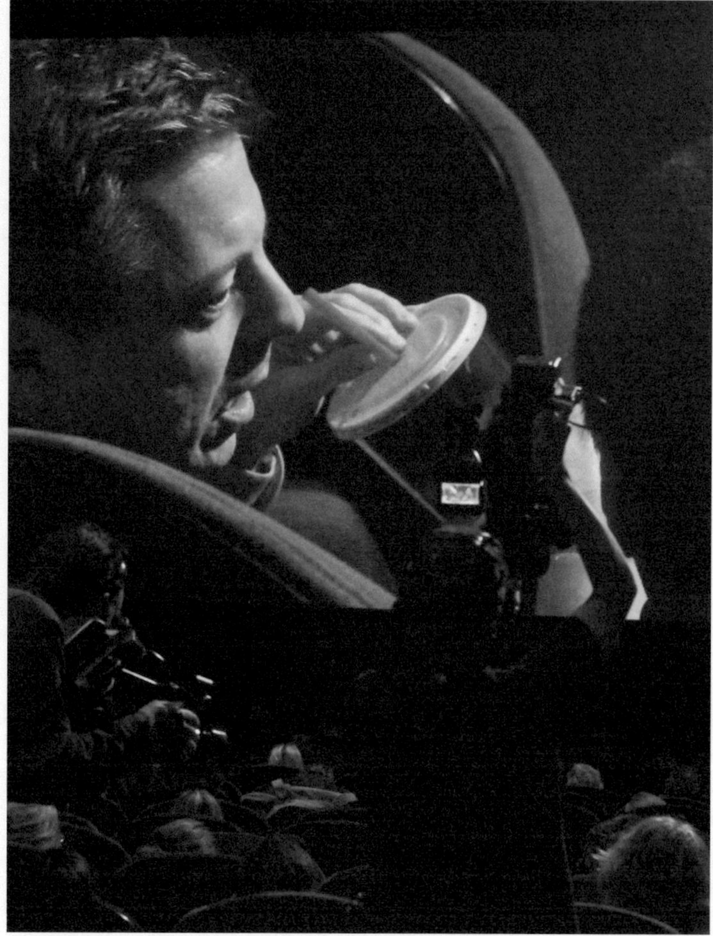

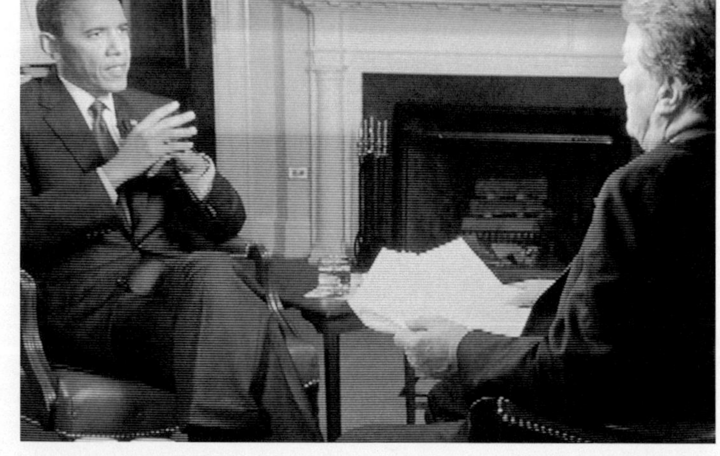
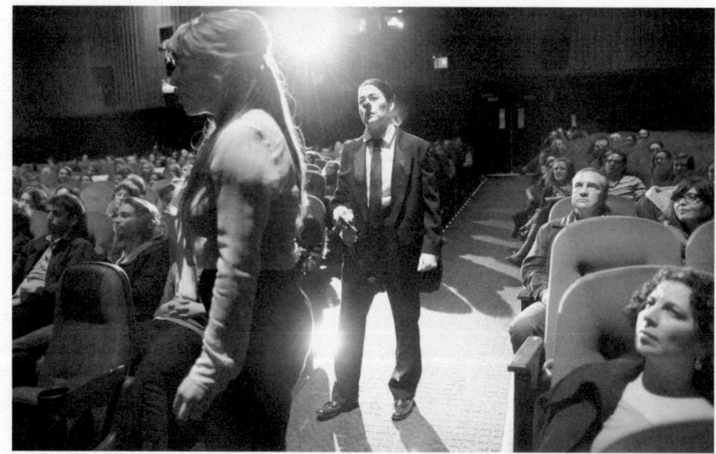

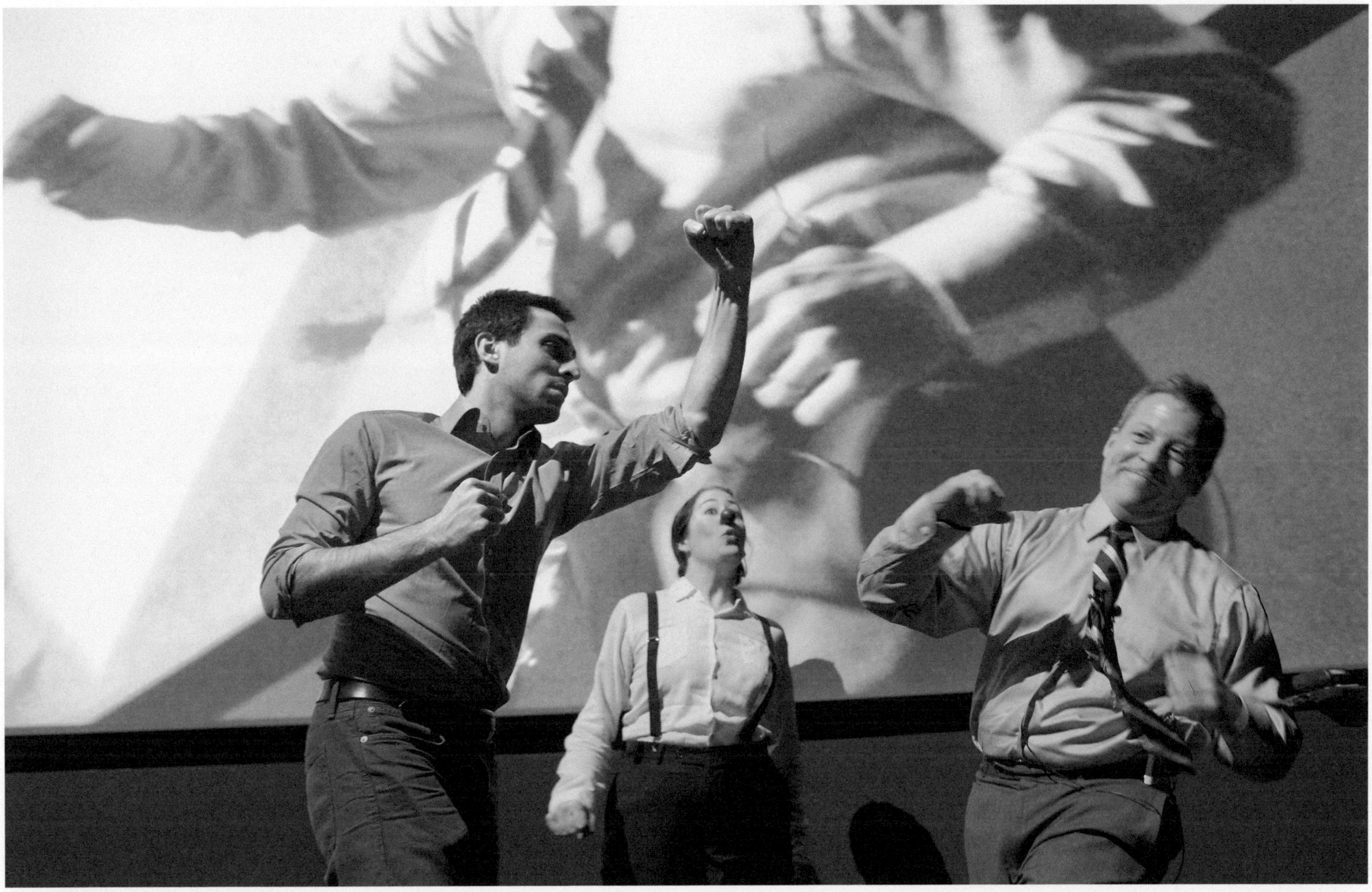

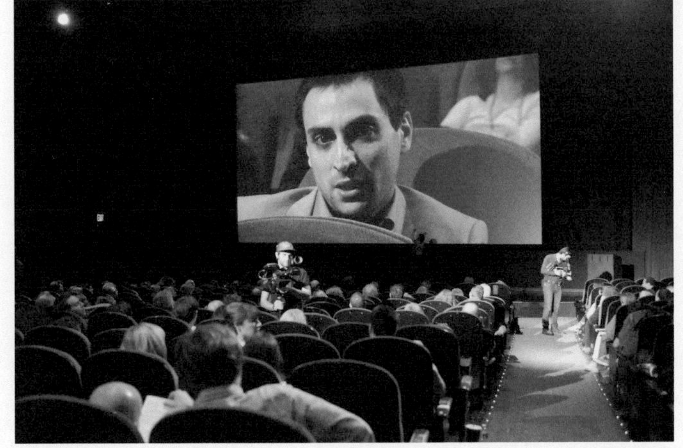

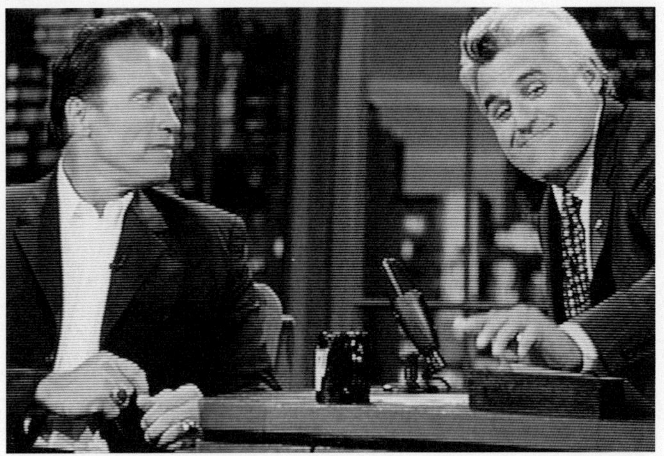

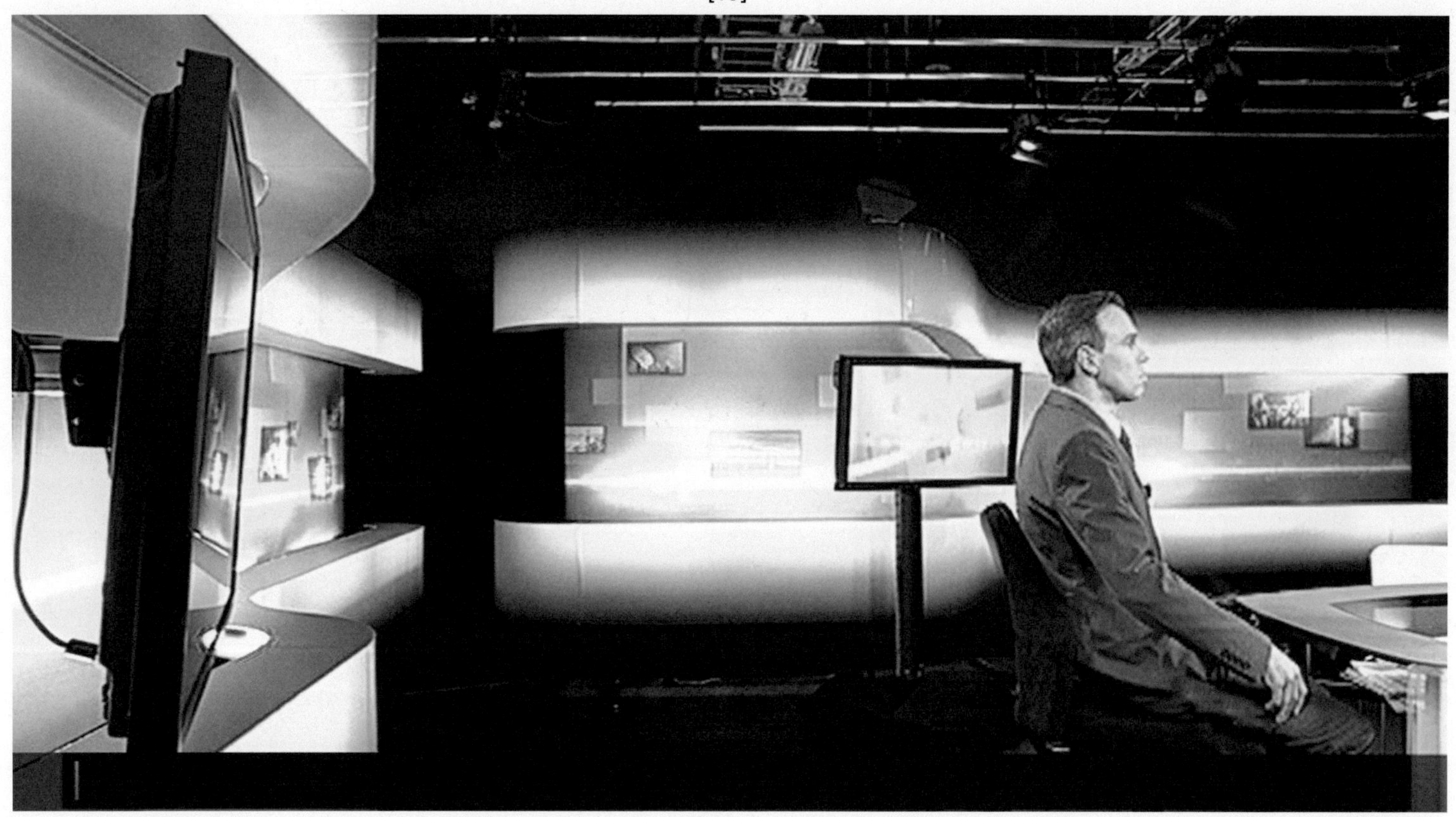

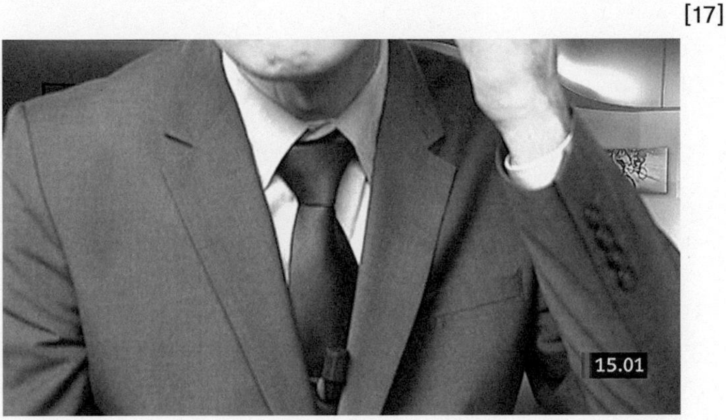
14.51

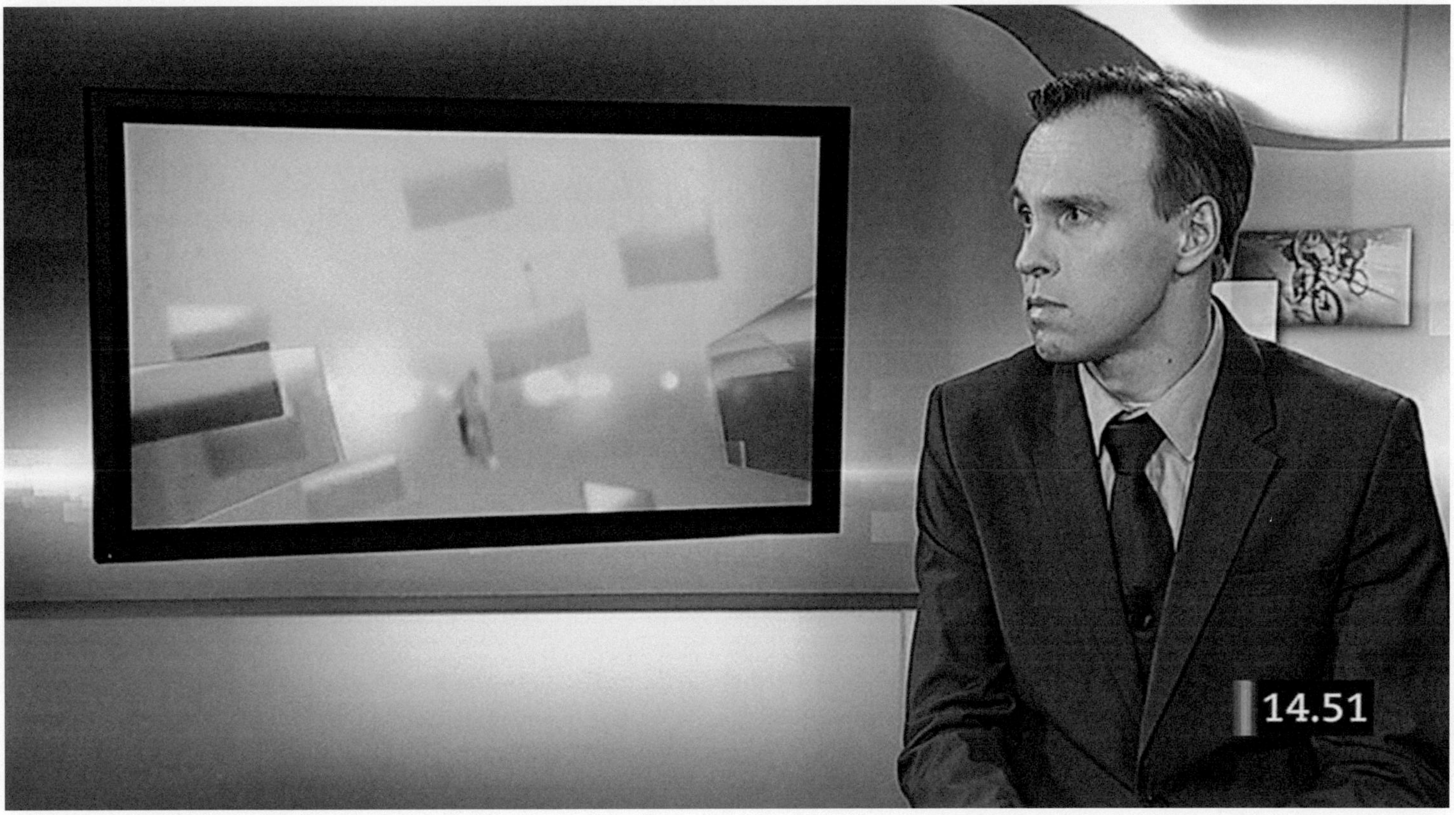

15.01

[18]

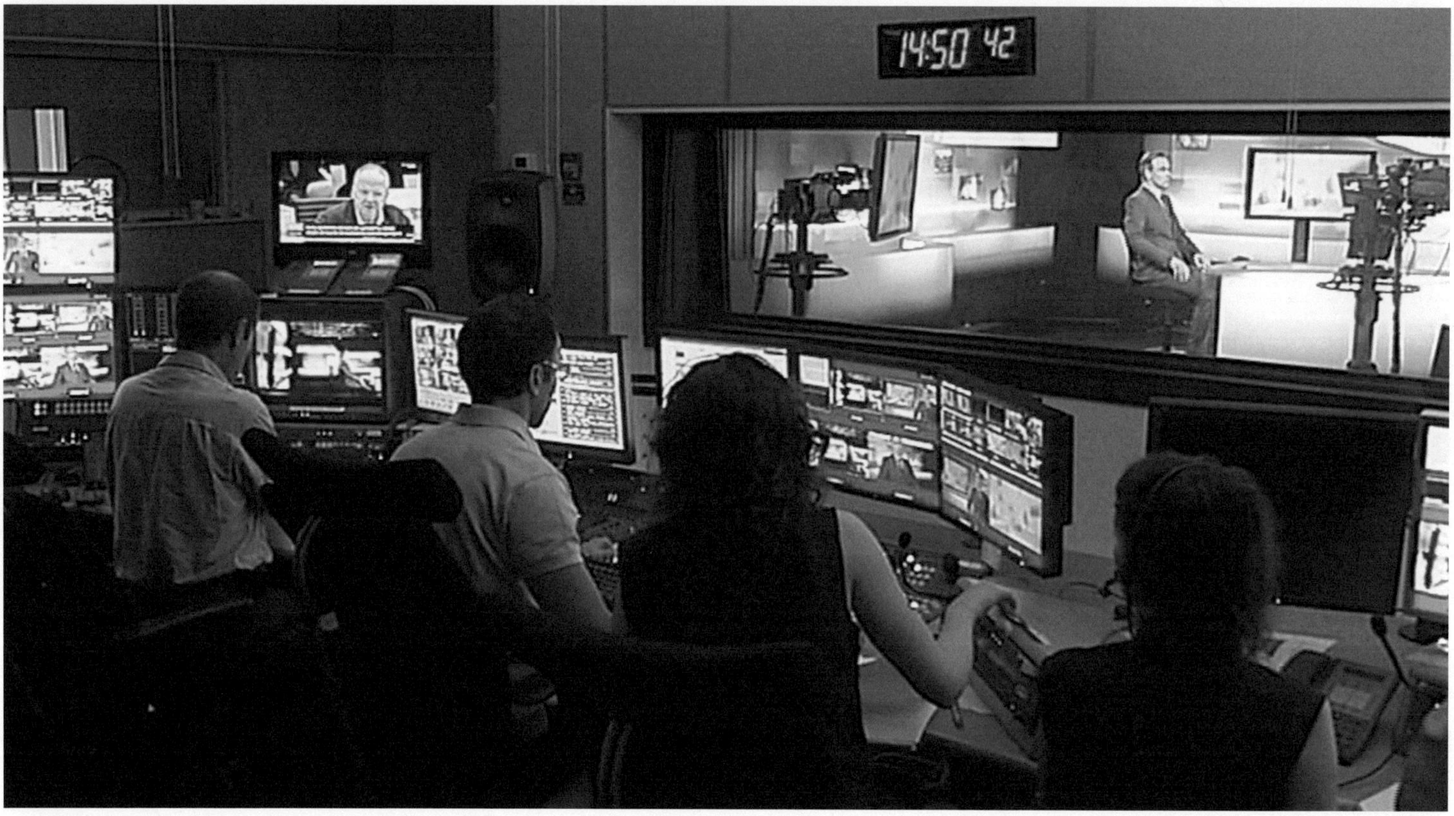

[19]

svt
15.01

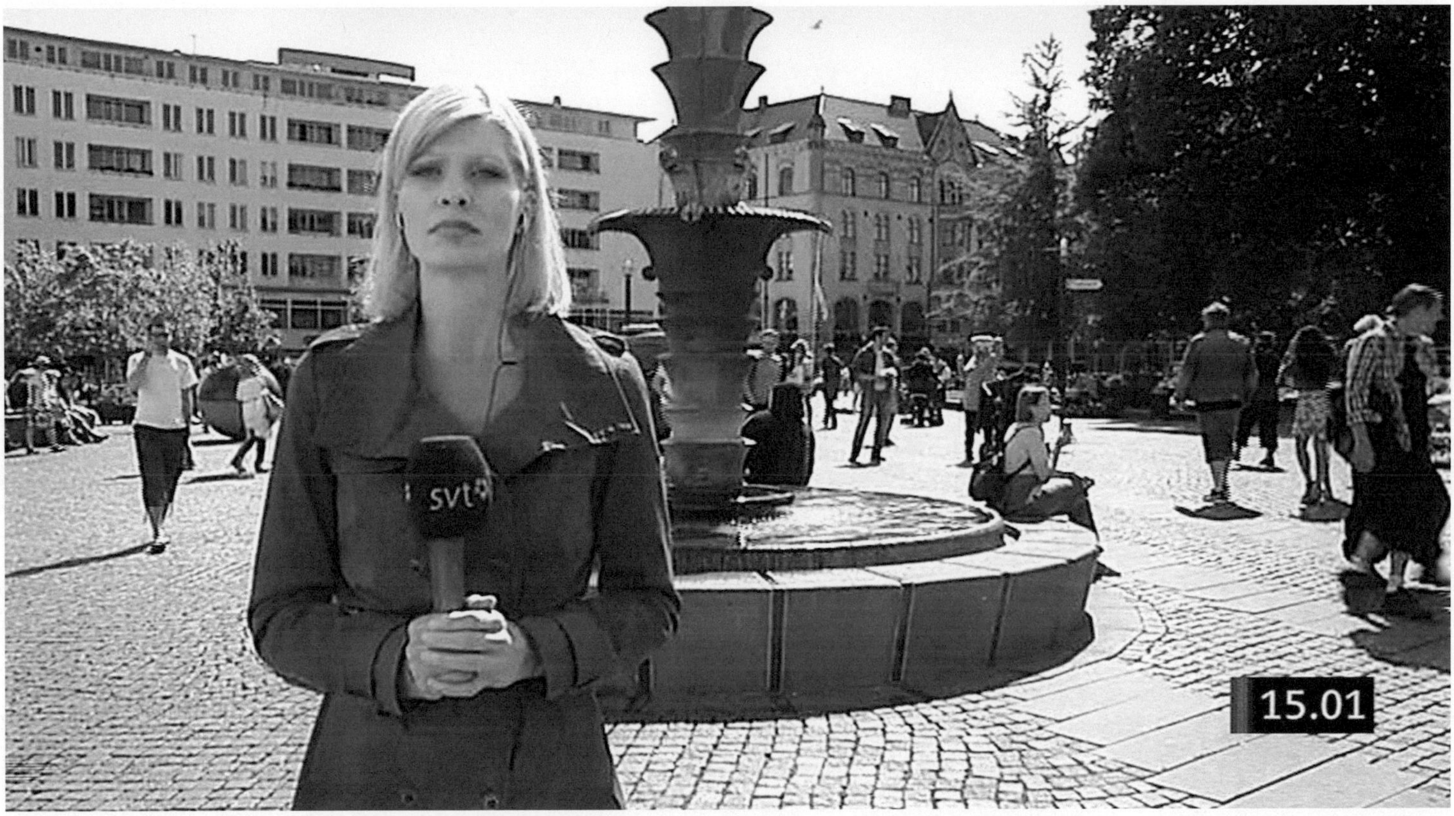

16.38

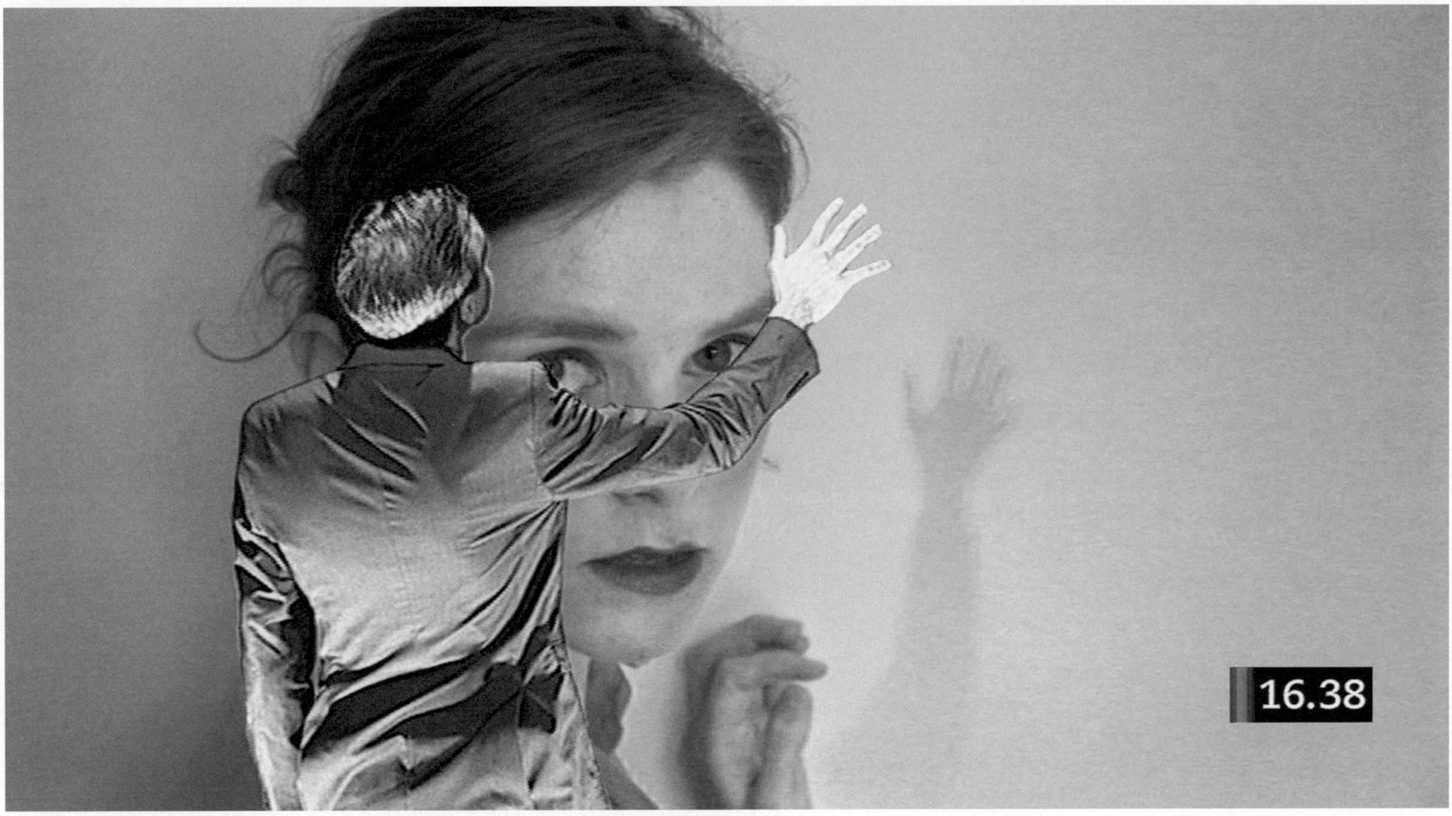

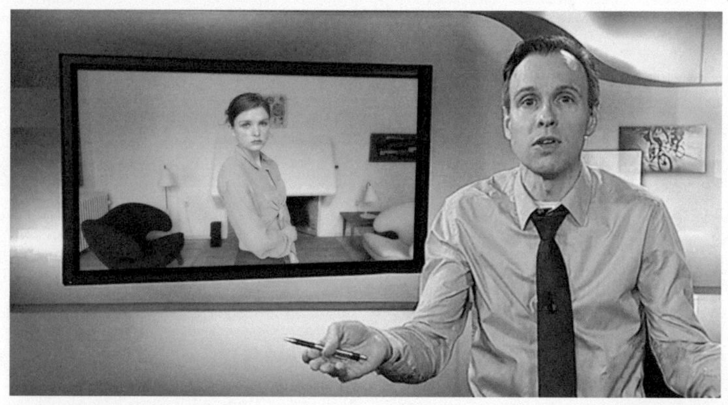

[23]

[24]

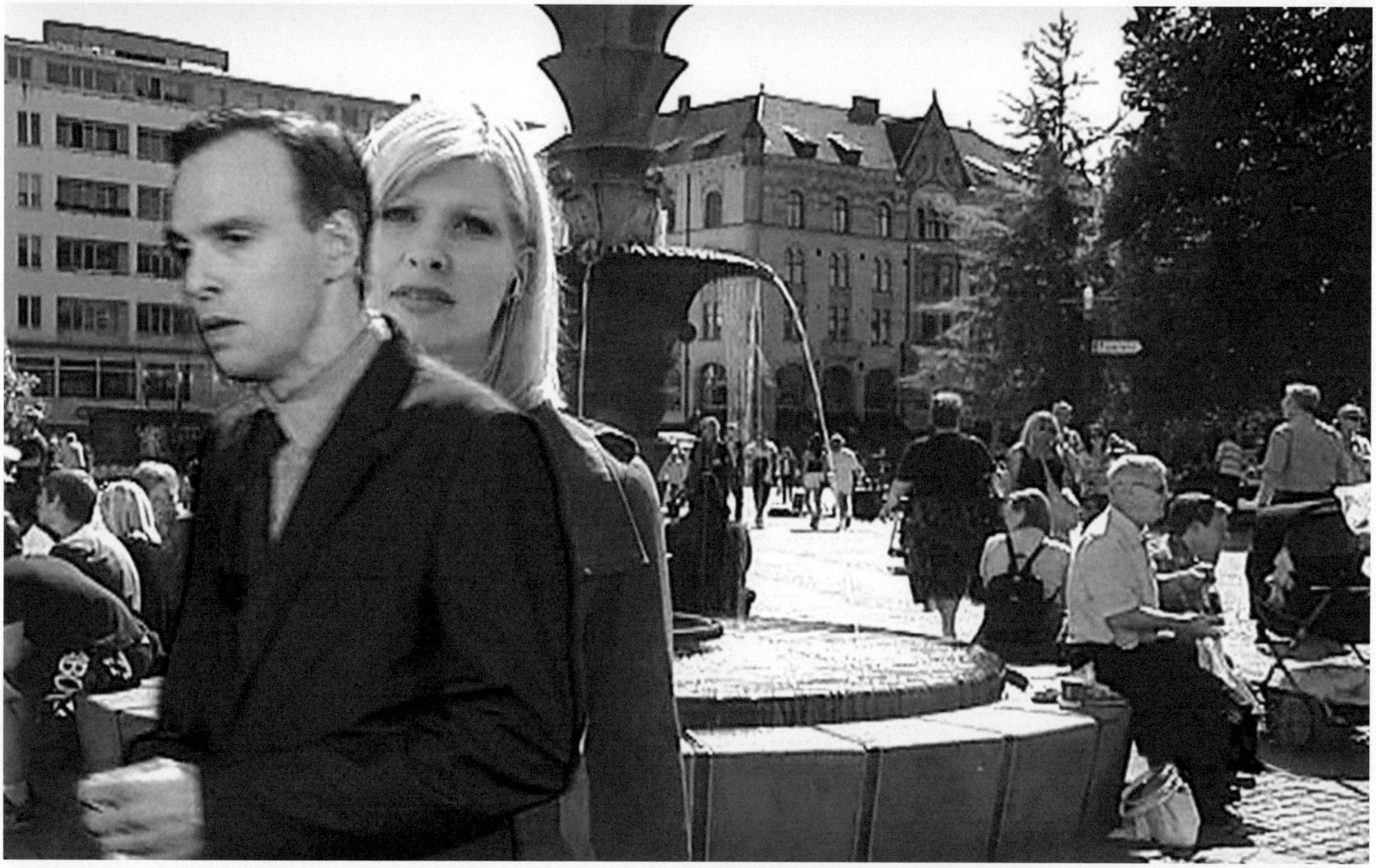

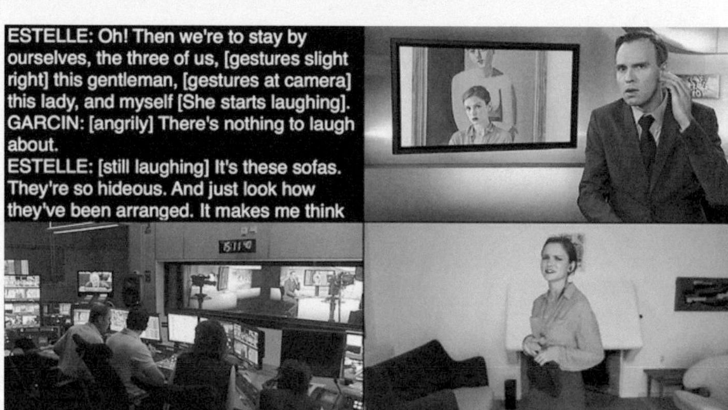
ESTELLE: Oh! Then we're to stay by ourselves, the three of us, [gestures slight right] this gentleman, [gestures at camera] this lady, and myself [She starts laughing].
GARCIN: [angrily] There's nothing to laugh about.
ESTELLE: [still laughing] It's these sofas. They're so hideous. And just look how they've been arranged. It makes me think

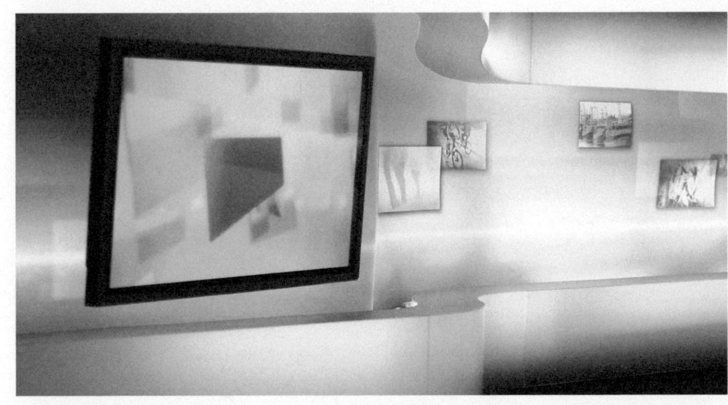 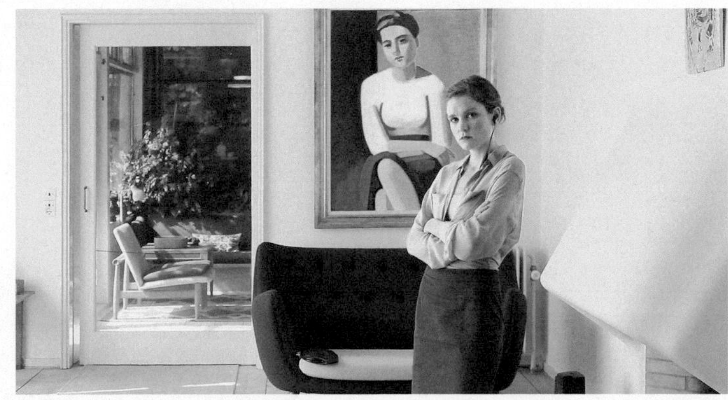

[27]

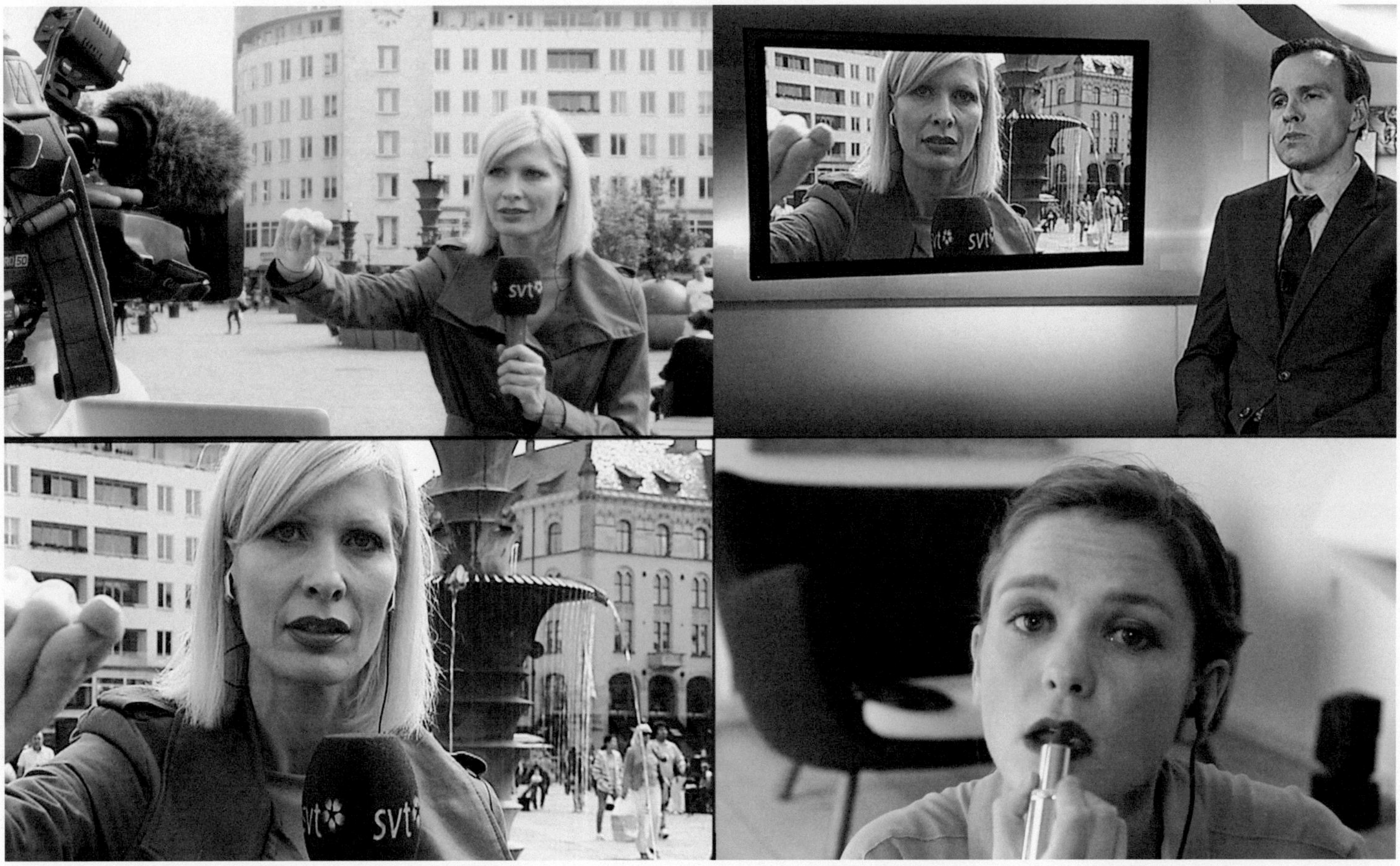

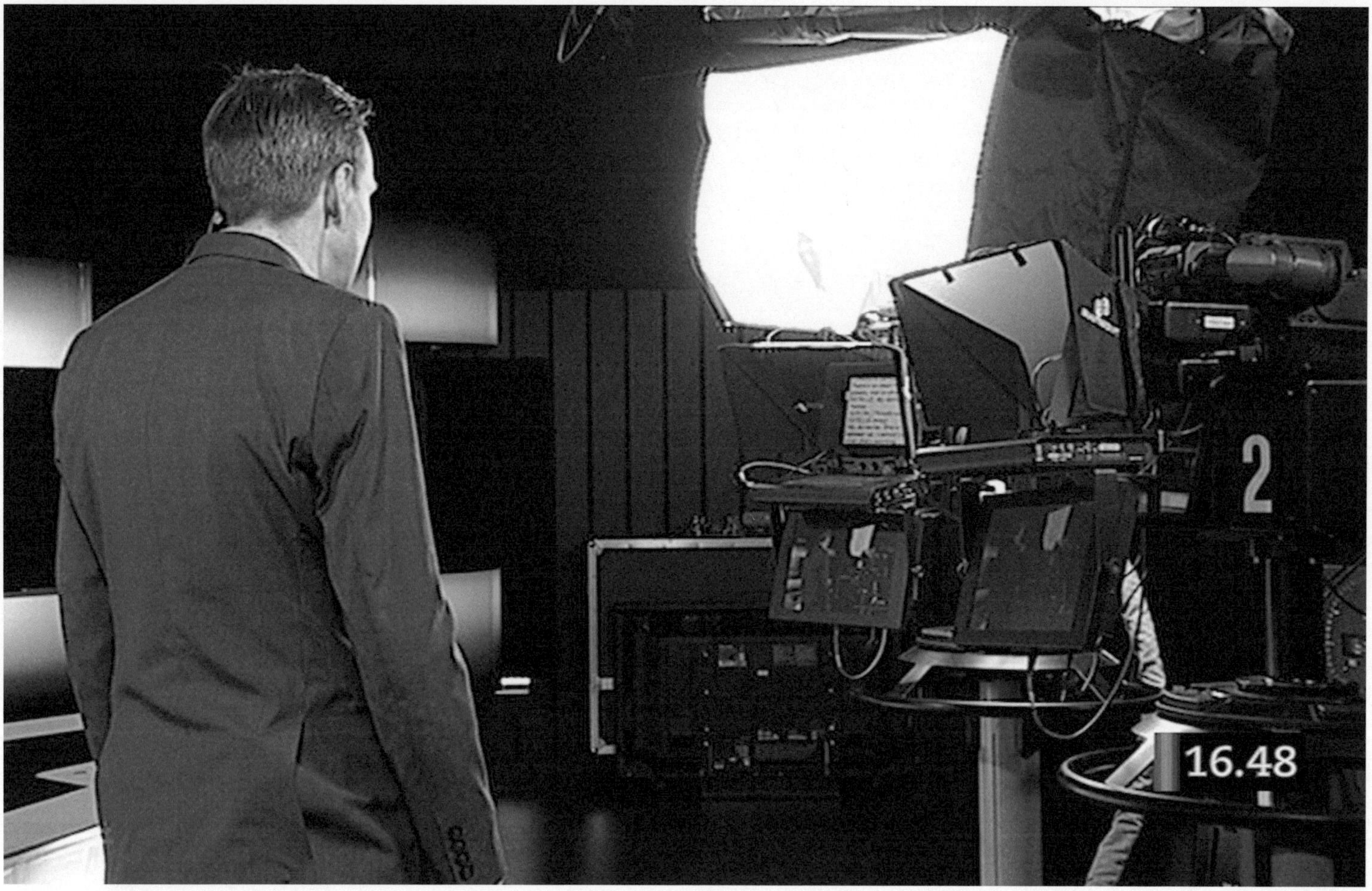

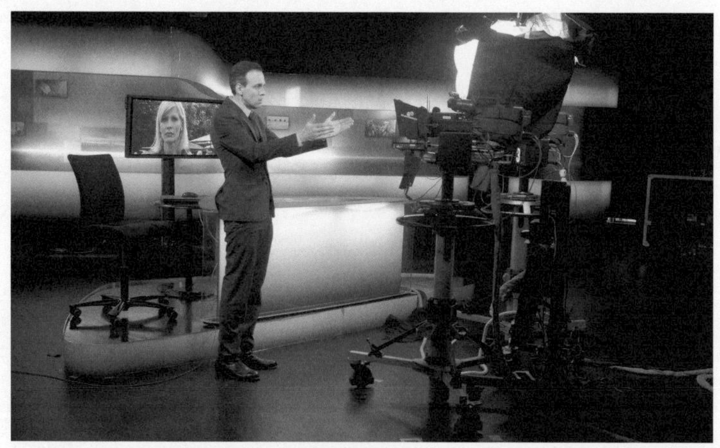

[29]

[30]

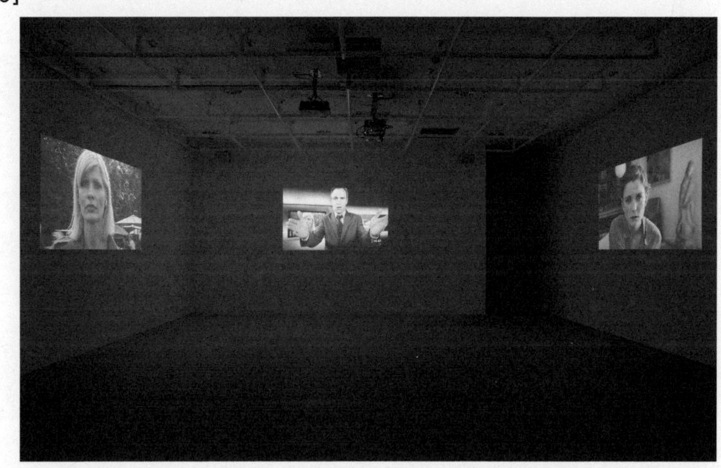

[31]

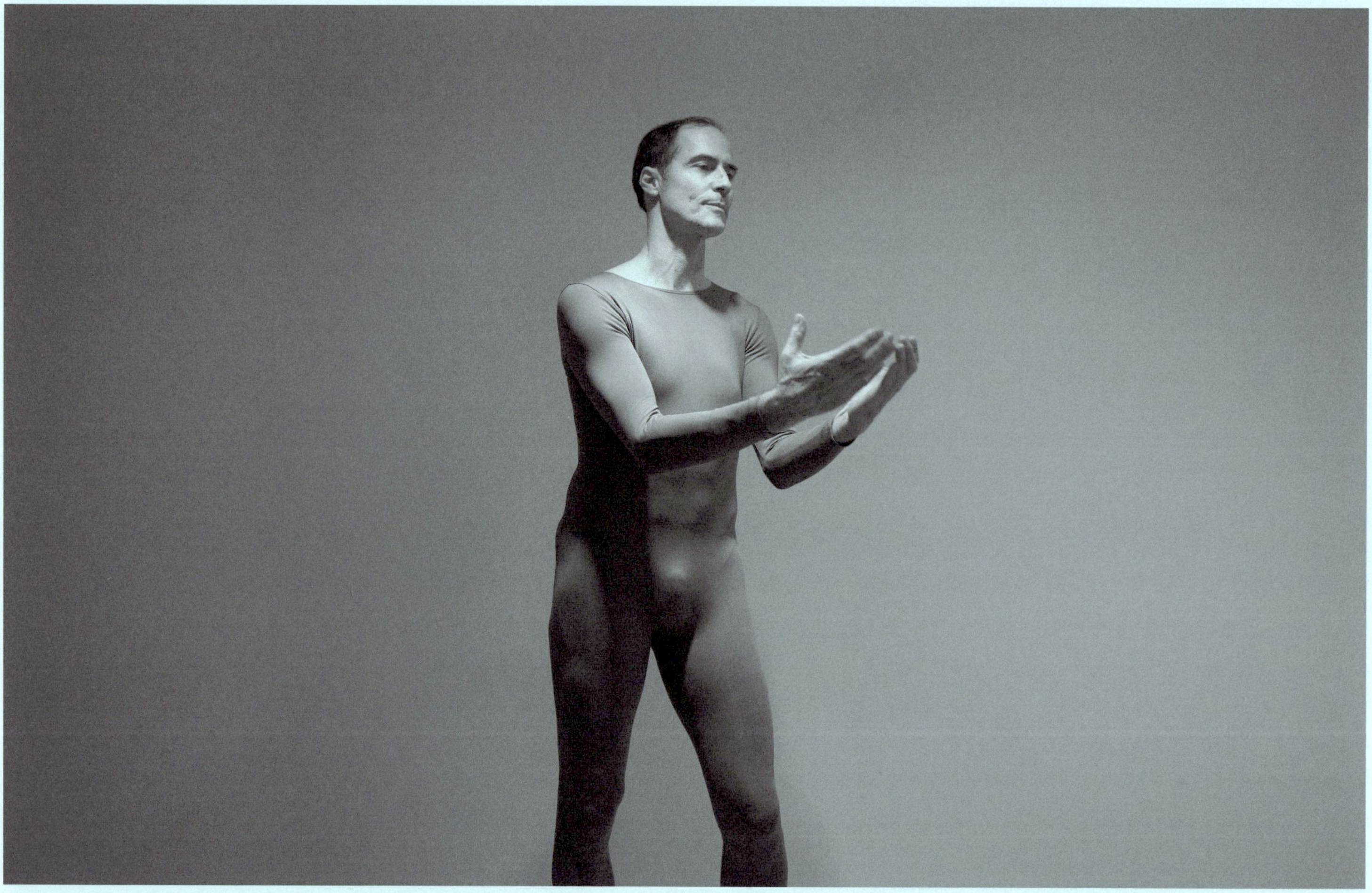

[32]

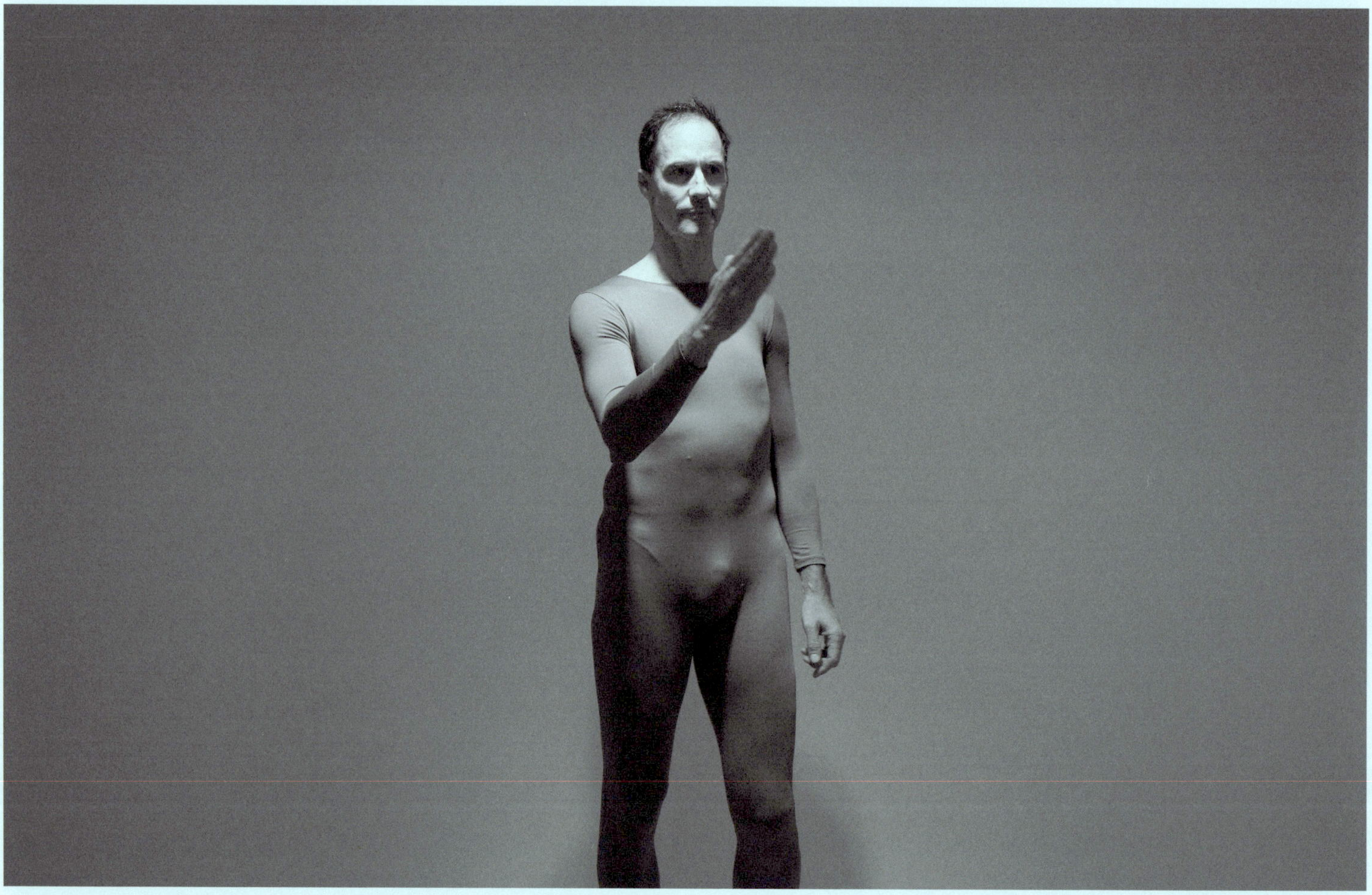

[33] [34]

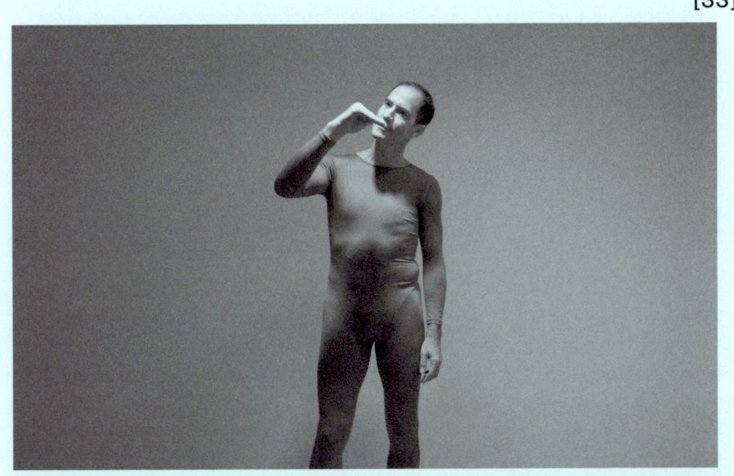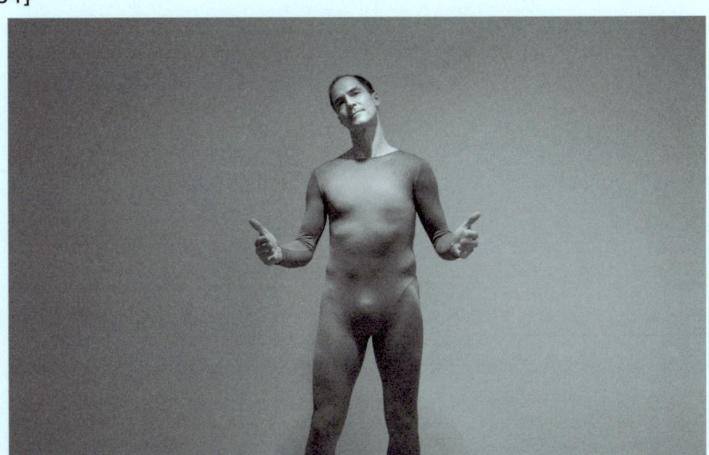

[35] [36]

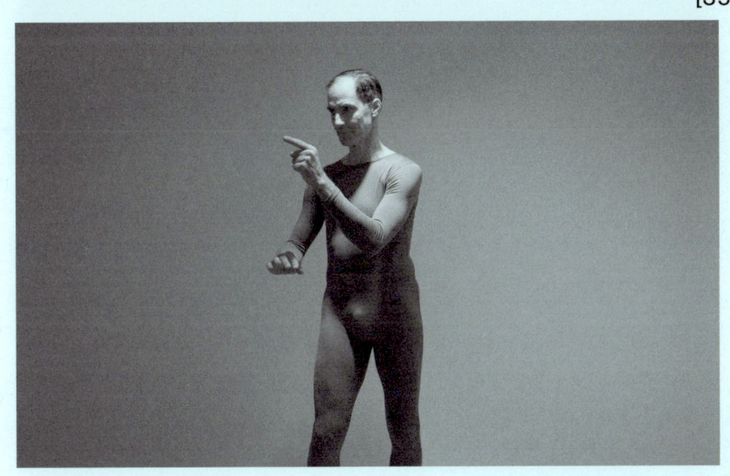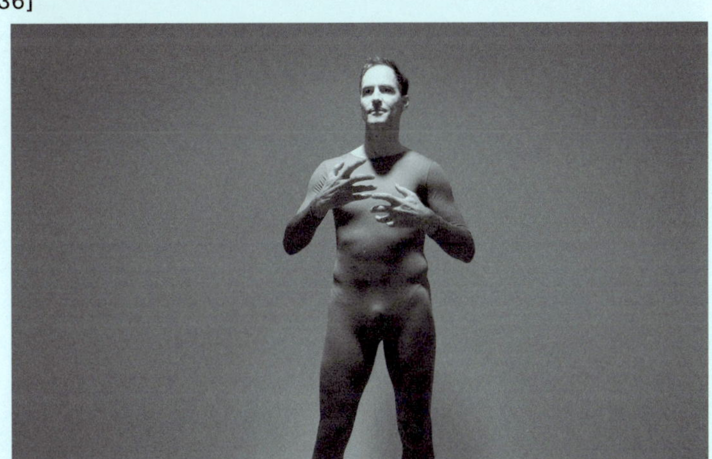

[37]

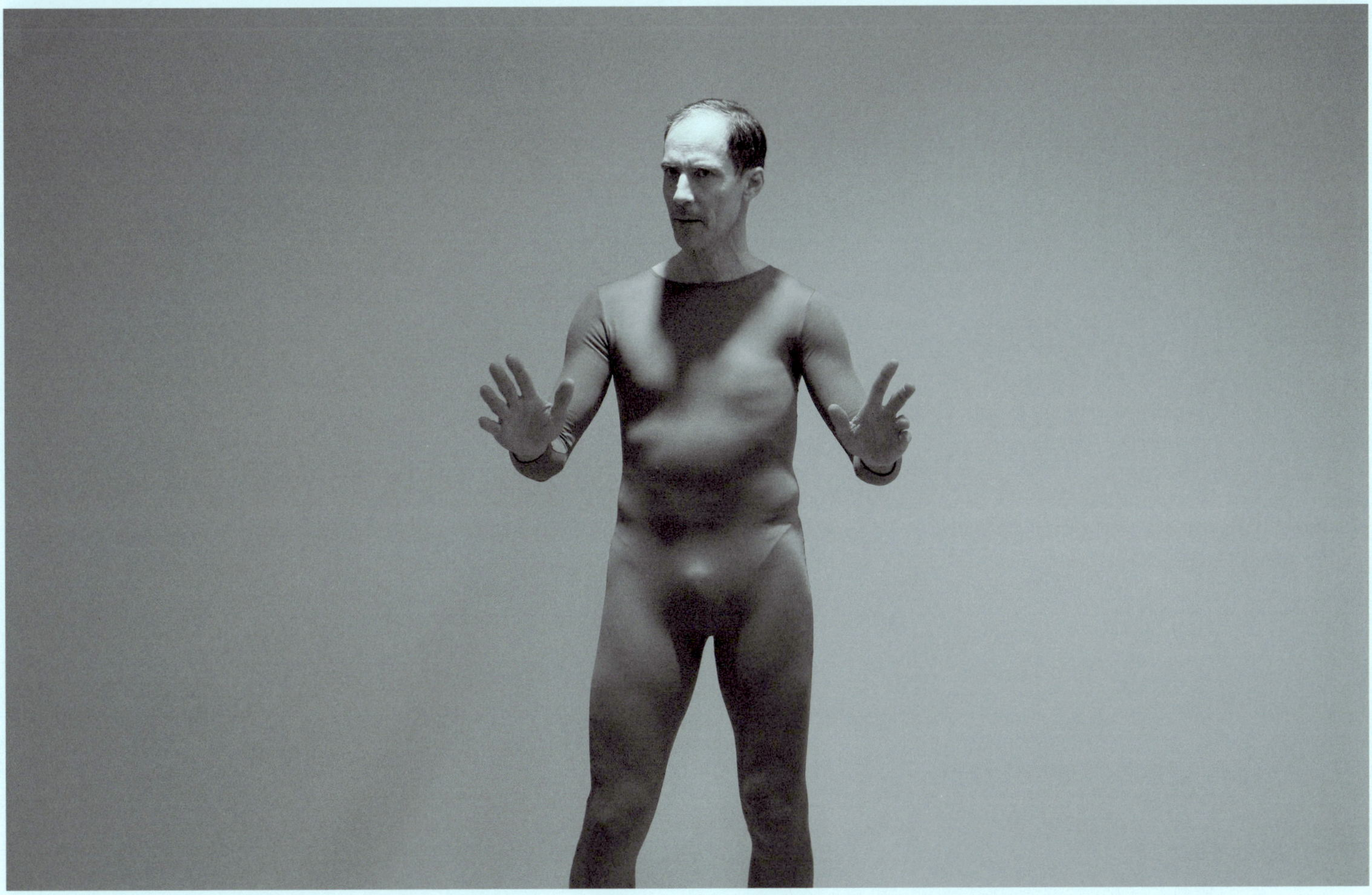

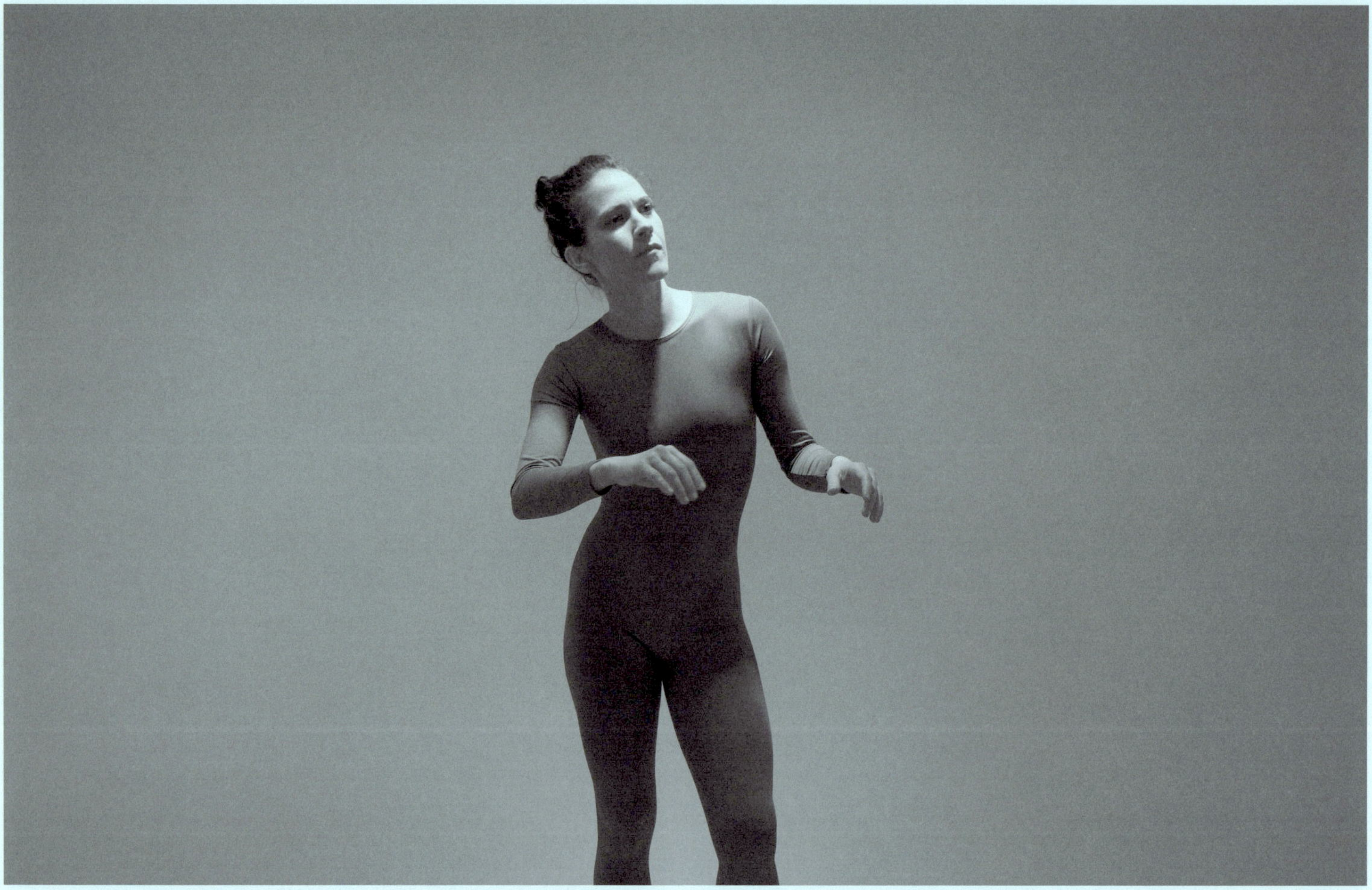

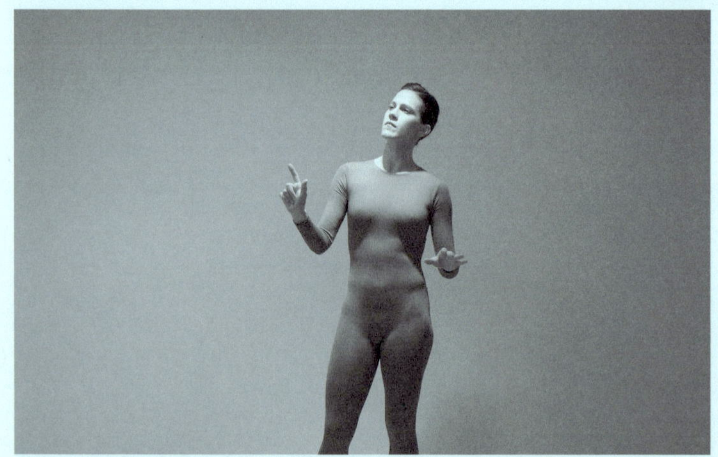

[39] [40]

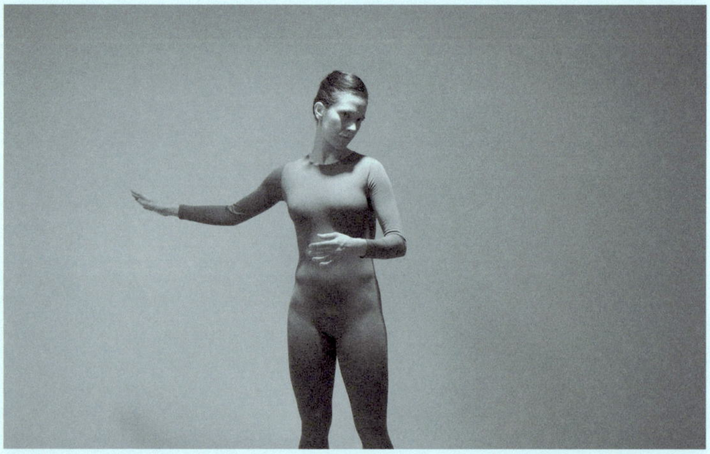

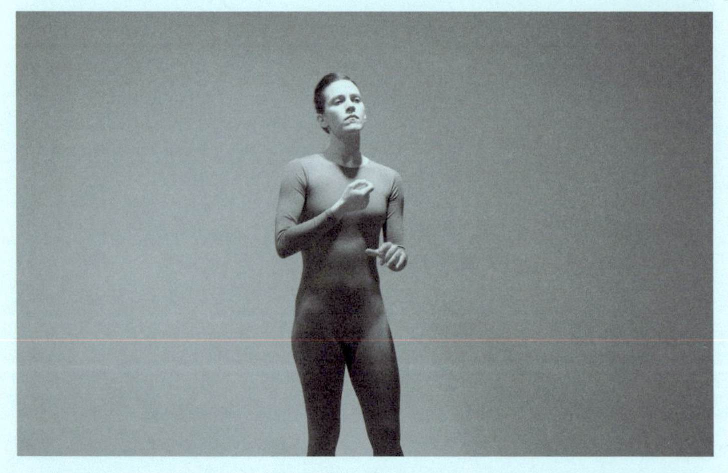

[41] [42]

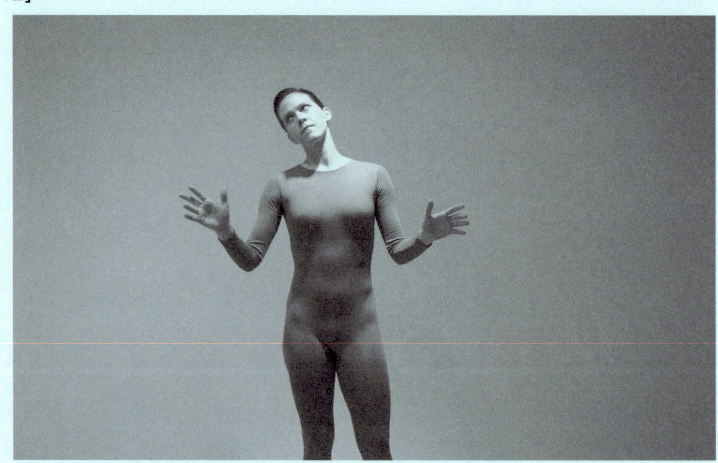

[43]

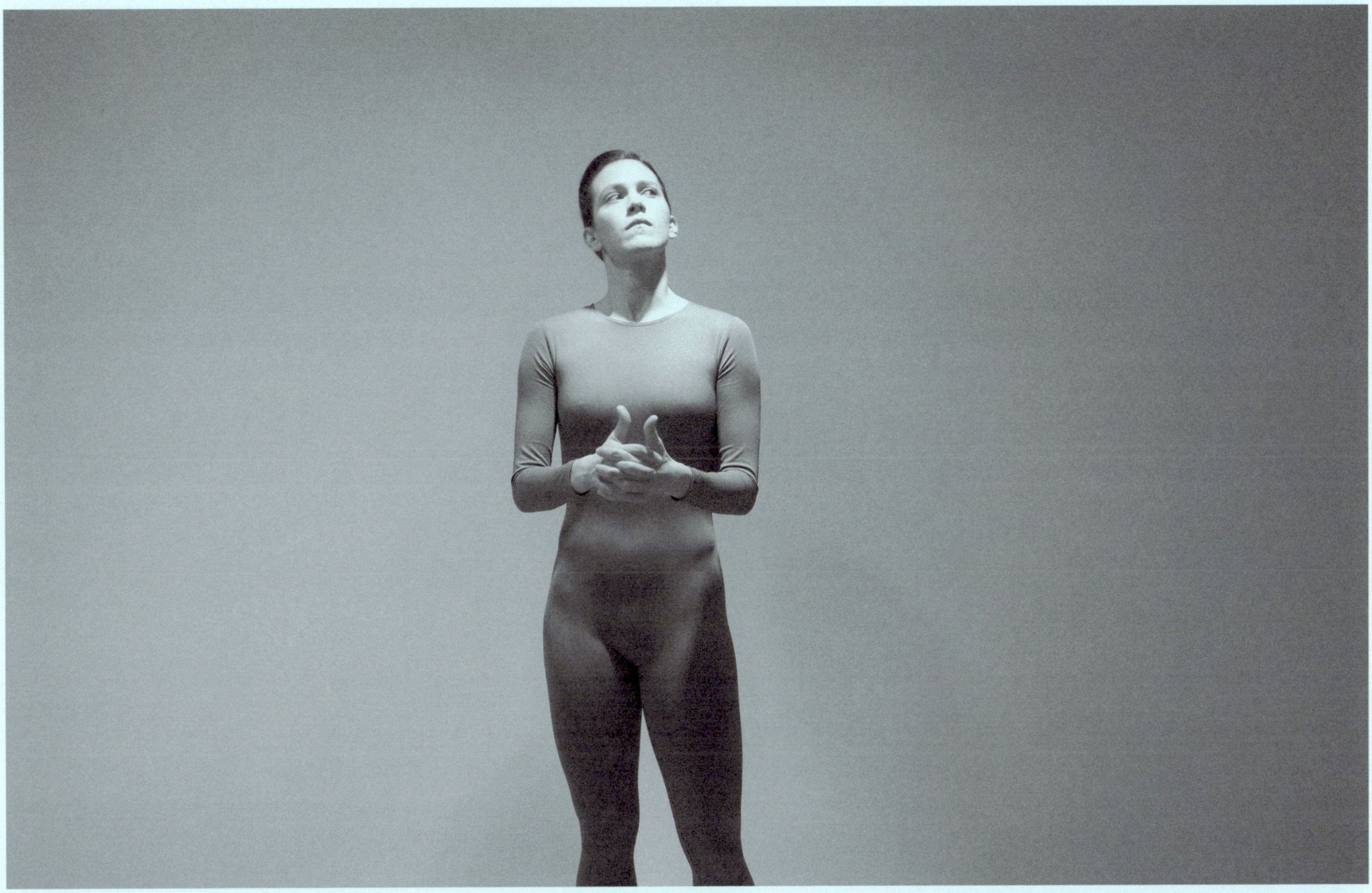

[44]

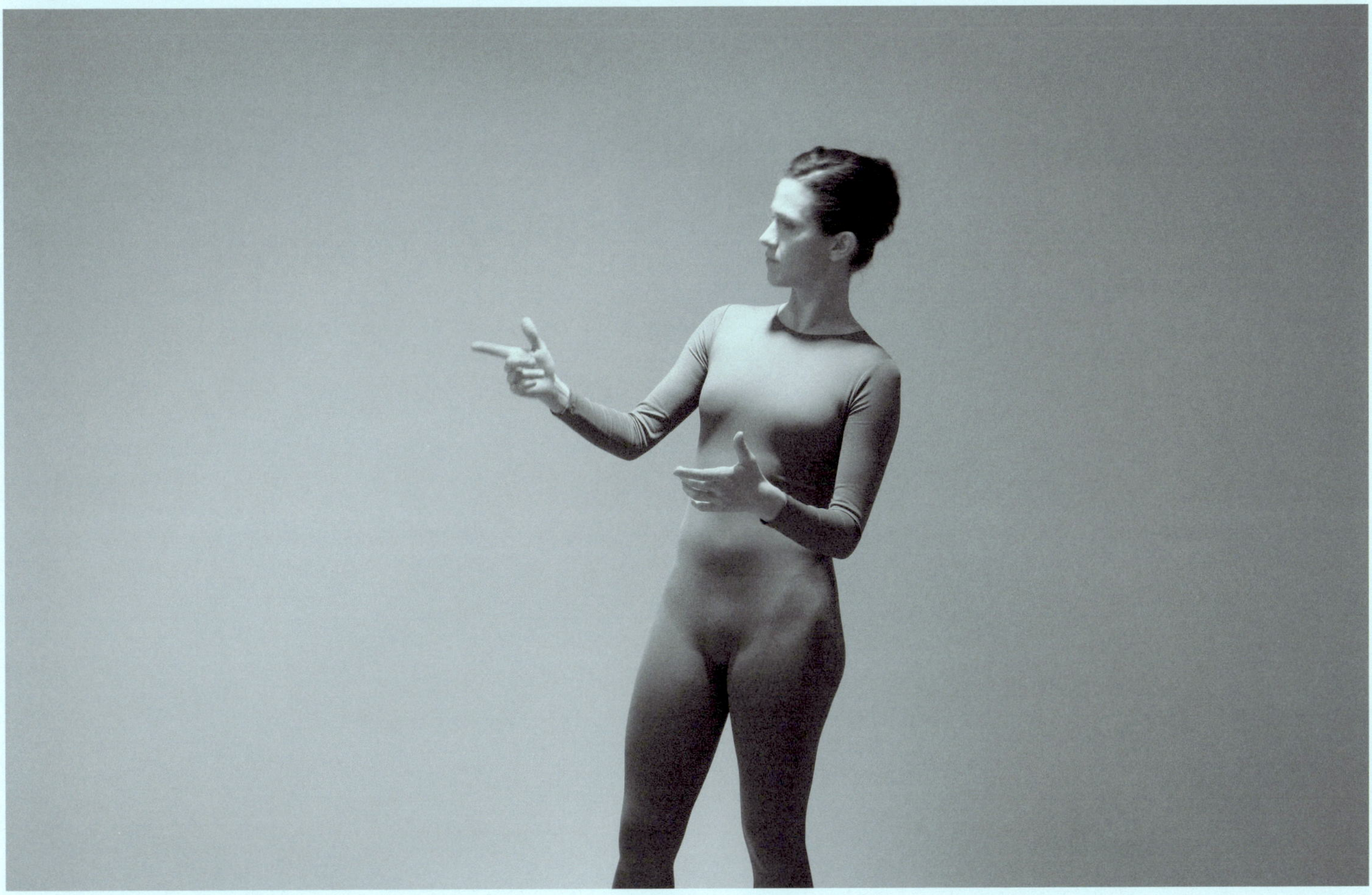

[45]

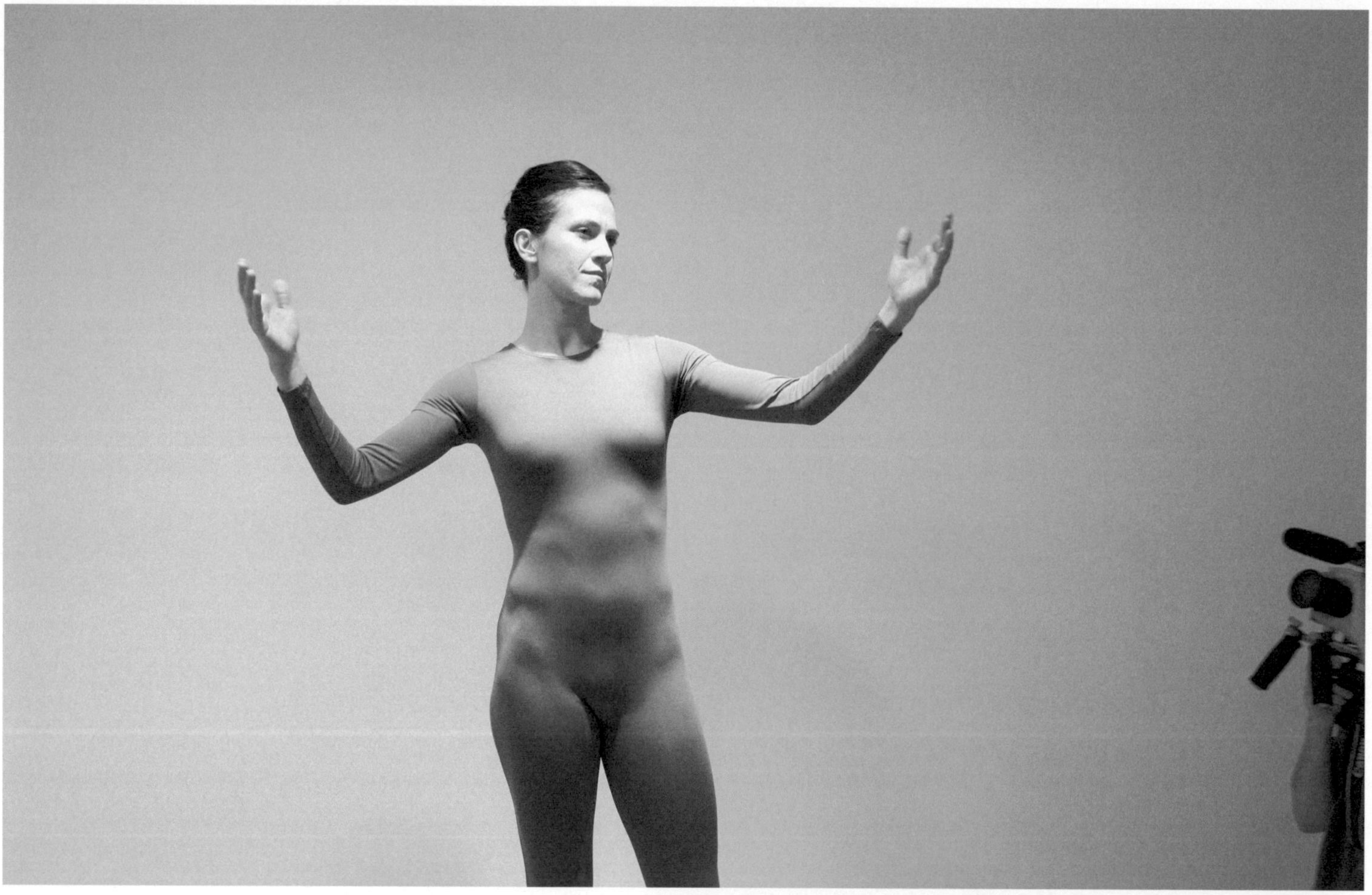

[46]

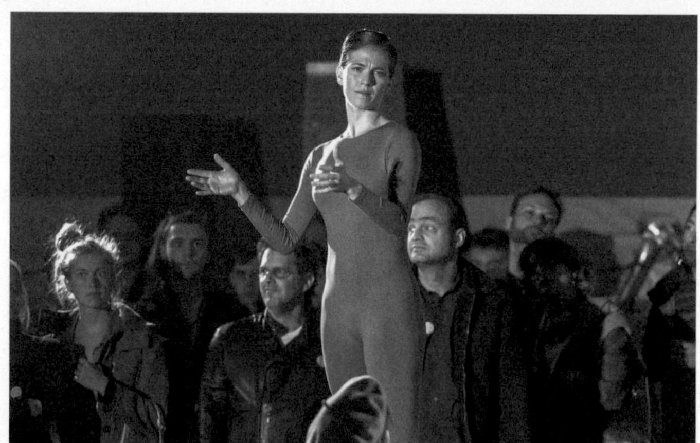

[47]

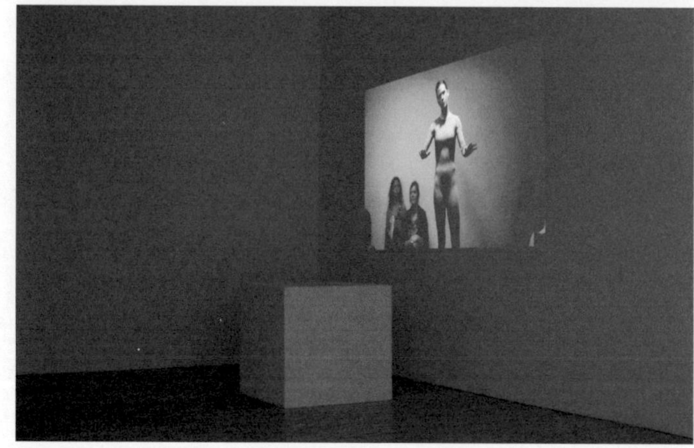

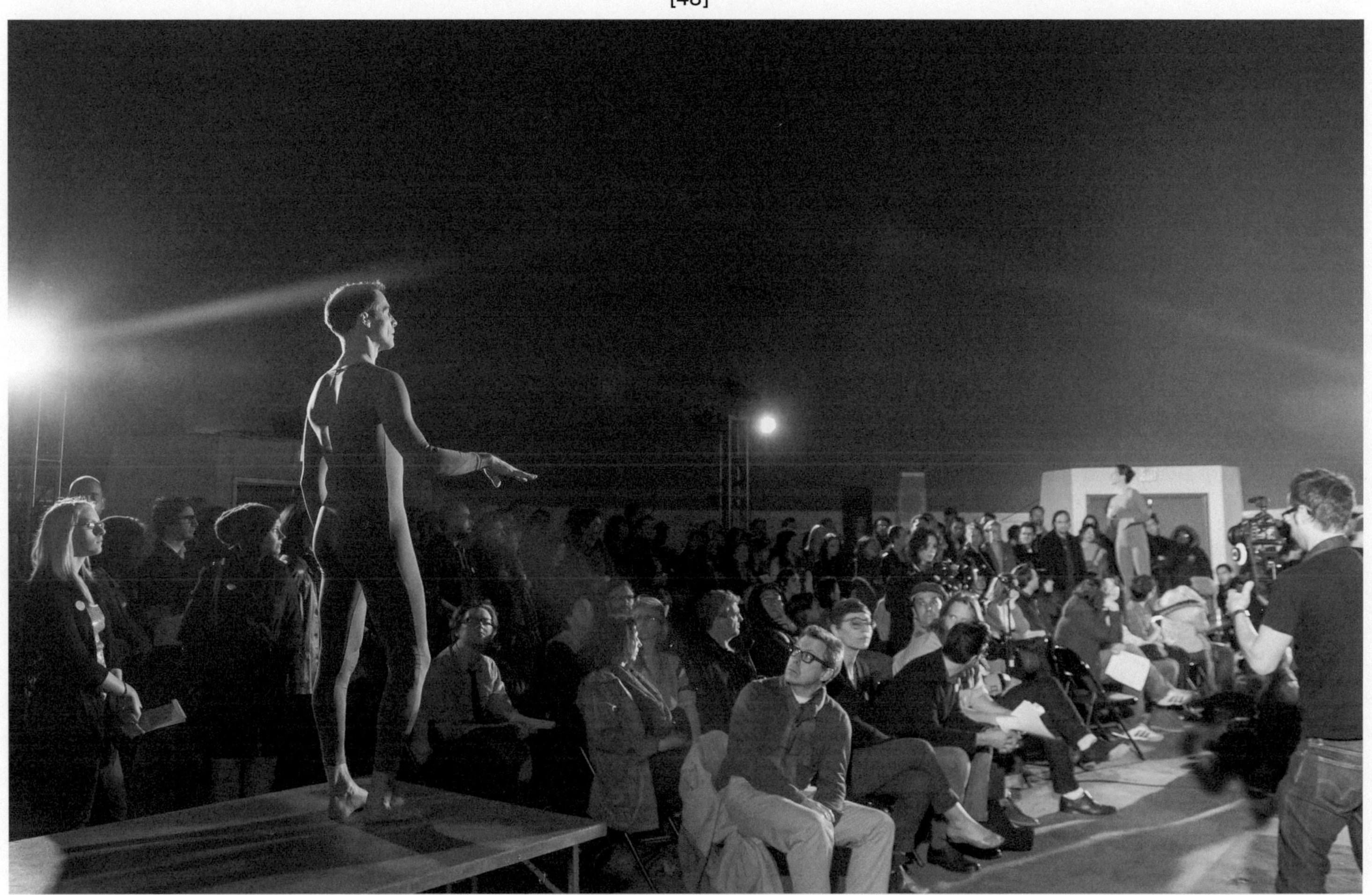

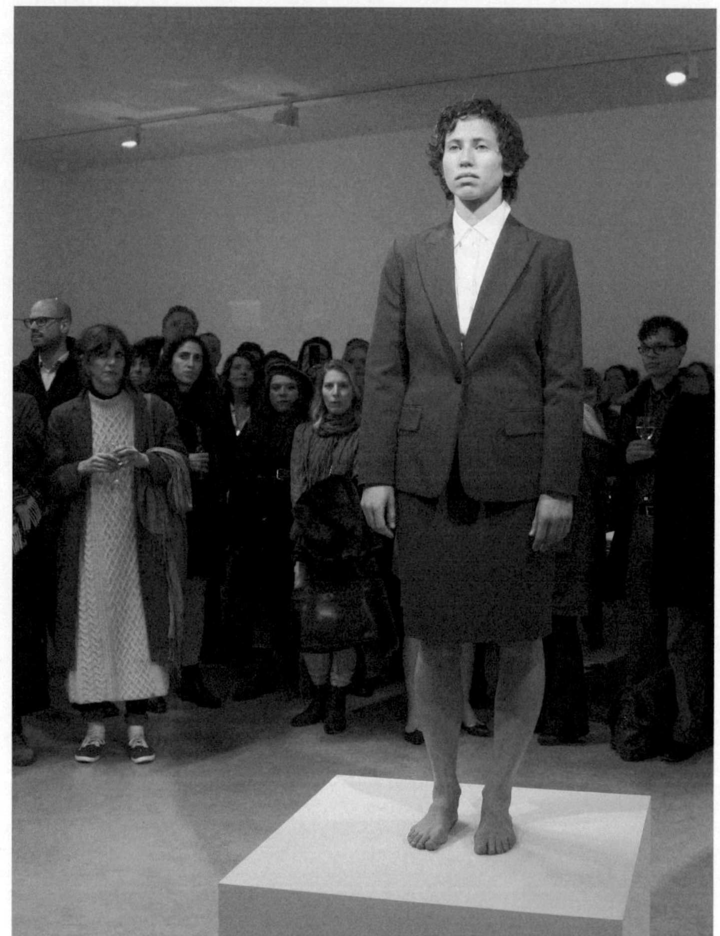

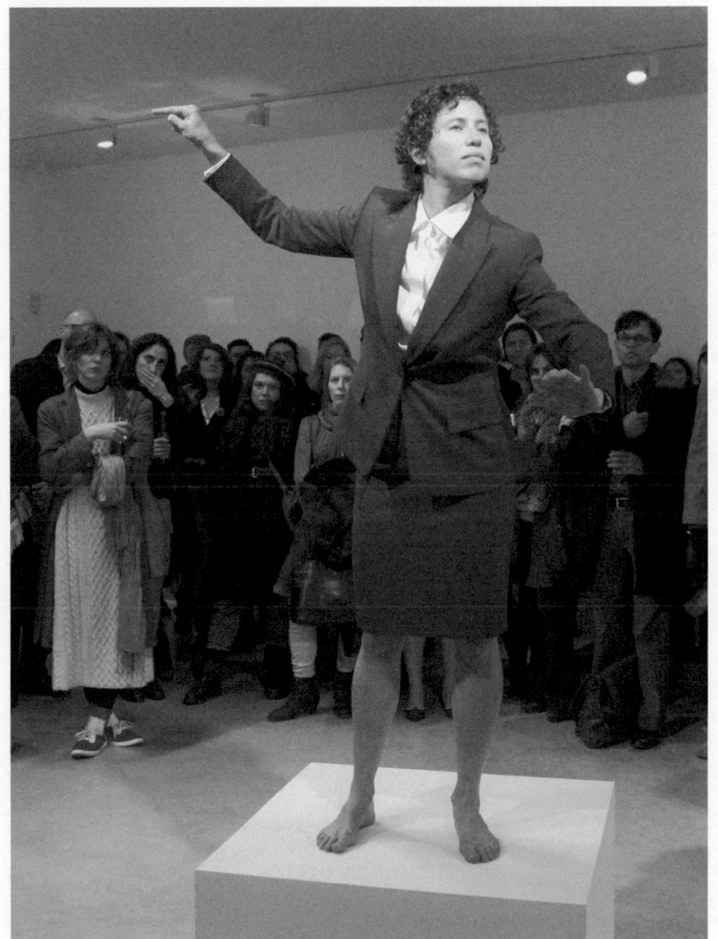

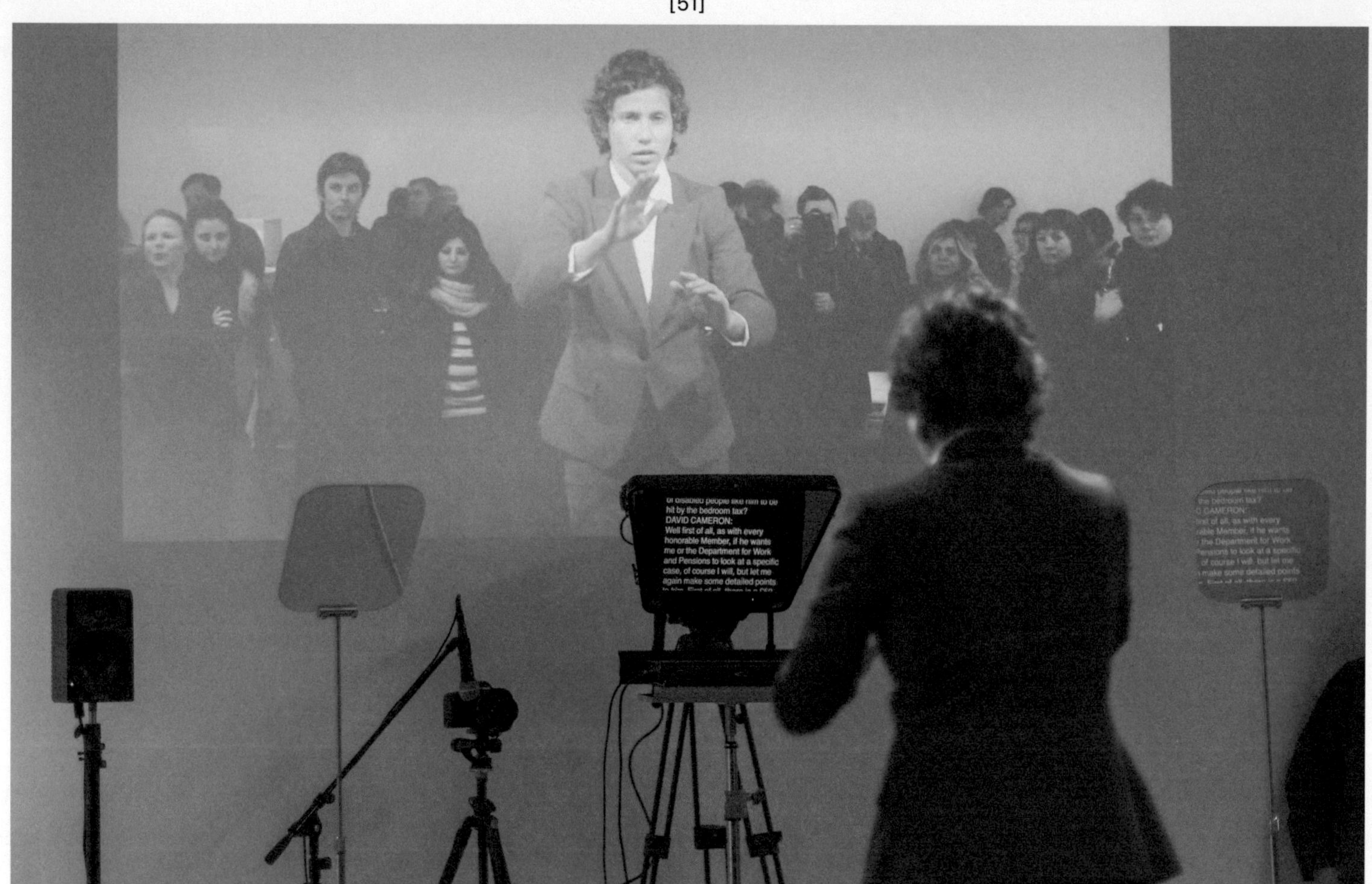
of disabled people like him to be
hit by the bedroom tax?
DAVID CAMERON:
Well first of all, as with every
honorable Member, if he wants
me or the Department for Work
and Pensions to look at a specific
case, of course I will, but let me
again make some detailed points.

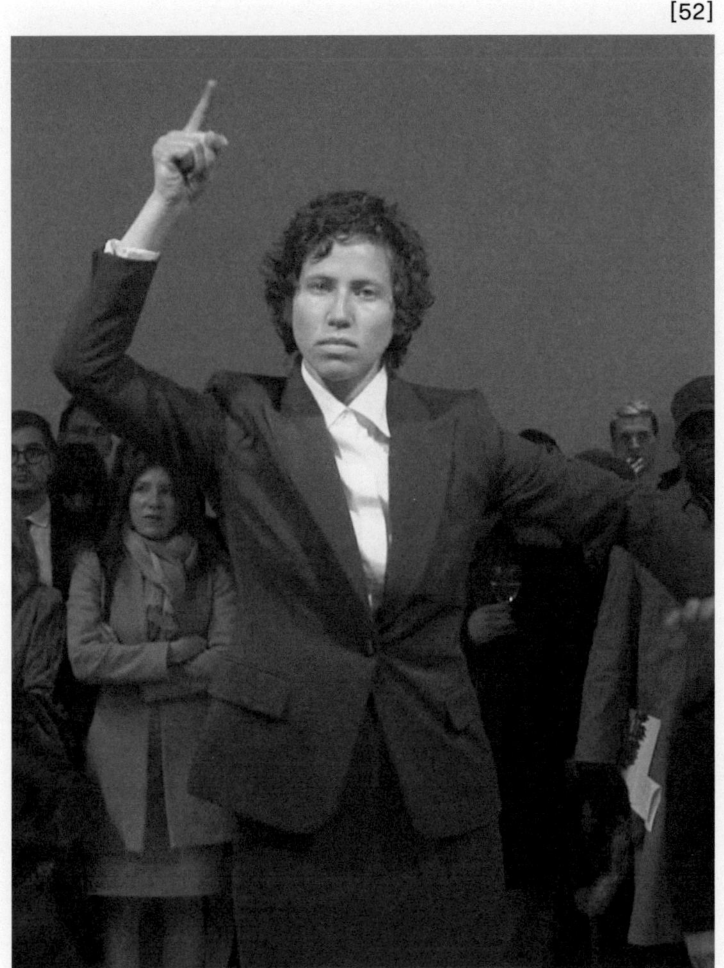

[53]

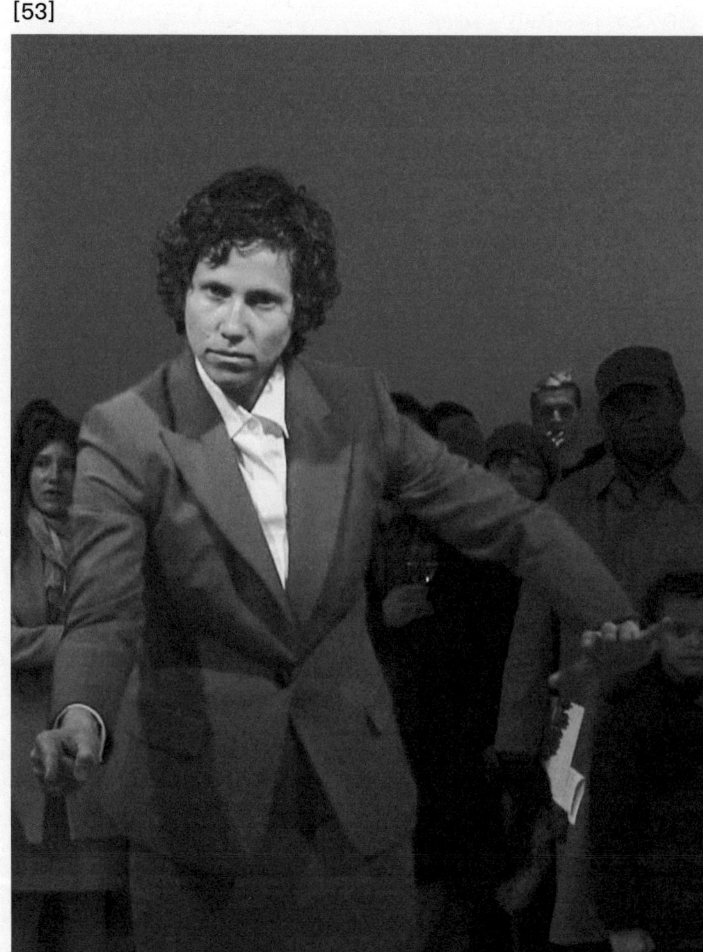

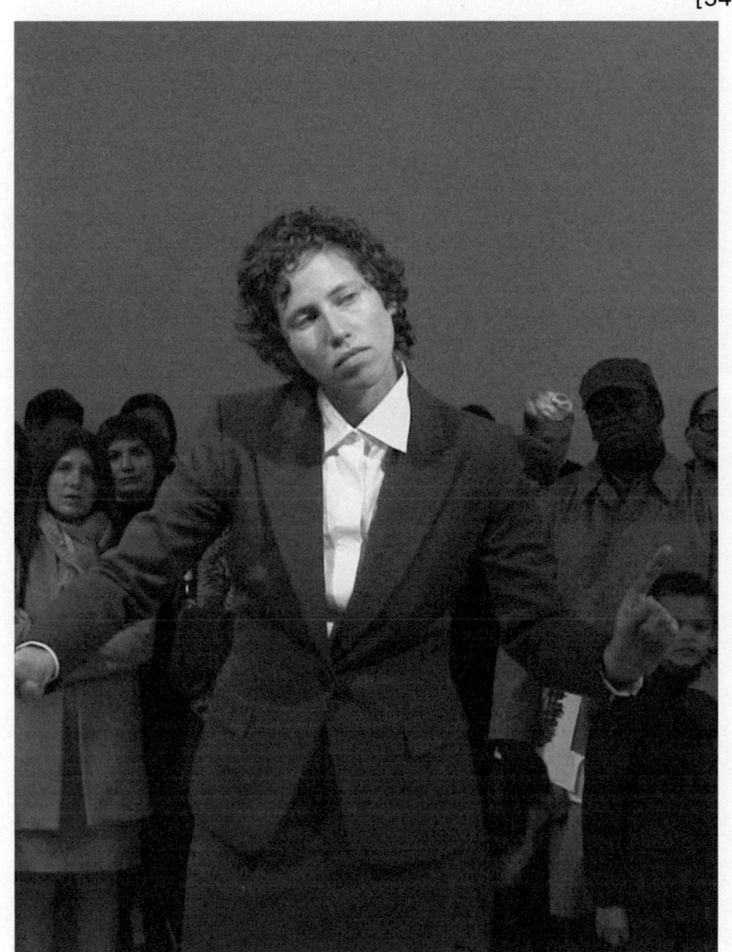 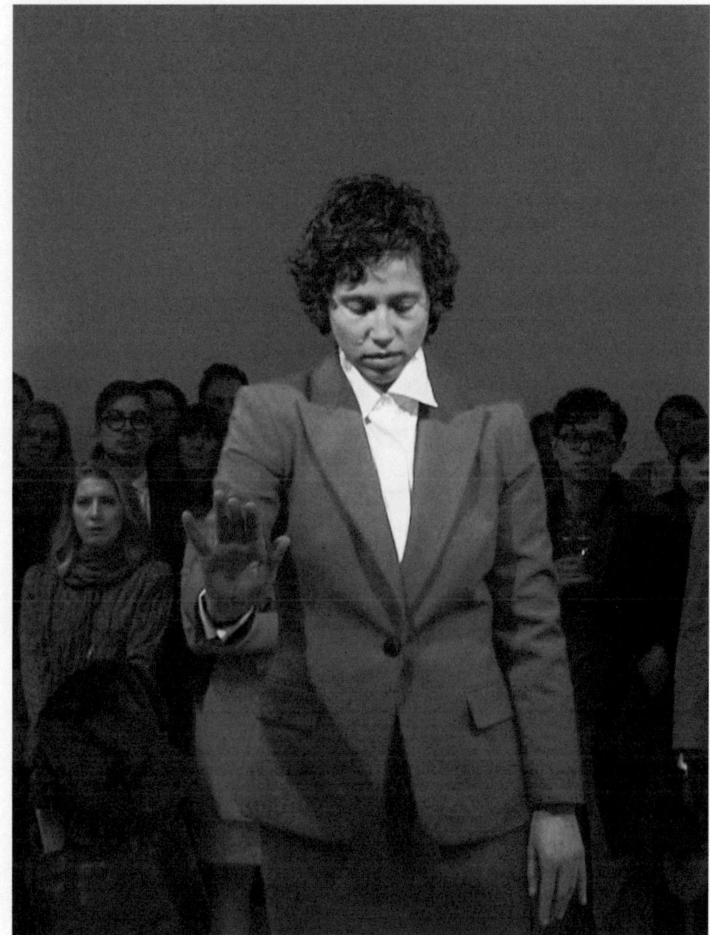

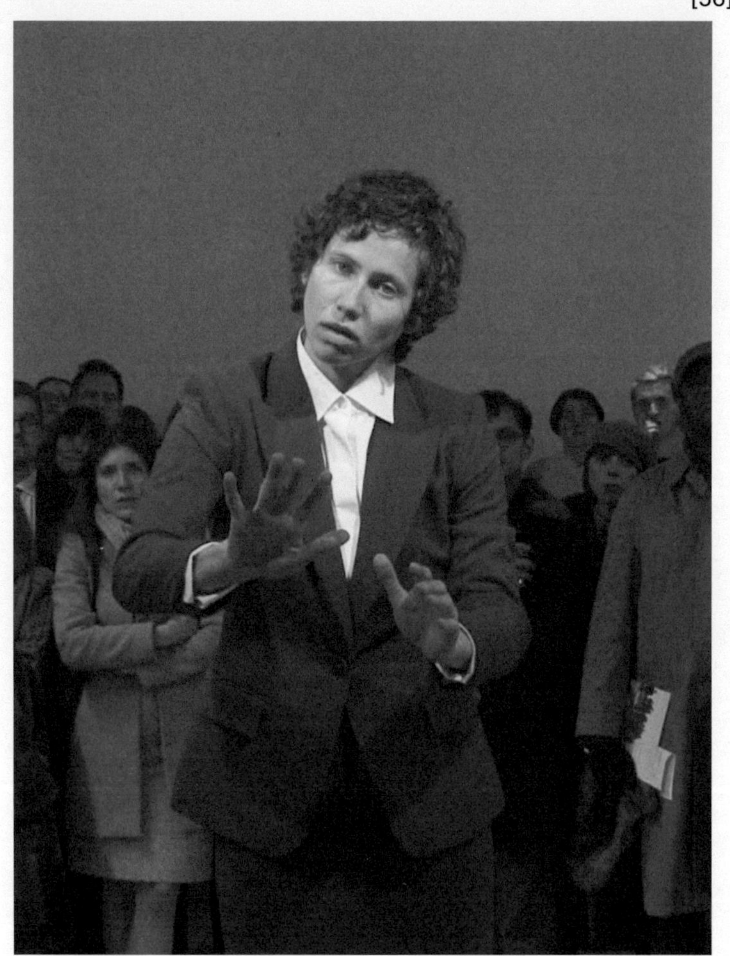 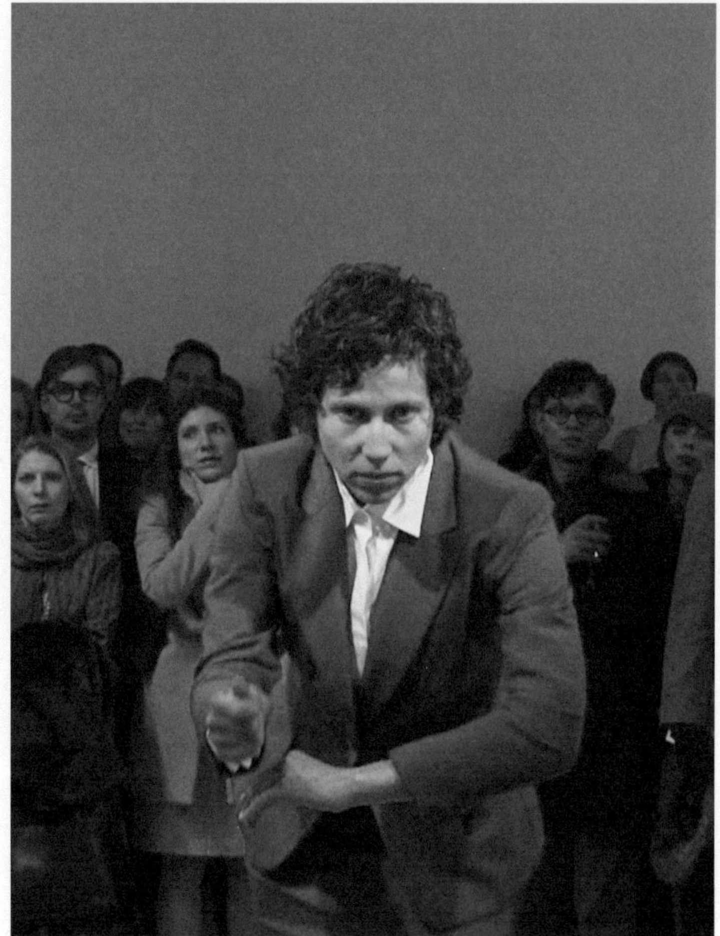

[58] [59]

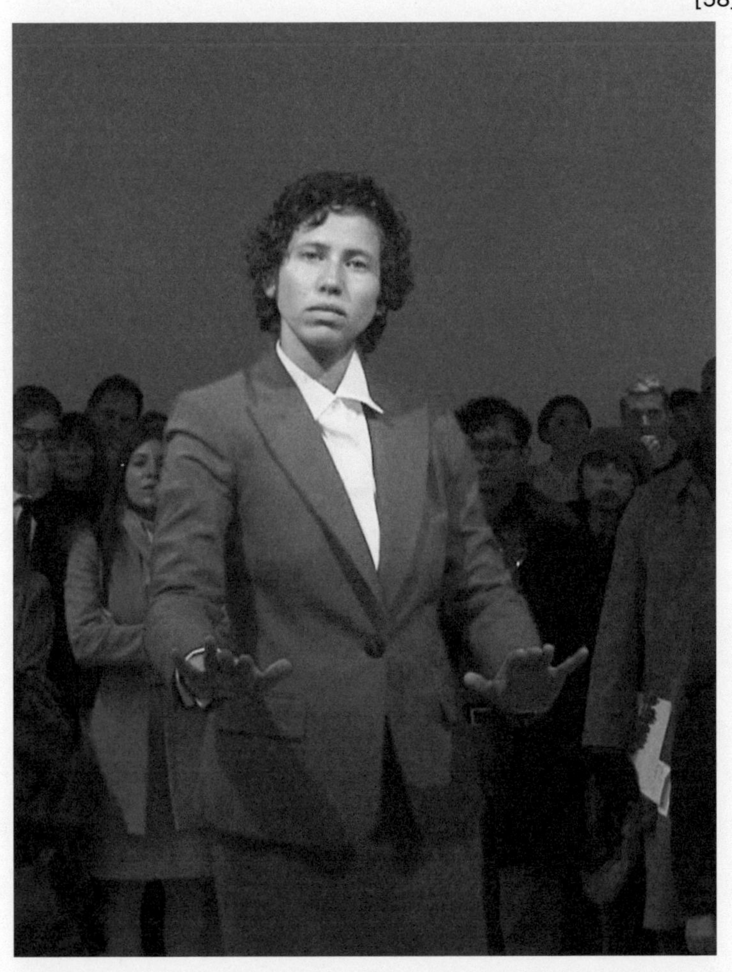 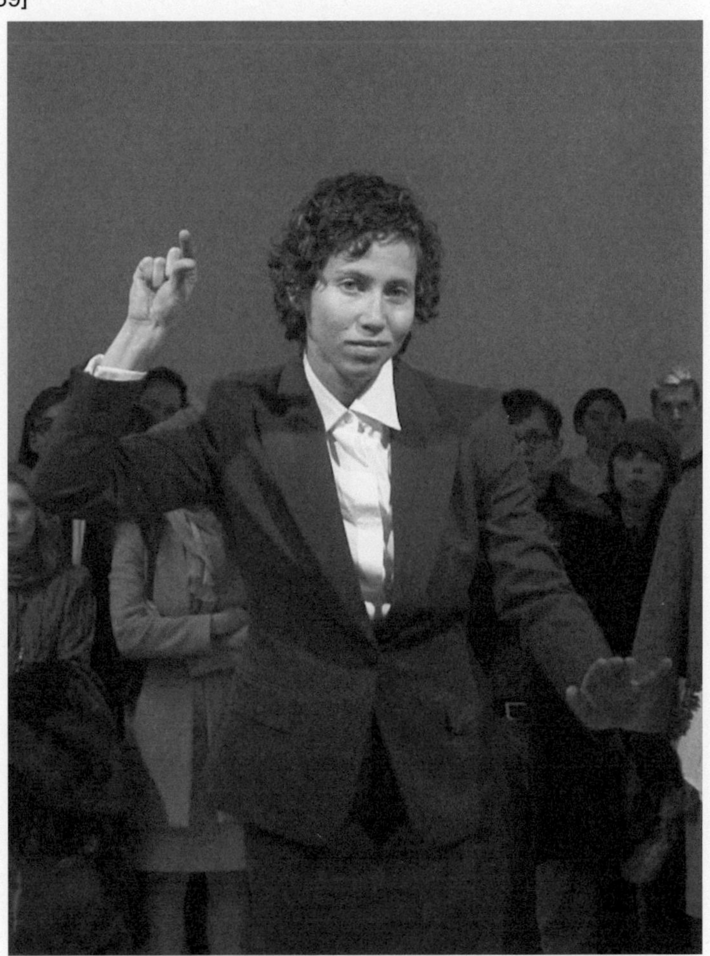

[60]

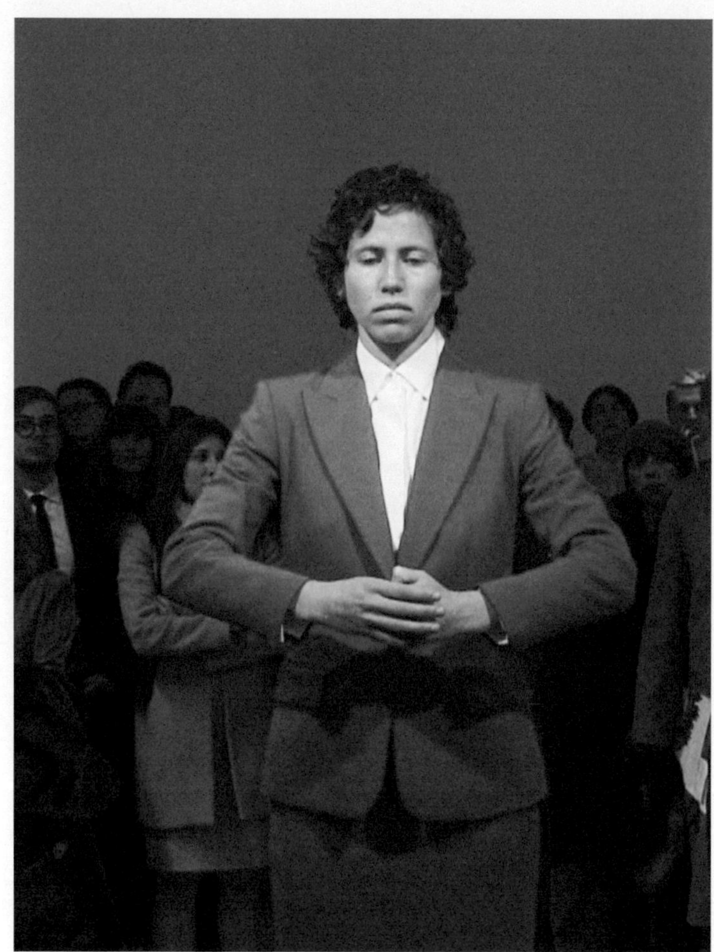

[61]

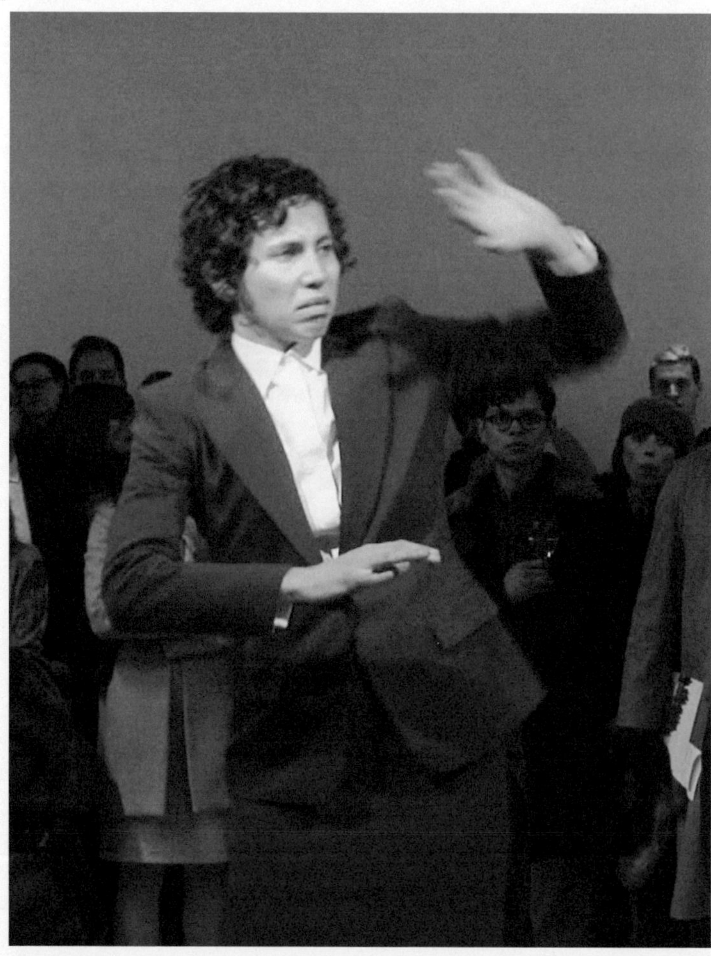

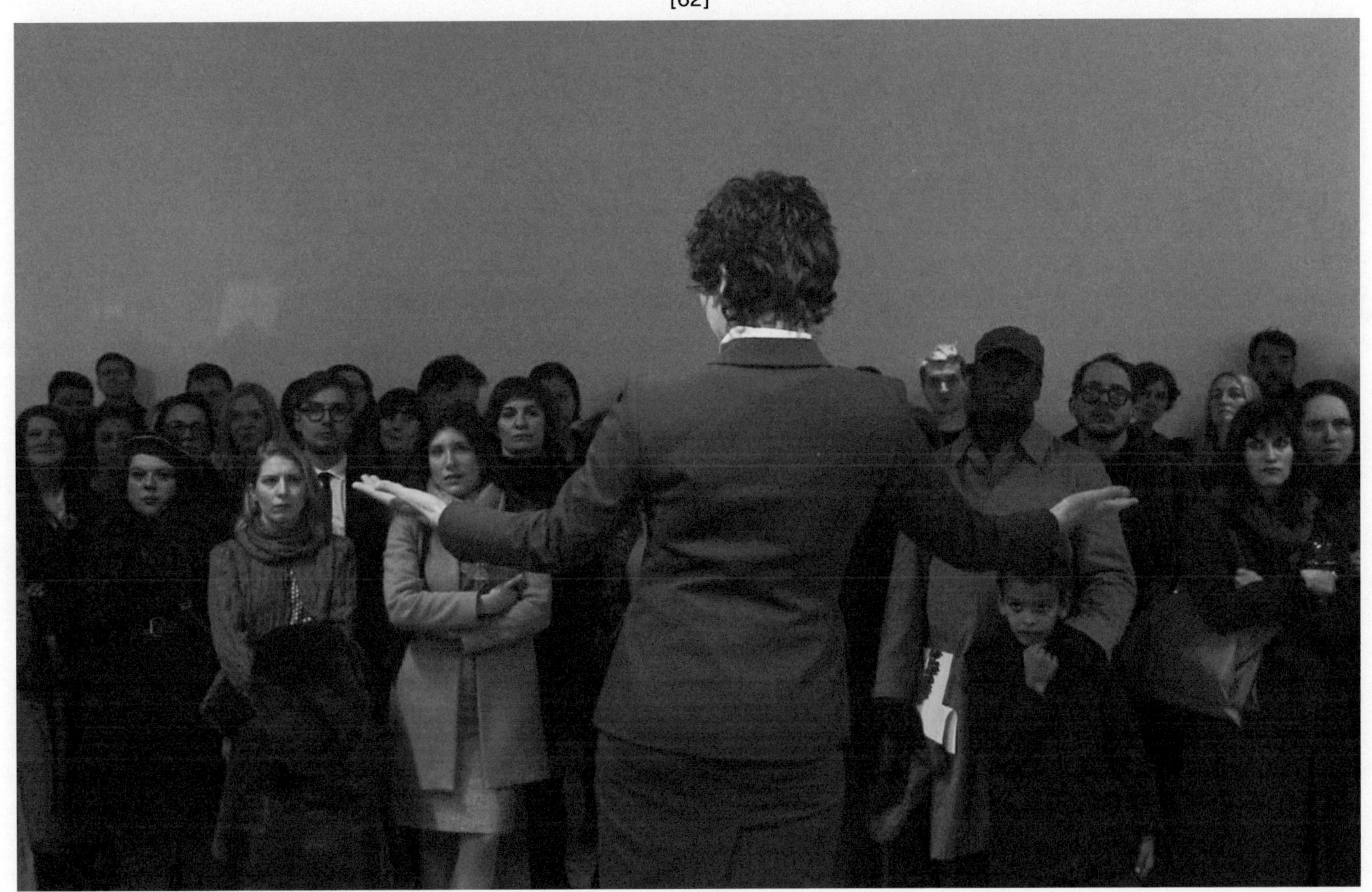

[63]

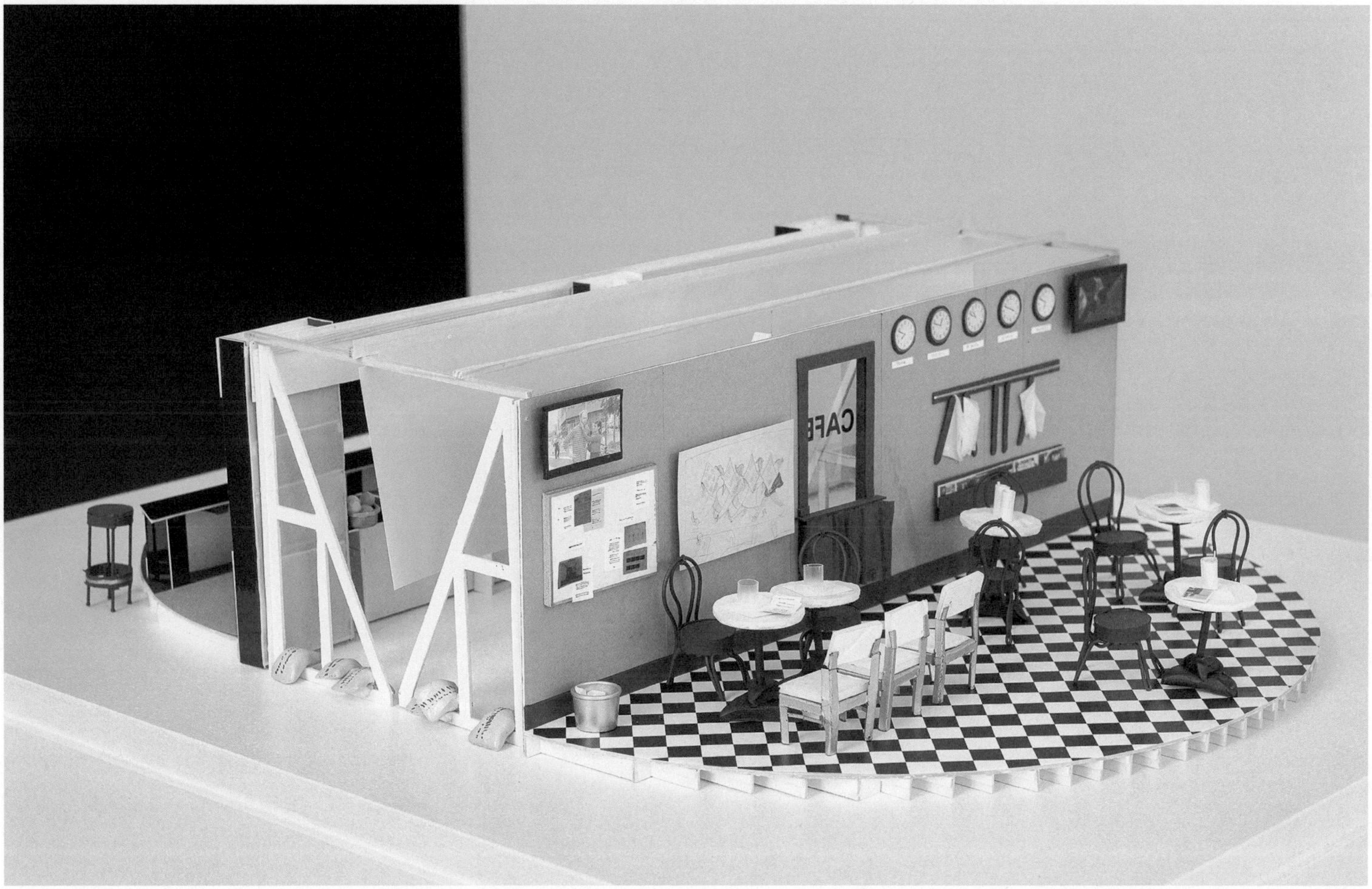

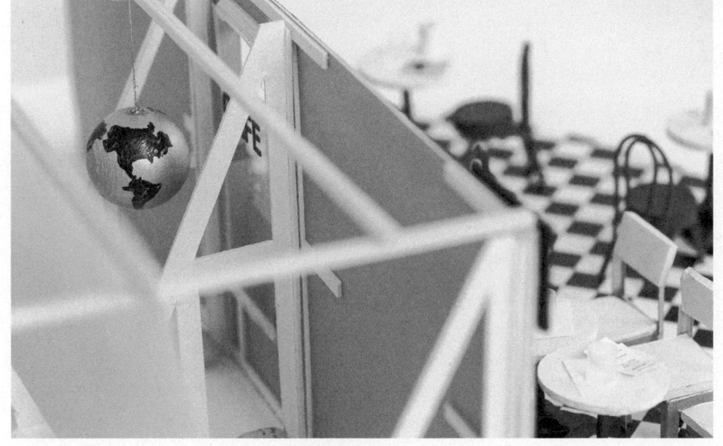

[64]

[65]

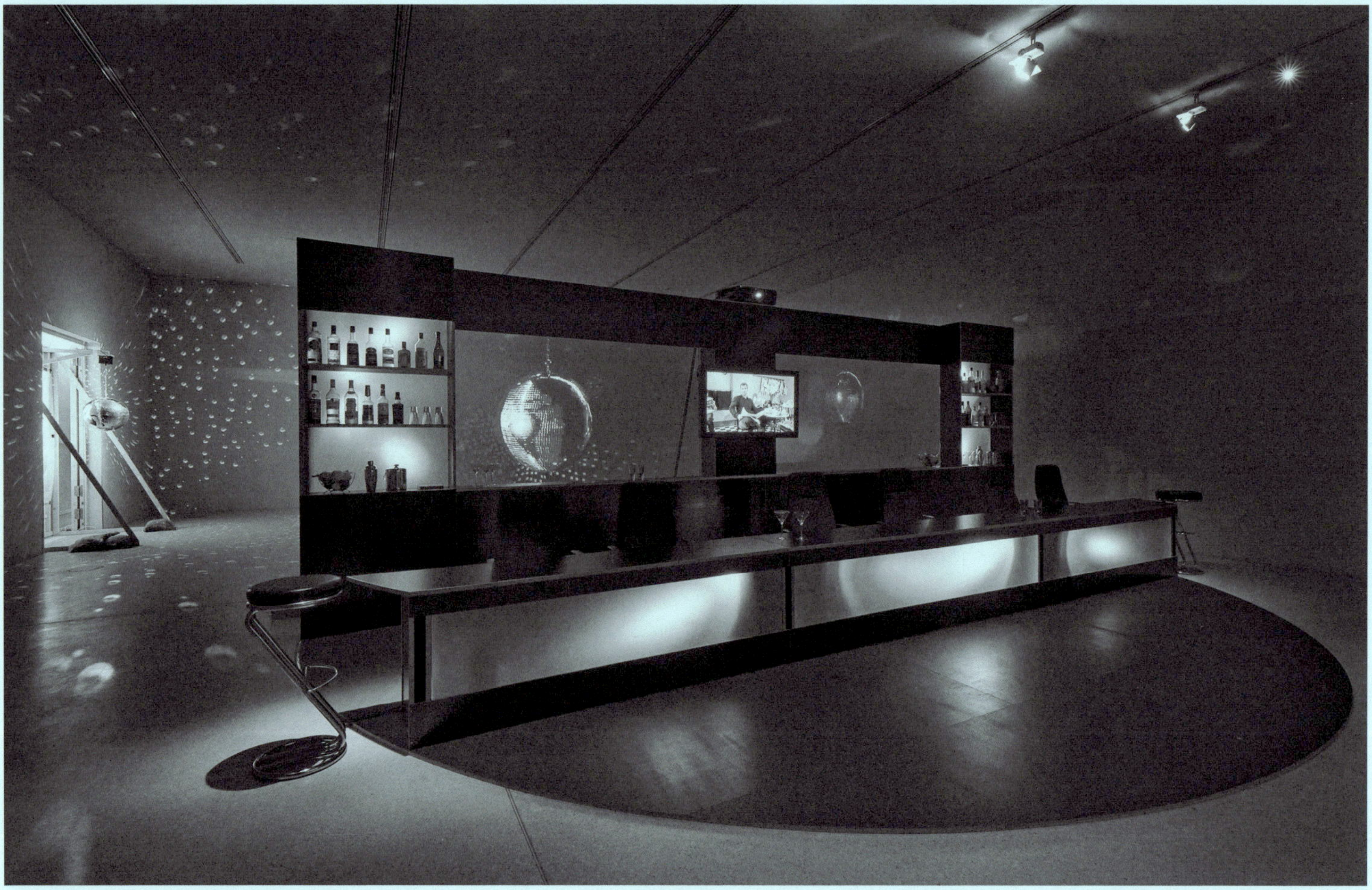

[66]

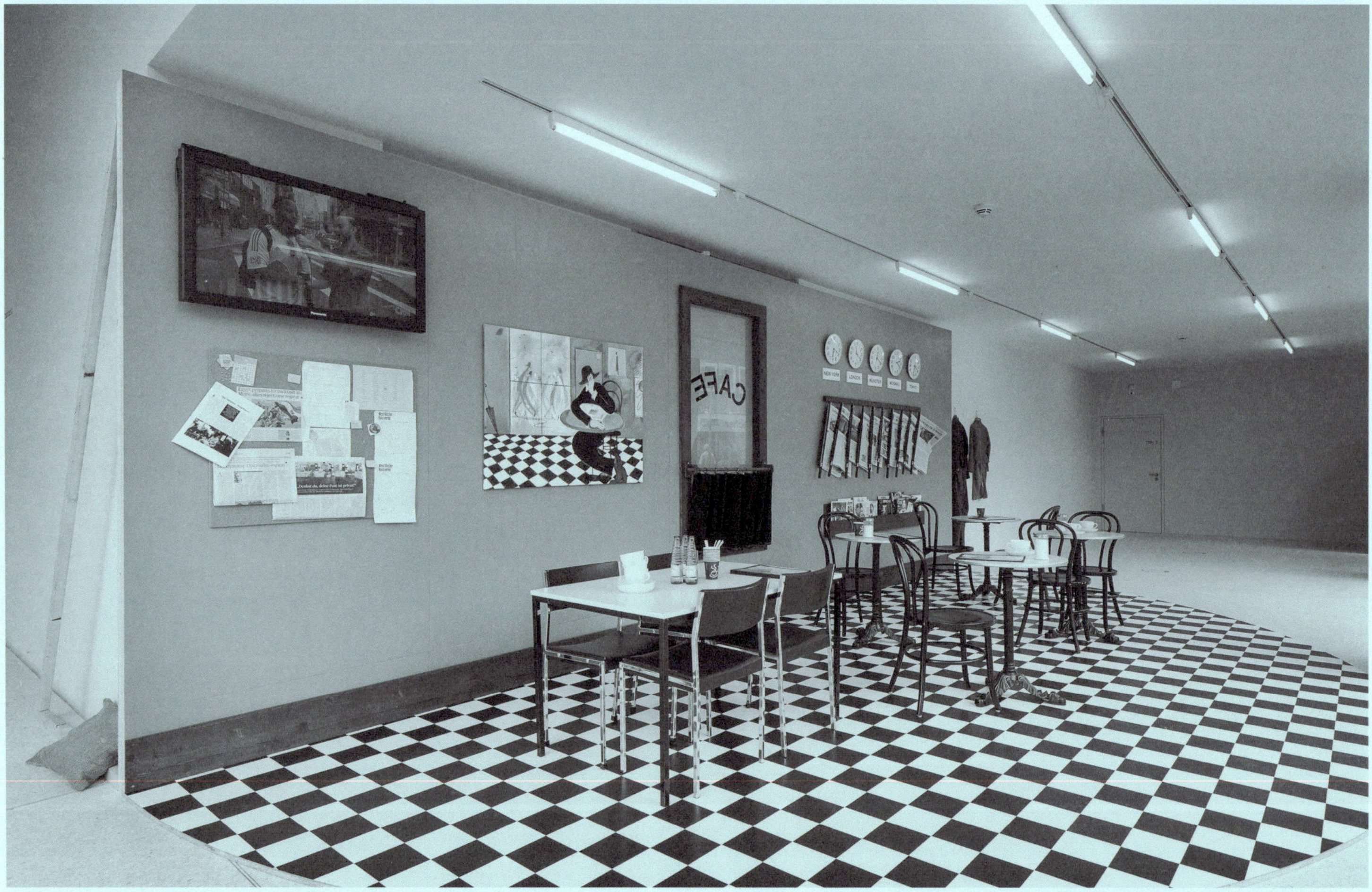

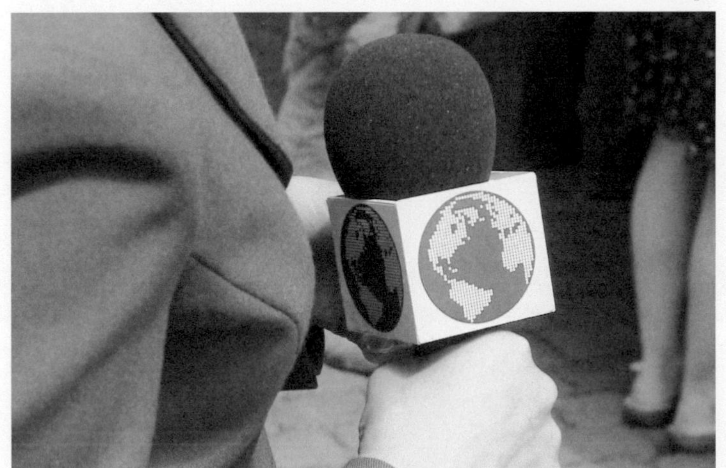 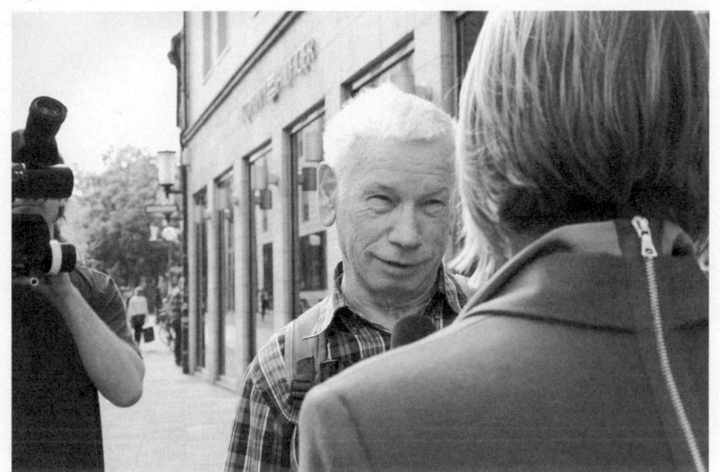

[69] [70]

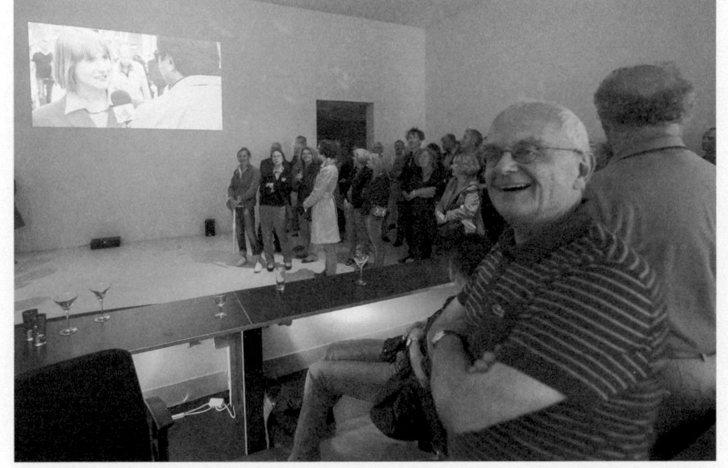 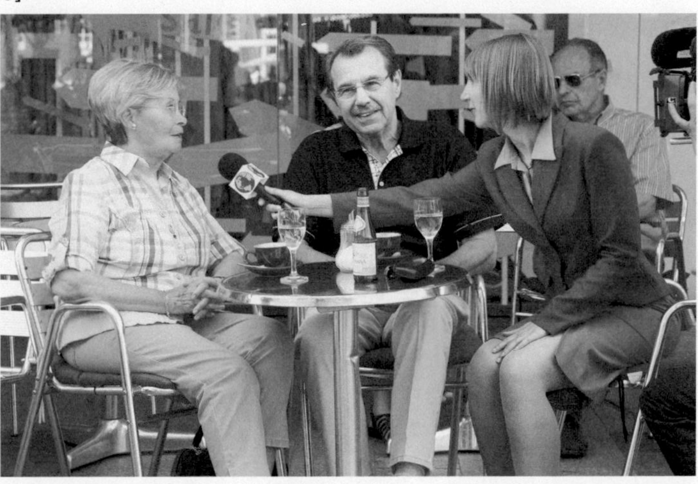

[71]

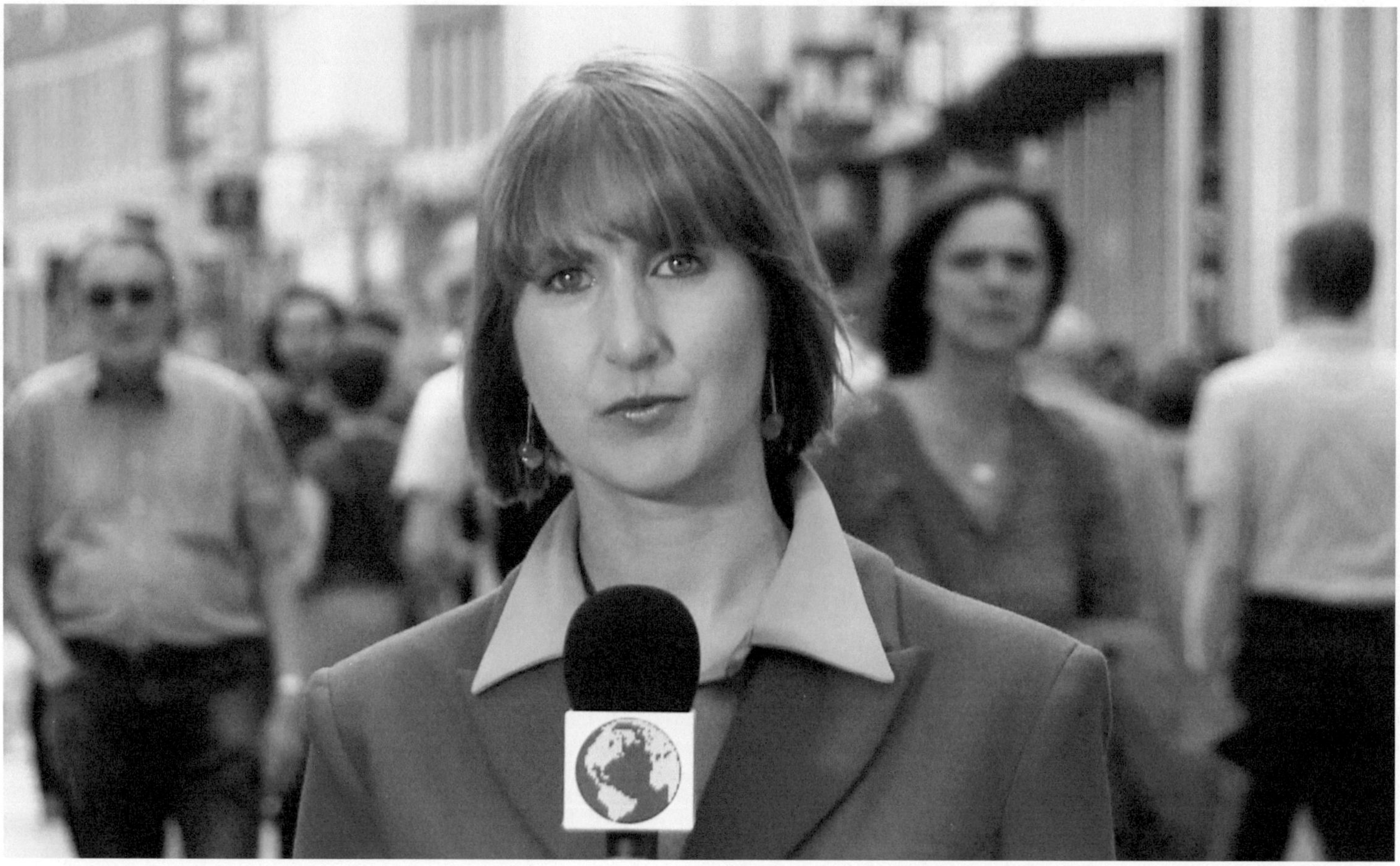

[72]

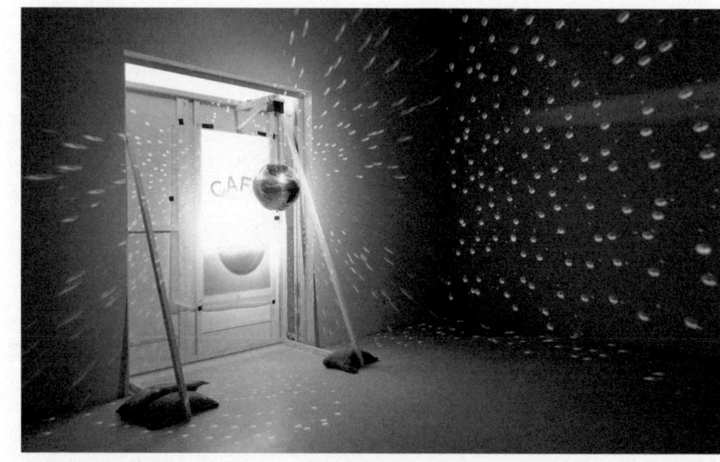

[73]

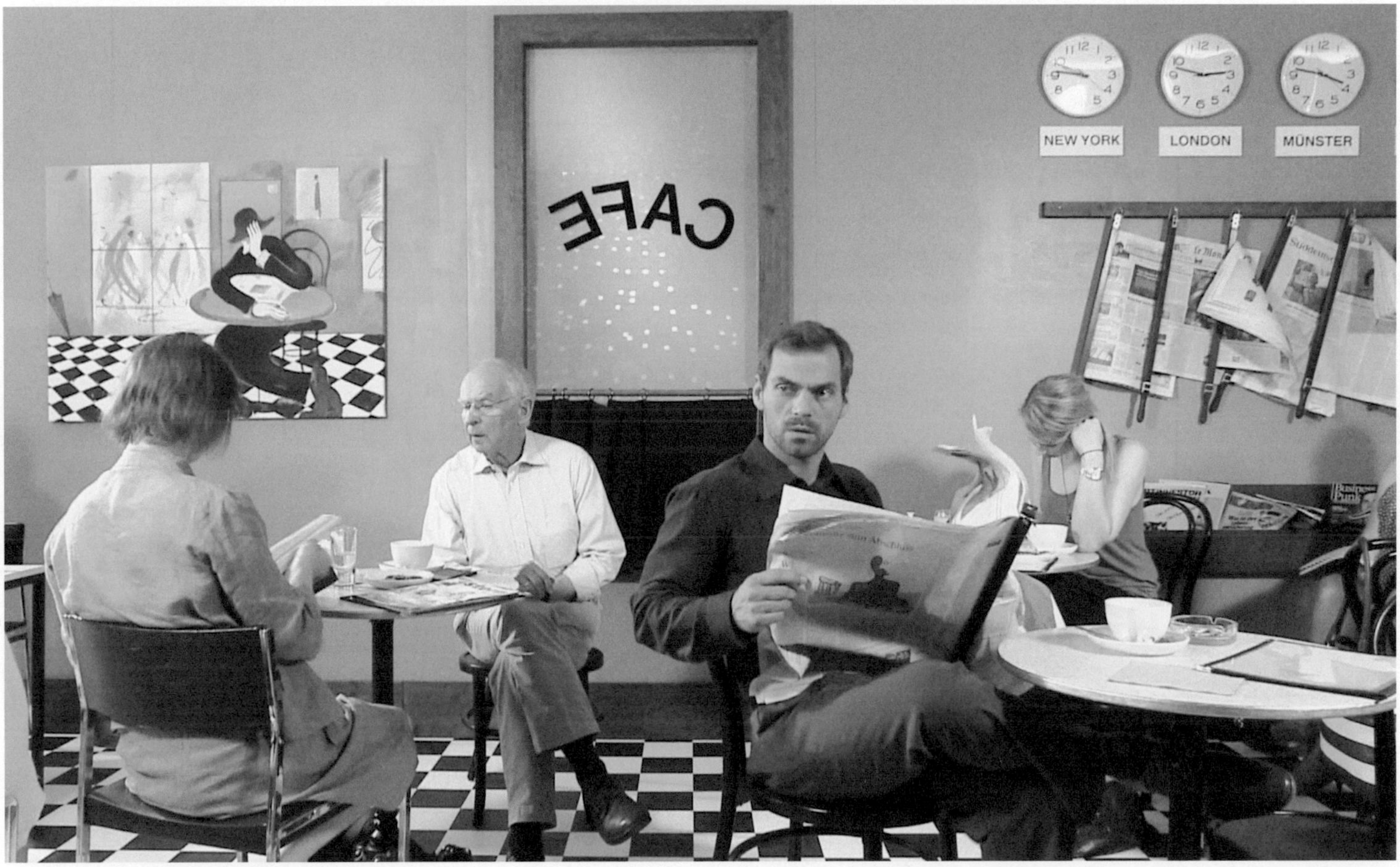

[74]

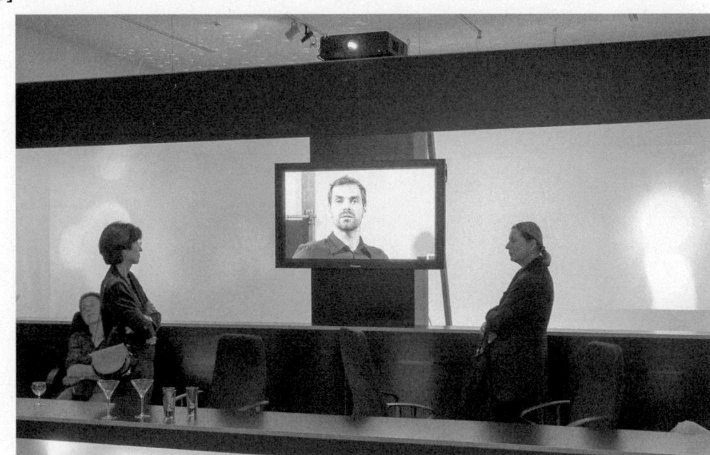

[75]

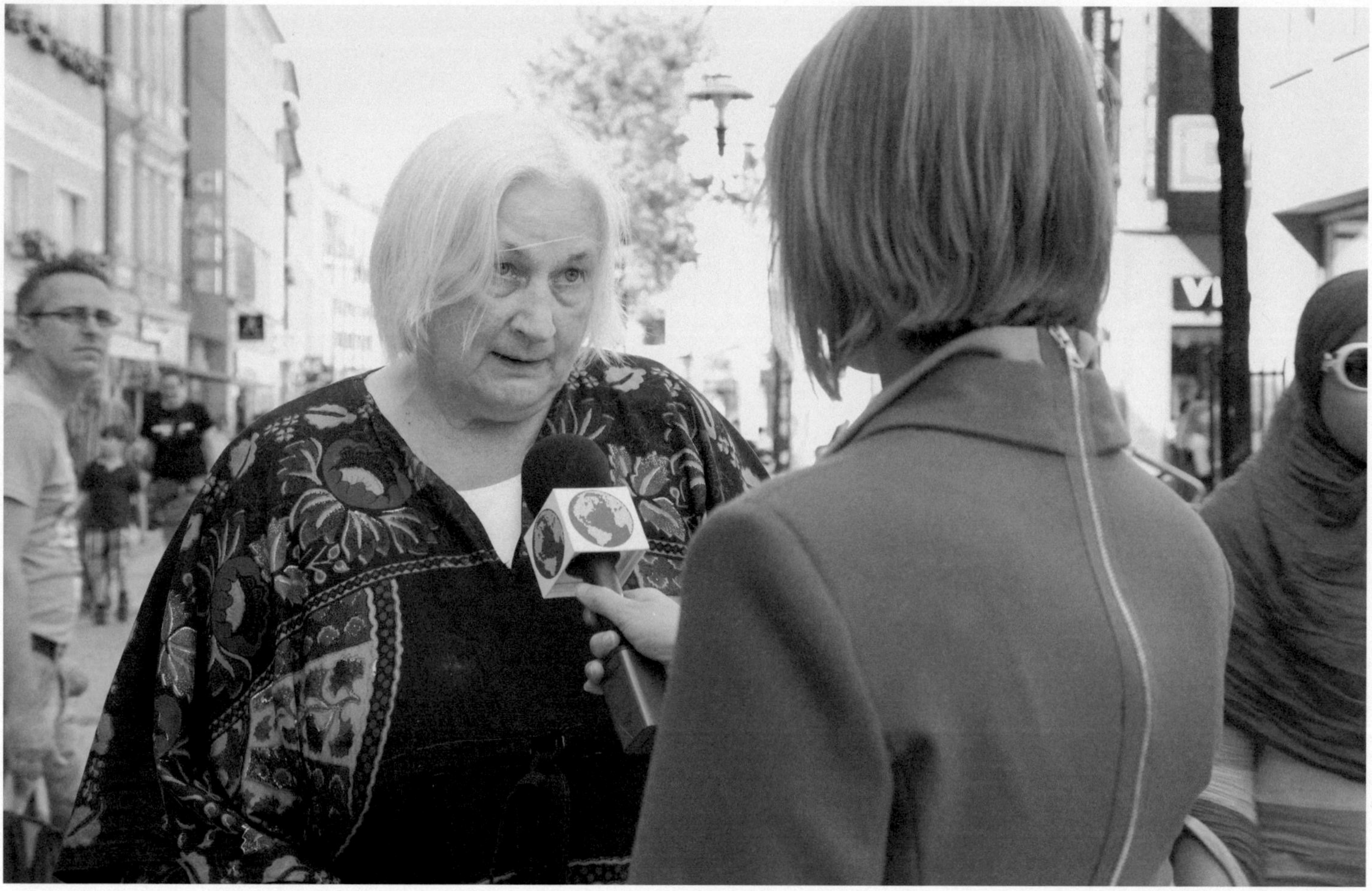

[76]

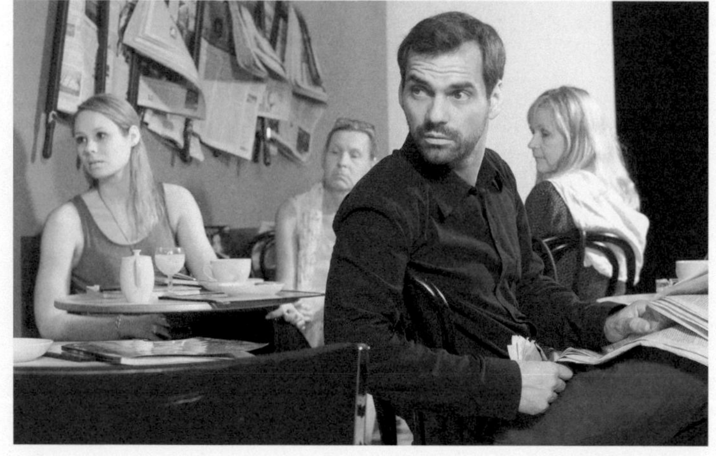

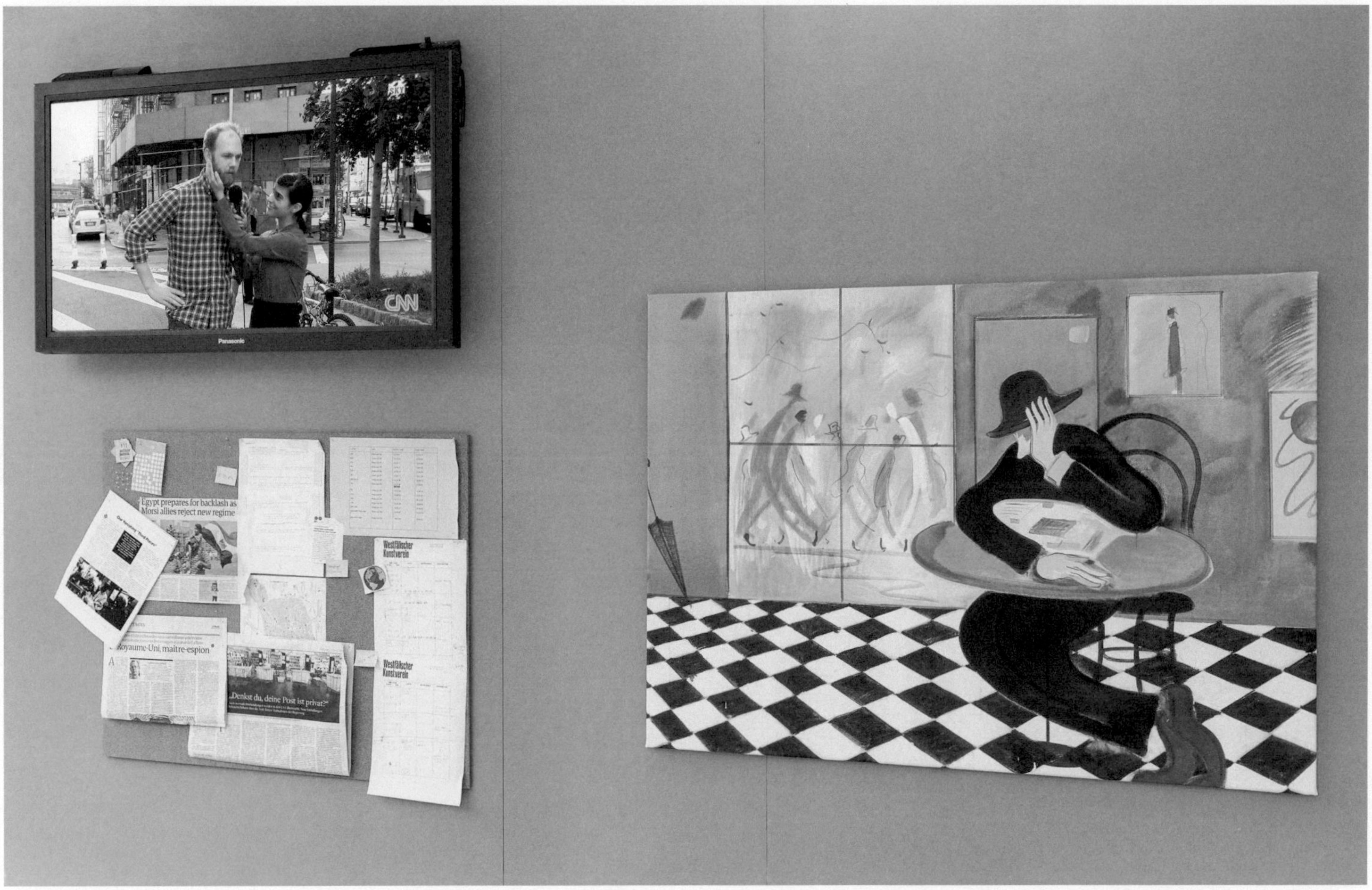

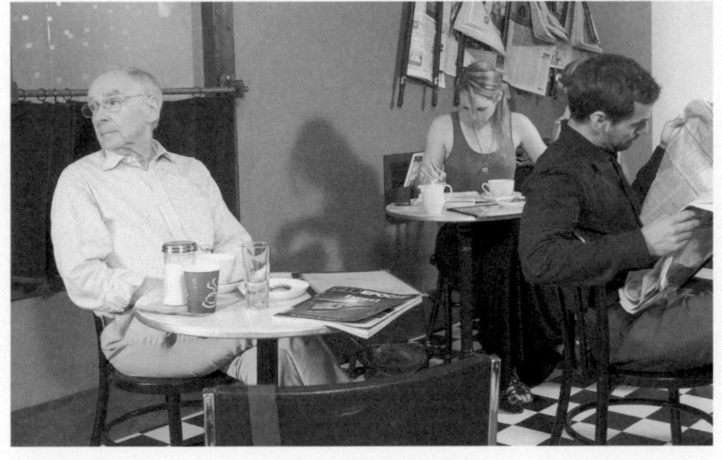

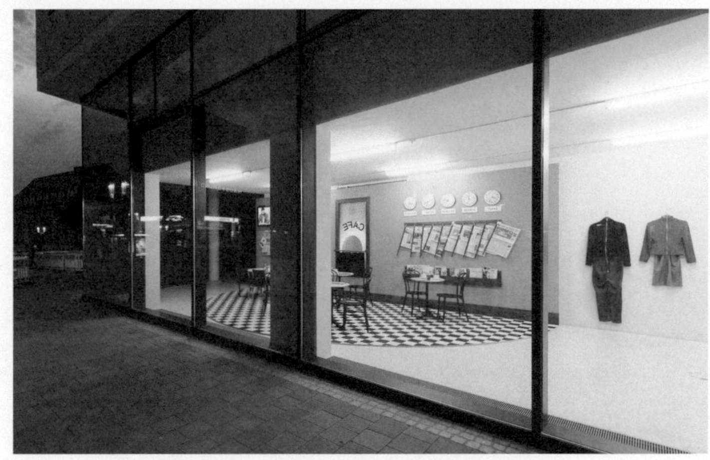

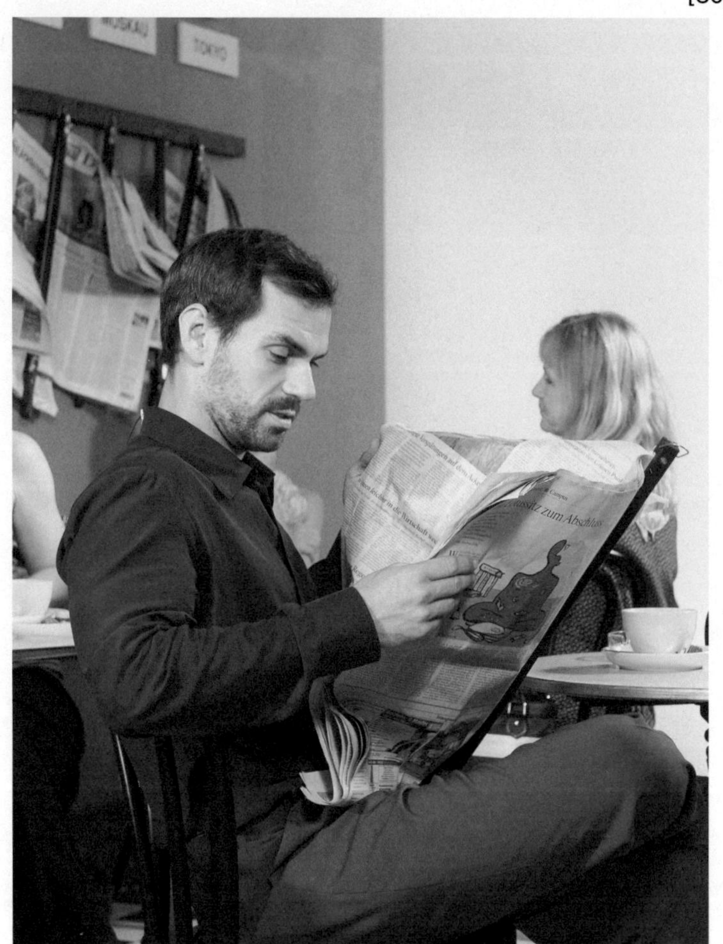

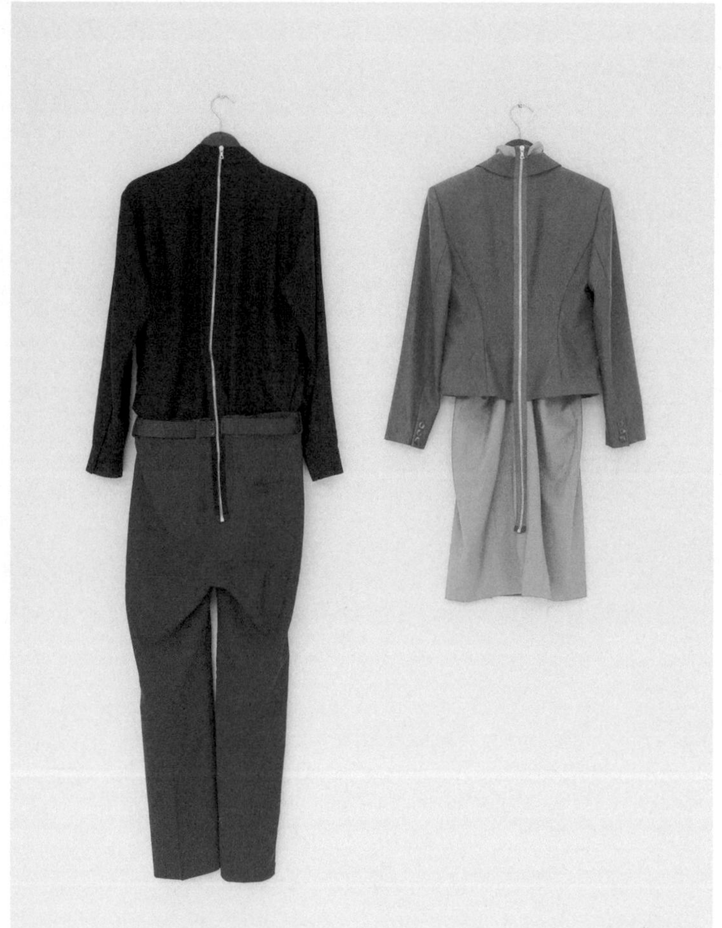

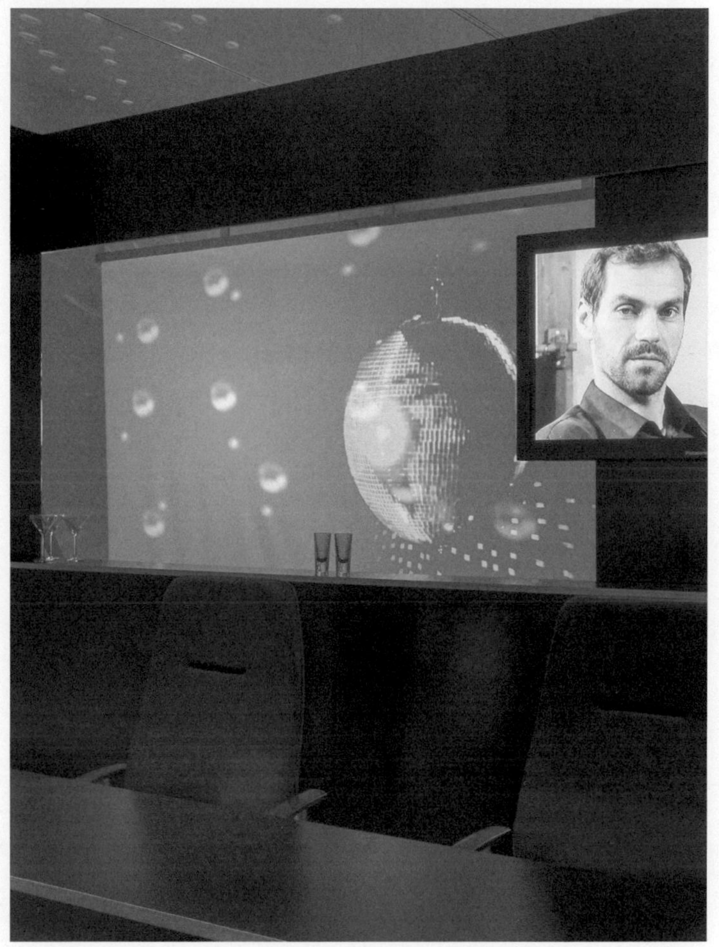

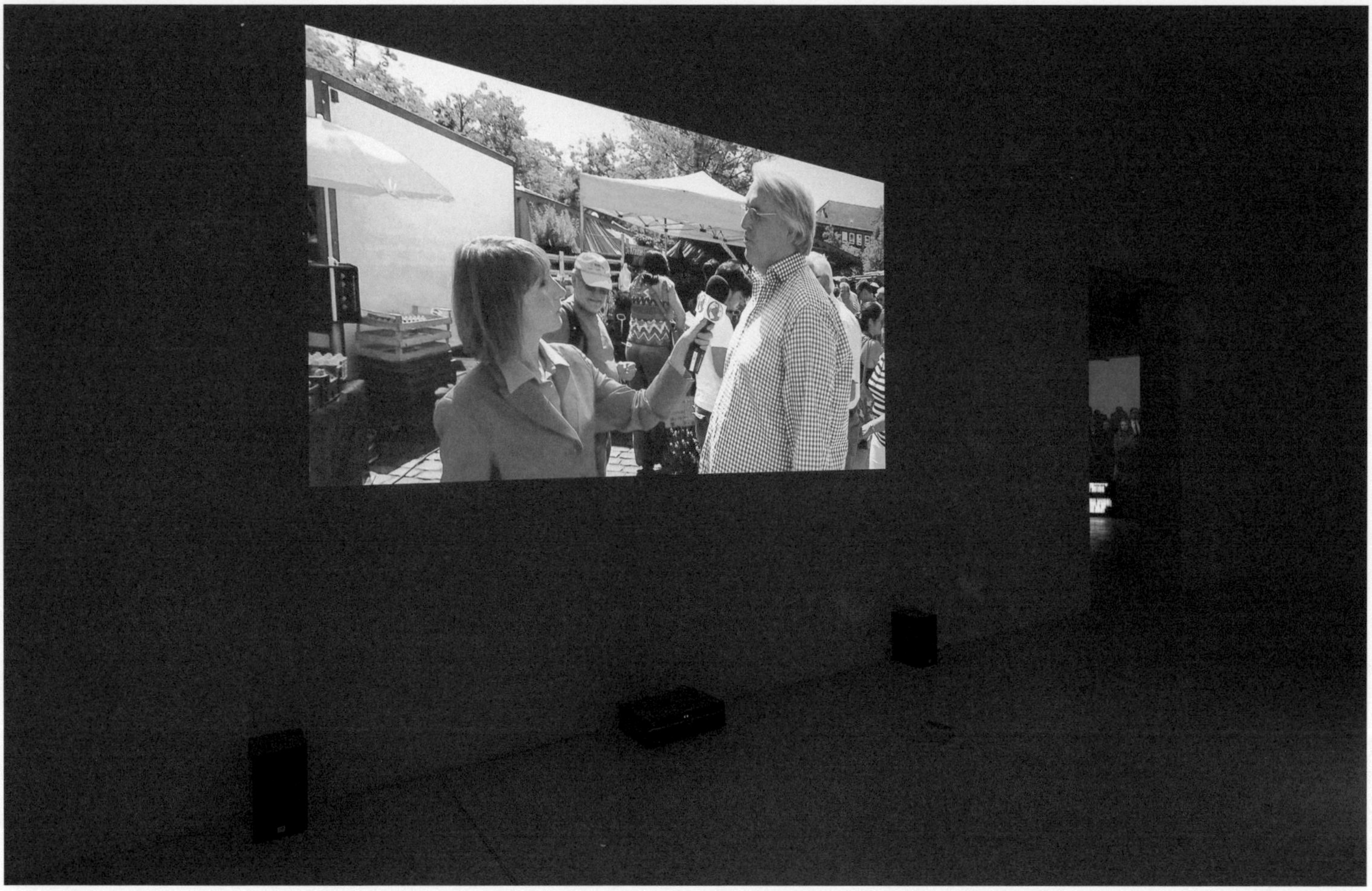

[84]

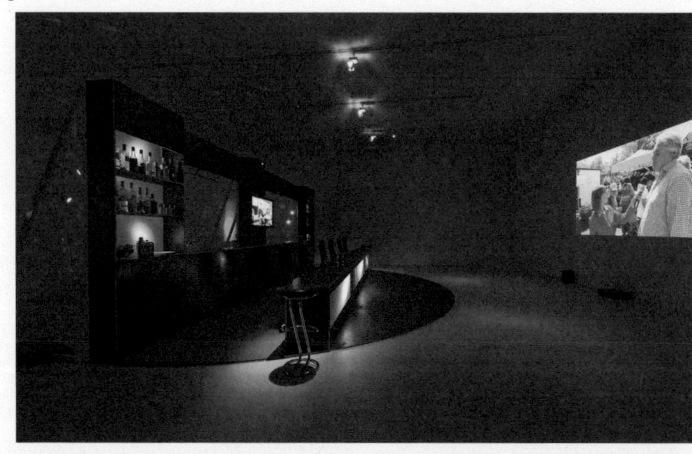

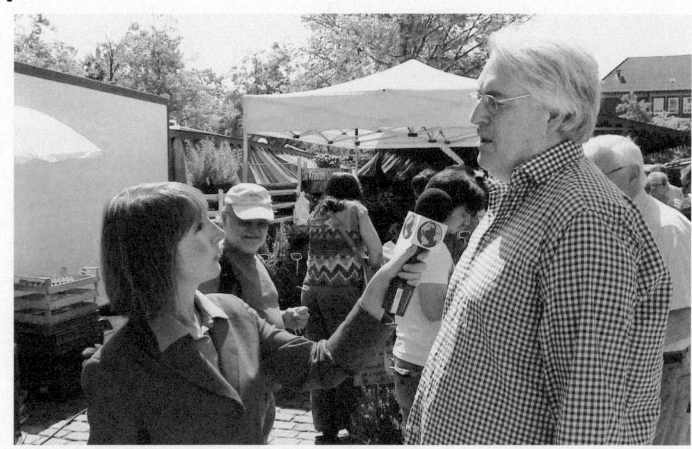

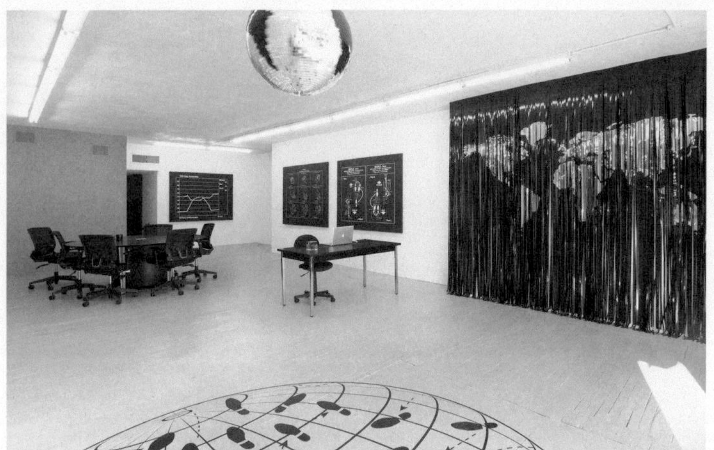

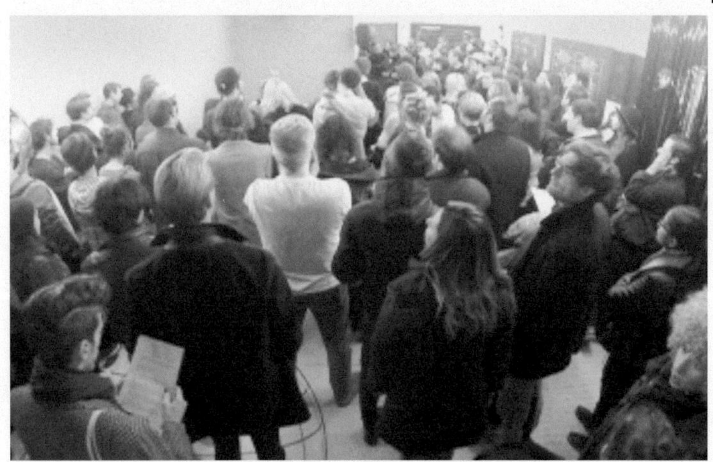

[88]

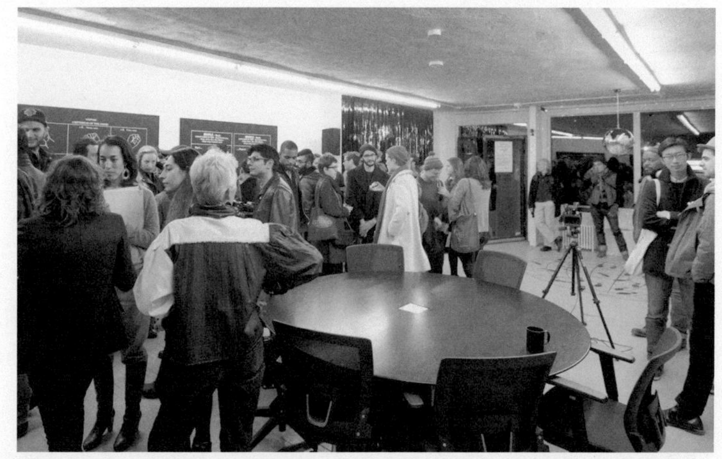

[89]

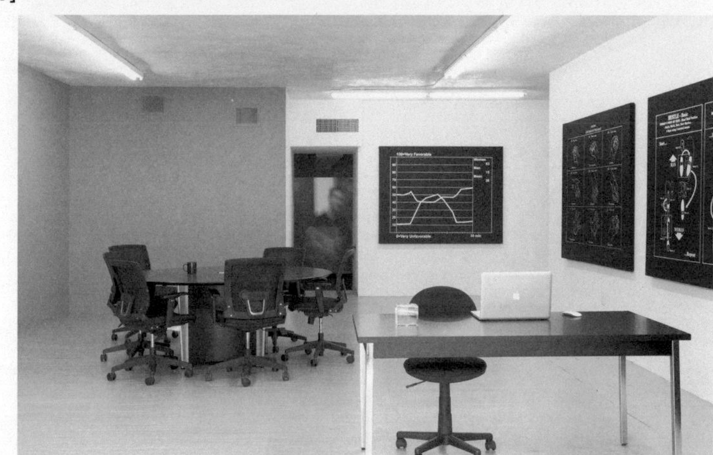

[90] [91]

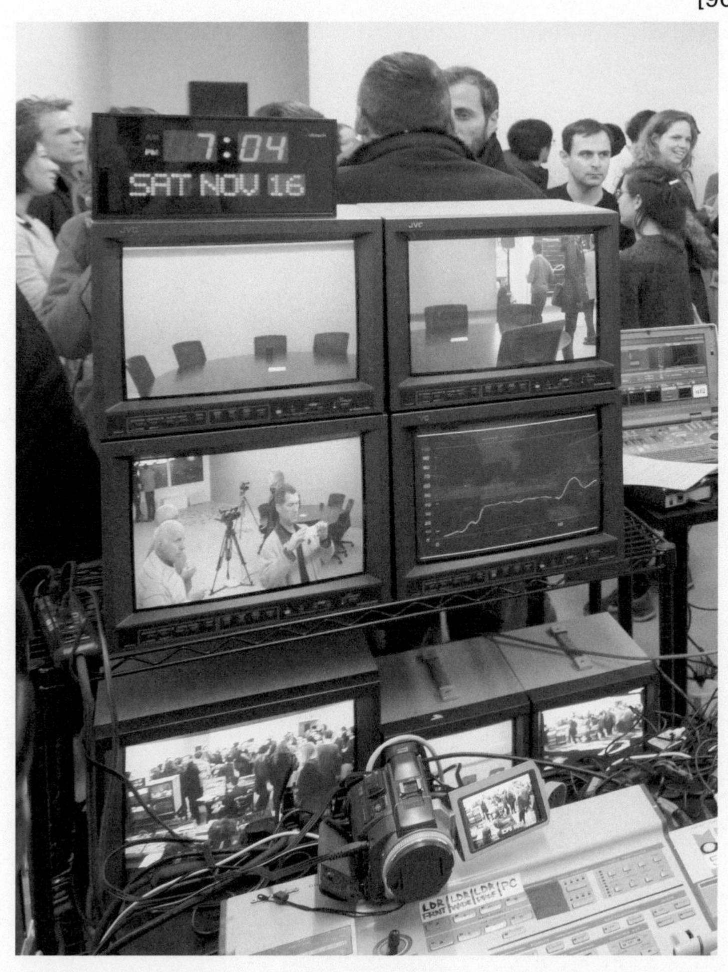

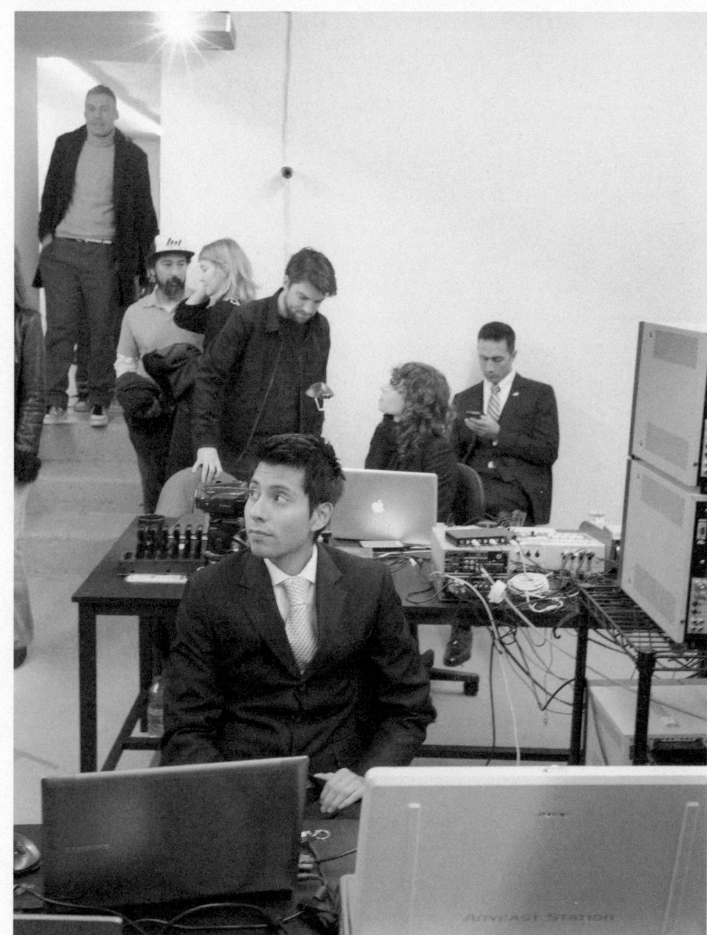

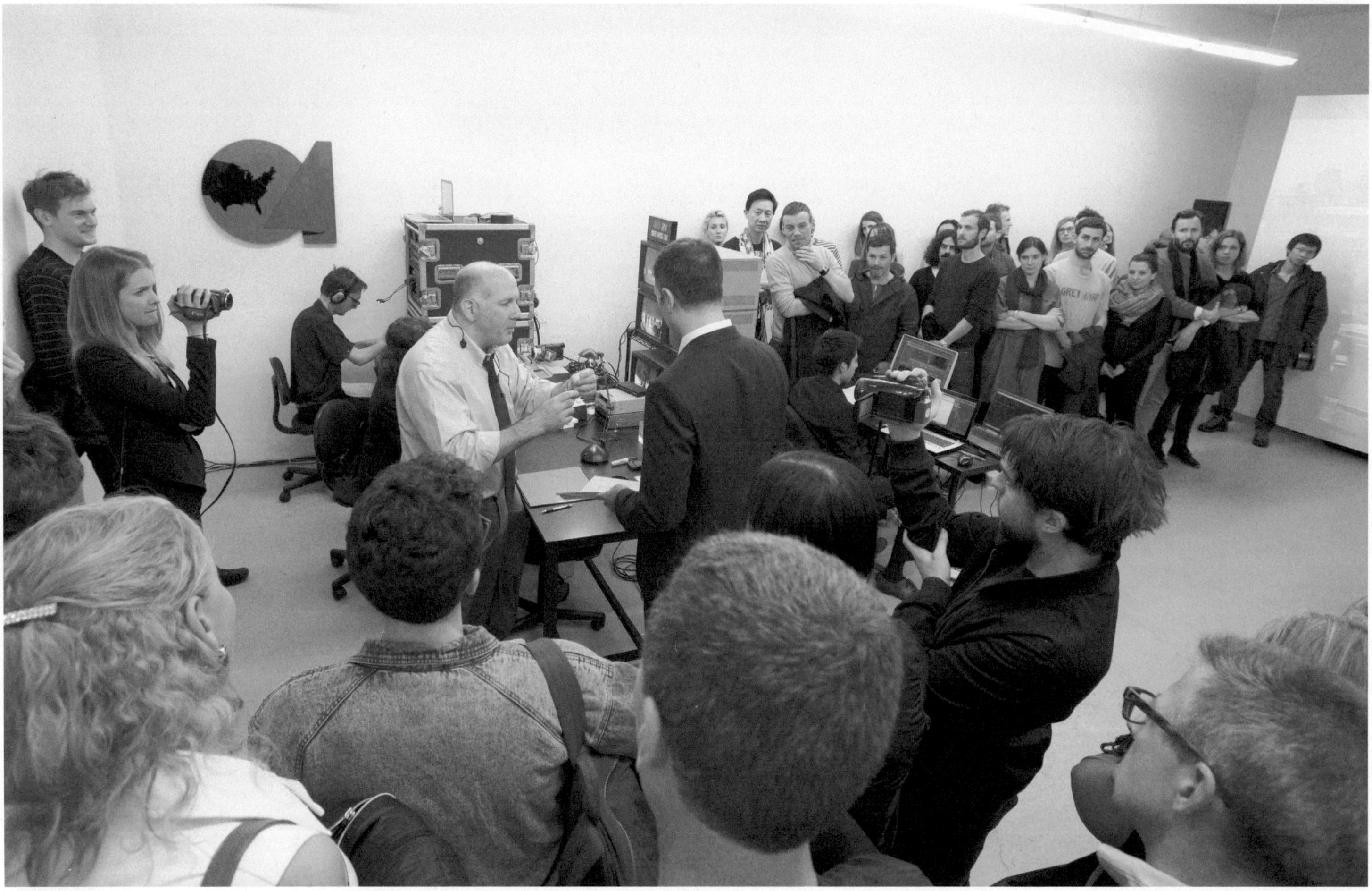

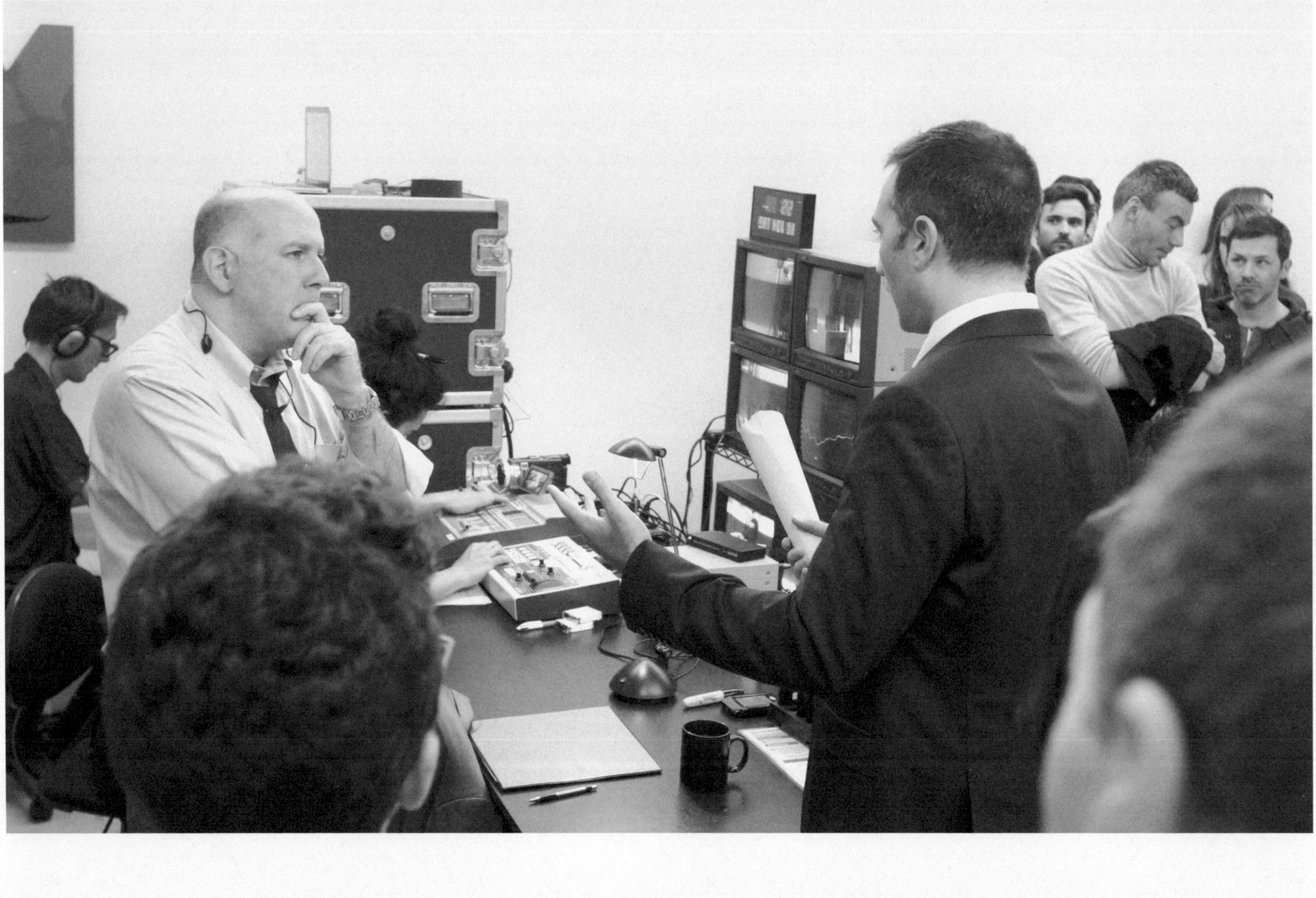

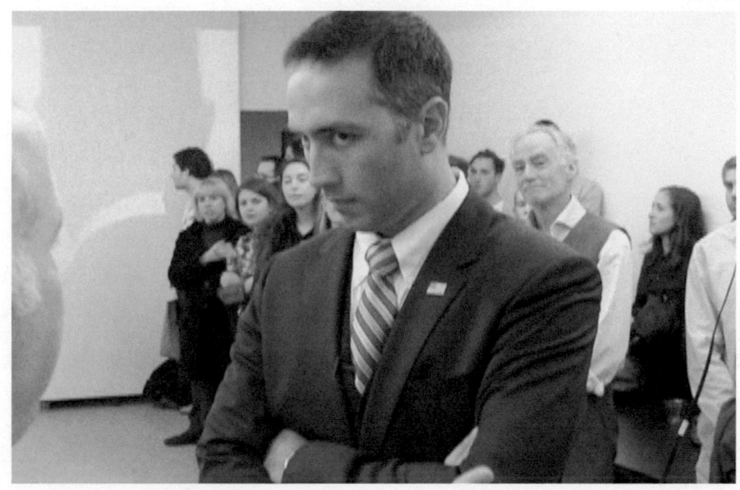

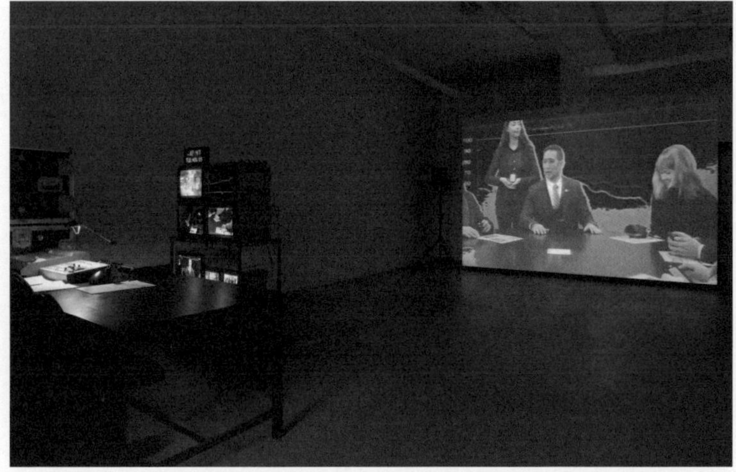

[96]

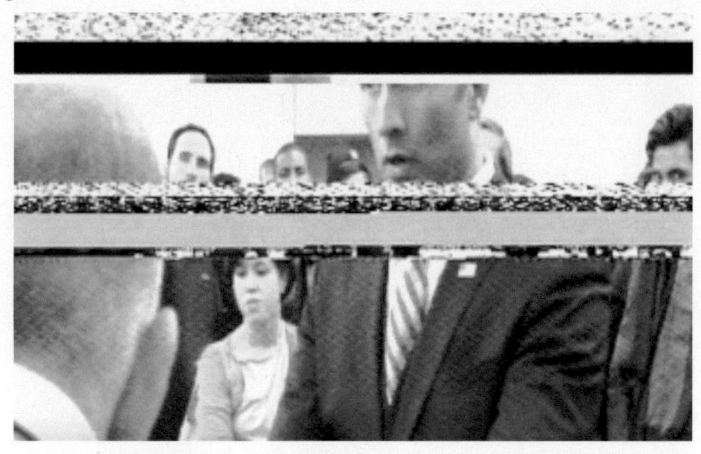

[97]

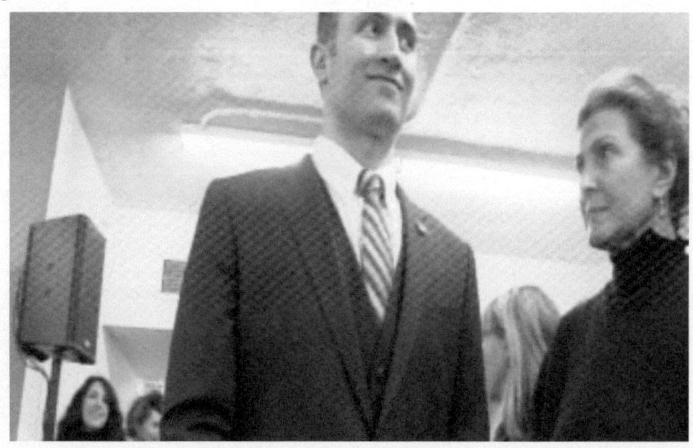

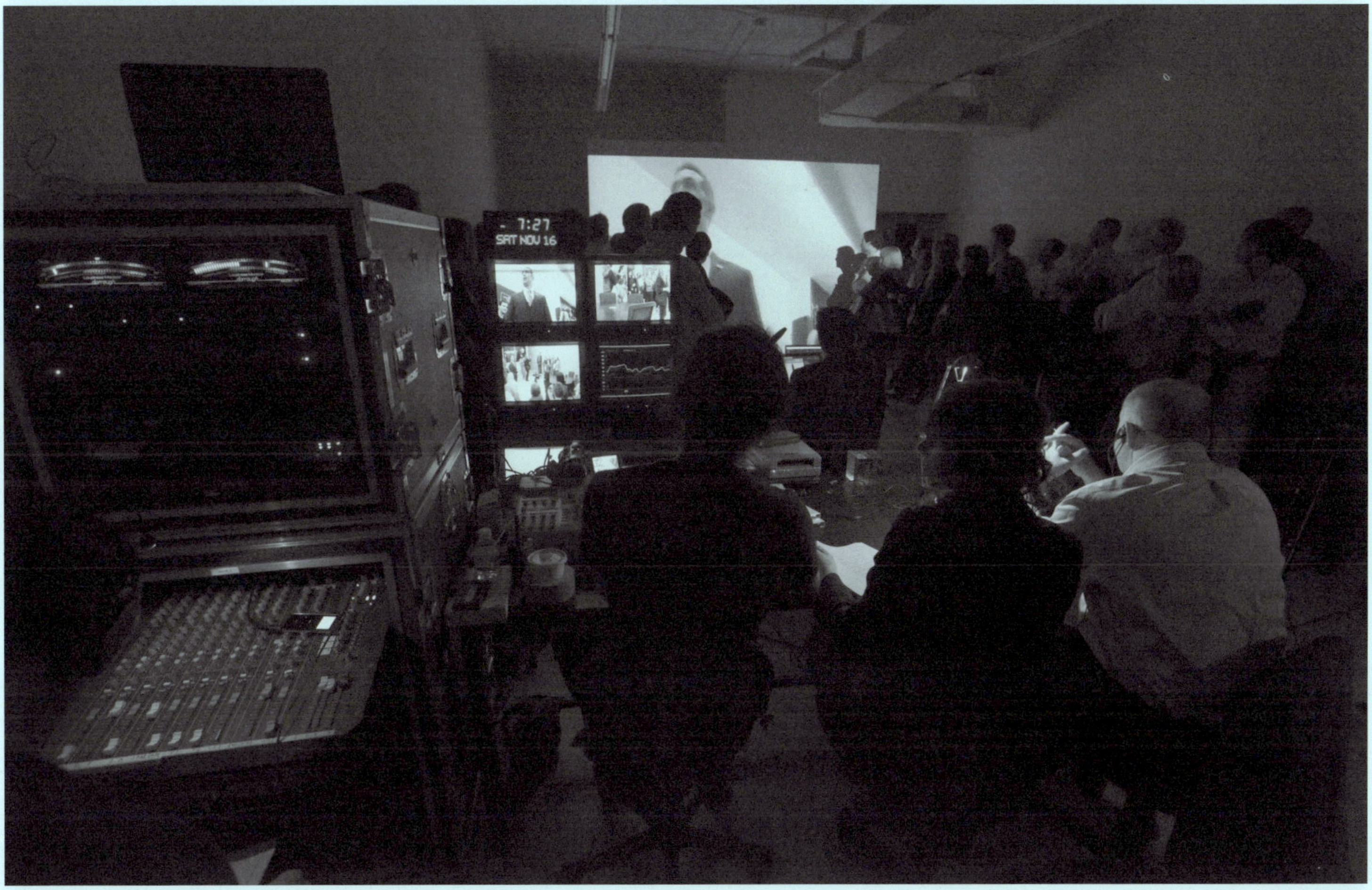

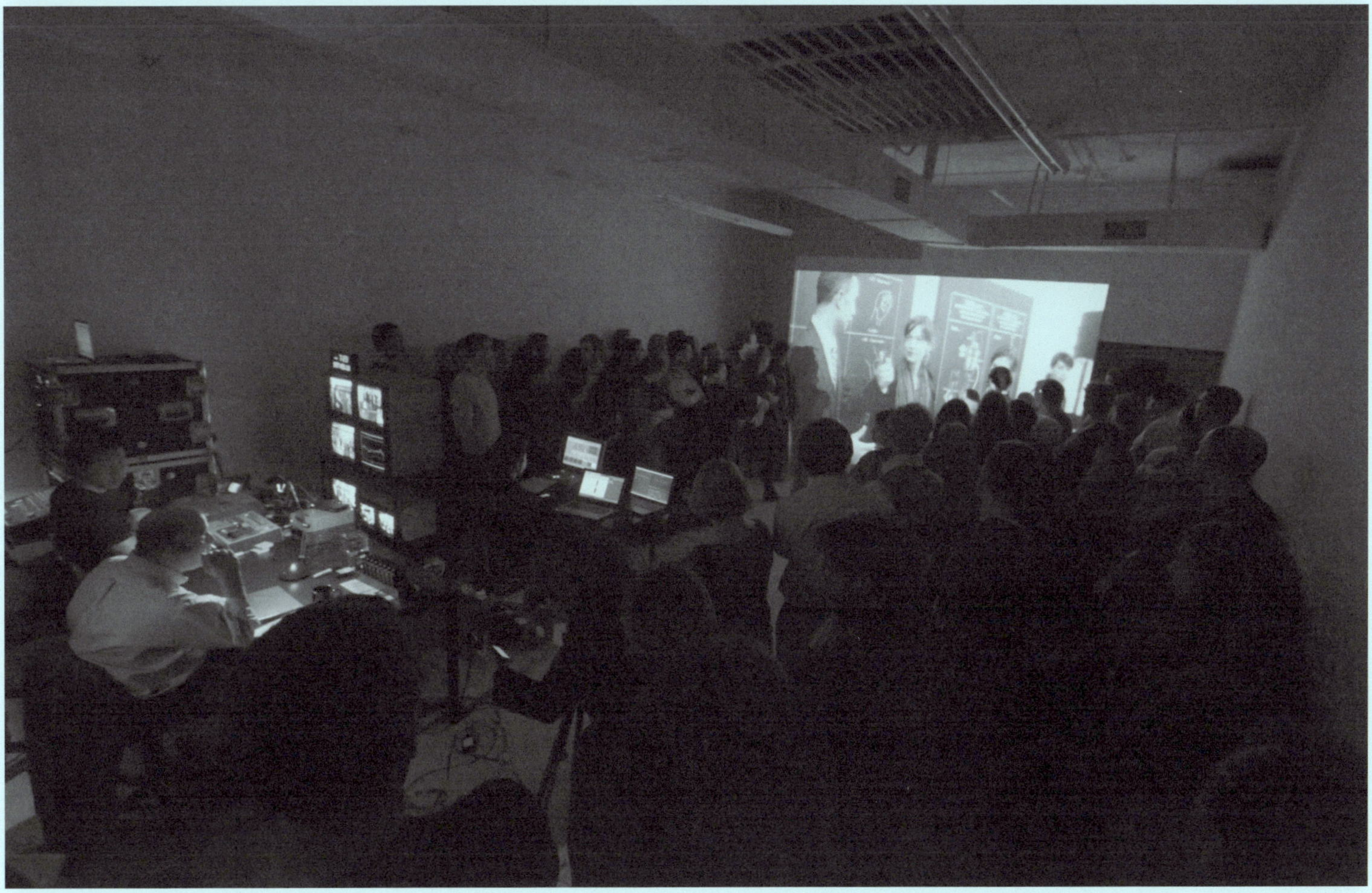

[100]

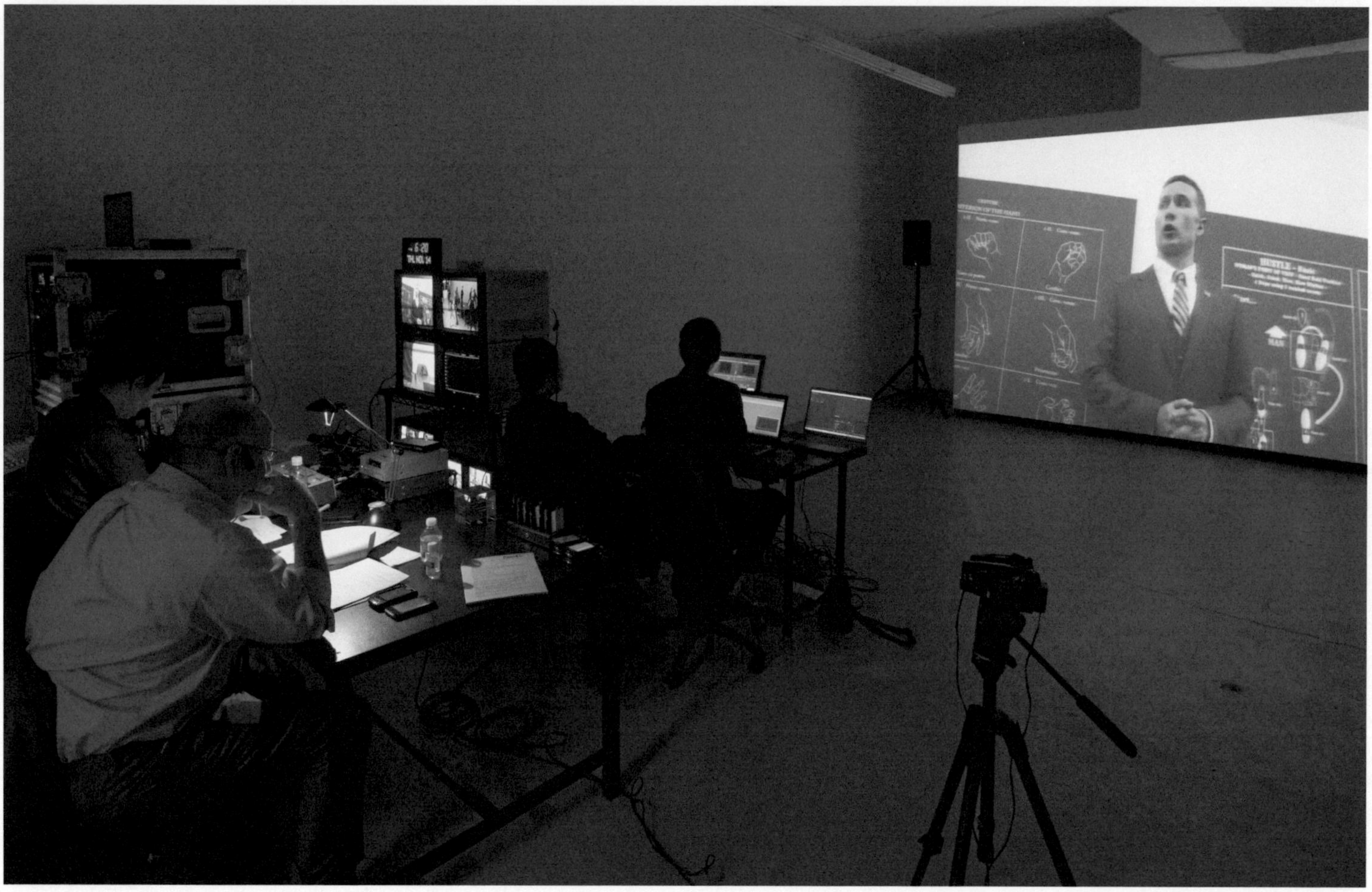

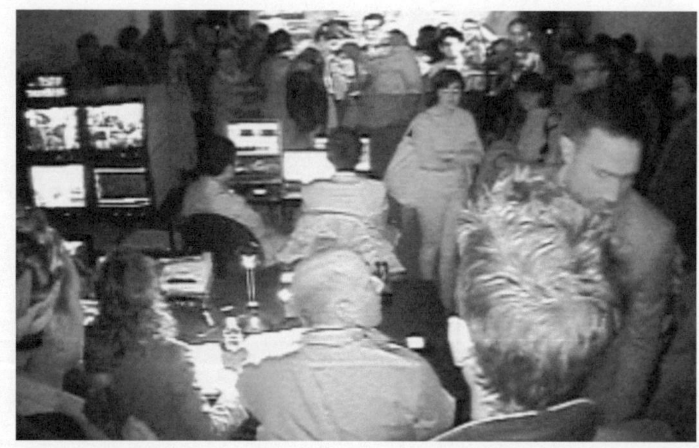

[101]

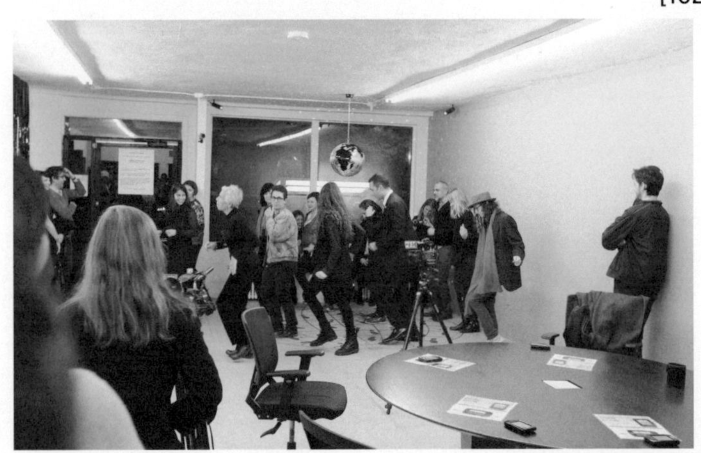
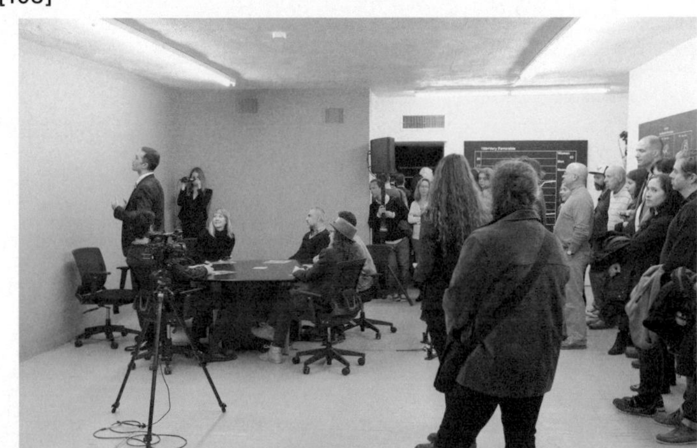

[102] [103]

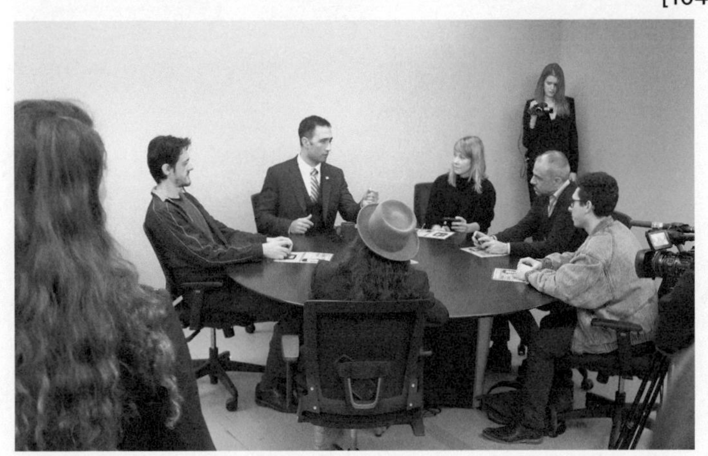
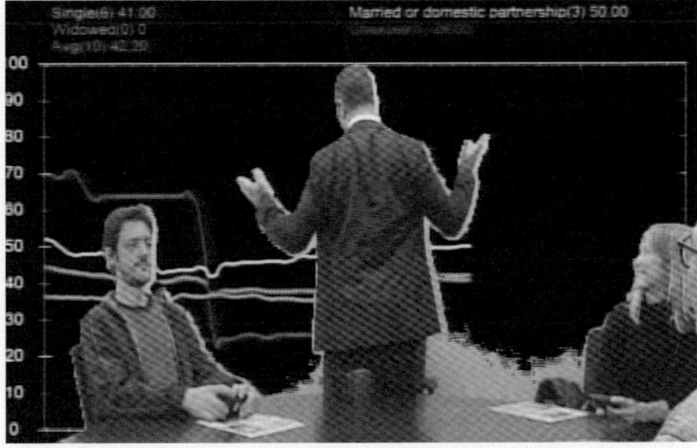

[104] [105]

[106] [107]

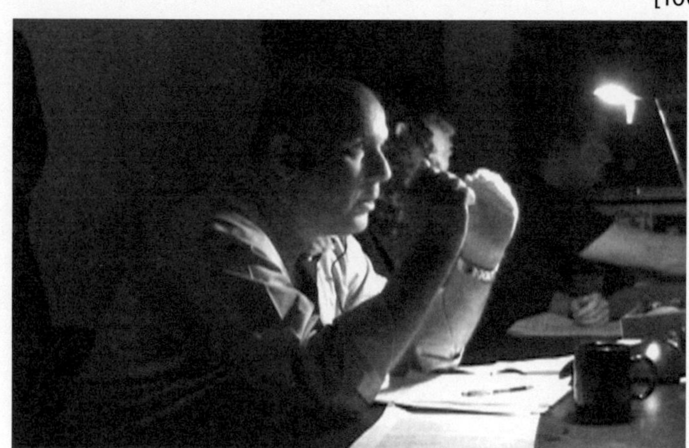
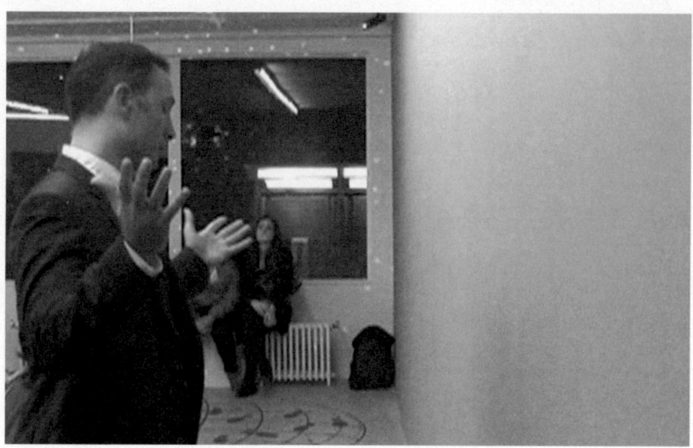

[108]

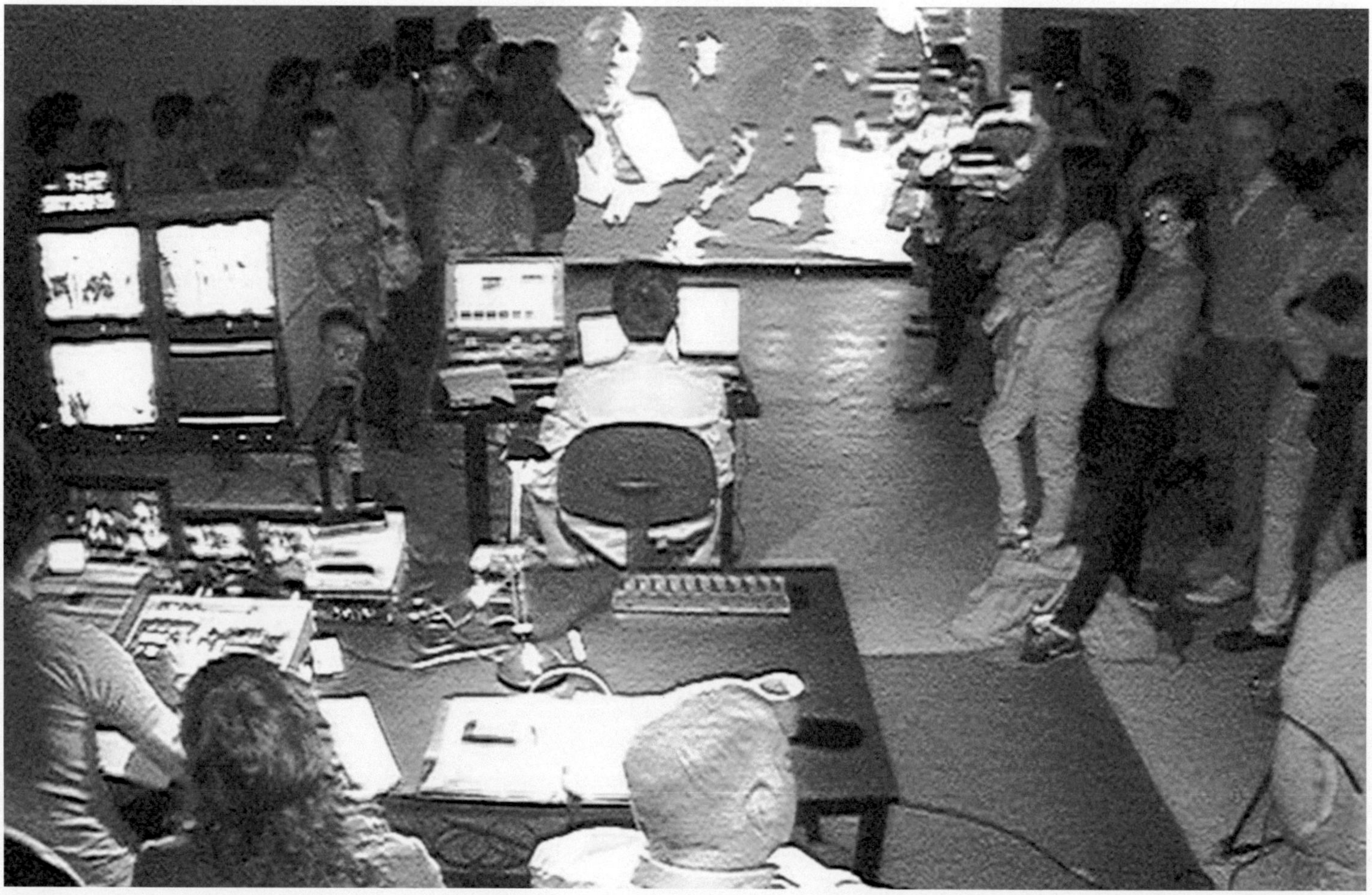

Scripts / Skripte

I Feel Your Pain, 2011
[Excerpts]

Synopsis

I Feel Your Pain was performed, filmed and edited in real-time in the midst of an audience in a movie theater. Eight actors performed a sequence of scenes that trace the progression of a relationship using dialogue adapted from political interviews with figures such as Glenn Beck, Hillary Clinton, Sarah Palin, Barack Obama, and John Boehner. As the actors performed, selected footage from three cinematographers was projected onto the screen in a continuous live-feed with Laser acting as live editor.

Act 1 Scene 1 – First Date

Dialogue adapted from
– Sarah Palin interview with Glenn Beck about the future of the Republican Party, Glenn Beck, Fox News, 14 Jan 2010[4]

Scenario

A teenage couple on a first date at the movies. They met through an online network and have been corresponding for two months, but have known who one another are for a longer time. They are flirtatious and physically engaged throughout much of scene. Both affect the idealism of youth with a radical edge.

RAFAEL (*pulls away from embrace*): Hey, can I read you what I wrote last night in my journal, (*pulls out journal*) it's about you. (*Reading from journal*) Tomorrow, I meet her for the first time. I'm actually a little nervous – as she is one of the only people that I can see that can possibly lead us out of where we are. I don't know yet if she's strong enough, if she's well enough advised, or if she knows she can no longer trust anyone. I don't know if she can lead us and not lose her soul (*emphasis*).
ANNIE: Yes. That trust thing, you nailed it, you know? Trustworthy people surrounding us, leading us, we've got to be able to *trust*. But it's very, very dangerous to trust anybody.
RAFAEL: You know, there's – a reason why I selected this particular location (*gesturing around theater*). There are very few places that inspire trust these days. If I say, think of the Capitol building, do you trust it?
ANNIE (*shrugs shoulders coyly*): No.[1]
[…]

Act 1 Scene 2 – Gratification

Dialogue adapted from
– Barack Obama interview with Steve Kroft about Osama Bin Laden's death, 60 Minutes, CBS, 4 May 2011[10]

Scenario

Man discussing his recent romantic/sexual conquest with his buddy. They are old friends. One holds popcorn, the other a jumbo soda.

RYAN (*elbowing him in the side*): Yeah, but you thought the advantages outweighed the risks, eh?

I Feel Your Pain, 2011
[Auszüge]

Synopse

I Feel Your Pain wurde in einem Kinosaal mit Publikum aufgeführt, aufgenommen und in Echtzeit geschnitten. Acht SchauspielerInnen spielten eine Folge von Szenen, die Entwicklungsstadien einer Beziehung in Dialogen nachzeichnen, Adaptionen von politischen Interviews mit Persönlichkeiten wie Glenn Beck, Hillary Clinton, Sarah Palin, Barack Obama oder John Boehner. Während der Performance wurde eine von Laser live bearbeitete Auswahl des von drei Kameraleuten aufgenommenen Materials in einem kontinuierlichen Live-Stream auf die Leinwand projiziert.

Akt 1, Szene 1 – Das erste Date

Adaptierter Dialog
– Sarah Palin im Interview mit Glenn Beck über die Zukunft der Republikaner, Glenn Beck, Fox News, 14. Jan 2010[4]

Szenario

Zwei Teenager gehen zum ersten Mal zusammen aus, ins Kino. Sie haben sich über eine Online-Plattform kennengelernt. Zwei Monate lang haben sie sich geschrieben, wussten aber schon länger, wer der andere ist. In der Szene turteln sie über weite Strecken, und sie kommen sich auch körperlich näher. Ihr jugendlicher Idealismus hat eine gewisse Radikalität.

RAFAEL (*löst sich aus der Umarmung*): Darf ich dir mal vorlesen, was ich gestern Abend in mein Tagebuch geschrieben habe, (*er holt sein Tagebuch hervor*) da geht's um dich. (*Liest aus dem Tagebuch*) Morgen treffe ich sie zum ersten Mal. Ich bin schon ein bisschen nervös – schließlich zählt sie zu den wenigen Leuten, von denen ich mir vorstellen kann, uns da wieder herausführen zu können. Ich weiß noch nicht, ob sie stark genug ist, ob sie gut genug beraten wird oder ob sie weiß, dass sie nun keinem mehr trauen kann. Ich weiß nicht, ob sie uns führen kann, ohne dabei ihre Seele aufzugeben (*betont*).
ANNIE: Ja. Das mit dem Vertrauen, weißt du, da hast du den Nagel auf den Kopf getroffen. Wir sind von vertrauenswürdigen Menschen umgeben, sie zeigen uns den Weg, wir müssen ihnen *vertrauen* können. Aber jemandem zu vertrauen, das ist sehr, sehr gefährlich.
RAFAEL: Weißt du, es gibt einen Grund, warum ich gerade diesen Ort hier ausgesucht habe (*weist mit einer raumgreifenden Geste auf den Kinosaal*). Nur ganz wenige Orte stärken heute unser Vertrauen. Na, denk' doch mal an das Gebäude des Kapitols – traust du dem?
ANNIE (*zuckt etwas verlegen mit den Schultern*): Nein.[1]
[…]

Akt 1, Szene 2 – Genugtuung

Adaptierter Dialog
– Barack Obama im Interview mit Steve Kroft über den Tod Osama bin Ladens, 60 Minutes, CBS, 4. Mai 2011[10]

RAY (*self-satisfied*): Oh it was worth it. We devoted enormous blood and treasure, we had to go for it.[9]

RYAN (*insinuating sexual innuendo*): Take me into the Situation Room. What was the mood in there?

RAY: Tense. (*speaks with royal 'we'*): Yeah, but we were doing a lot of listening as well, cause we were able to monitor the situation in real time (*acknowledges screen*). There were big chunks of time in which all we were doin' was just waiting. Longest 40 minutes of my life. (*Stands up to take off blazer as if hot, puts it on back of seat.*)

[…]

Act 2 Scene 3 – How did you meet?

Dialogue adapted from
– John Boehner interview with Lesley Stahl, 60 Minutes, CBS, 12 Dec 2010[6]
– George W. Bush speaking about Vladimir Putin, BBC News, 16 Jun 2001
– Ronald Reagan speaking about Mikhail Gorbachev, in interview with Mike Wallace, 60 Minutes, CBS, 15 Jan 1989

Scenario
Kathryn is friend of Lizzie's and is meeting her new beau for the first time and is asking questions about him.

KATHRYN: Do you know what's happening over here (*gesturing to Ryan on screen*).

RYAN: No, no. My nose is running.

KATHRYN: No it's not. What set you off that time? Is it cause she's proud of you? Does he cry all the time?

LIZZIE: No, but he's going through an emotional period. I mean, this isn't you know, as you say this is not an ordinary job. Whoever would have thought that he'd be in this position. He was a janitor when I met him. (*Laughter*) He's come a long way.

KATHRYN: Somebody who's gone from mopping the floors to running them.

LIZZIE: Yeah. Doesn't happen every day.

RYAN: Welcome to America (*sniffling*).

[…]

Act 4 Scene 2 – Coming To Blows

Dialogue adapted from
– George W. Bush interview with Candy Crowley, State of the Union, CNN, 14 Nov 2010
– Gubernatorial candidate Carl Paladino's altercation with reporter Frederic Dicker in Bolton Landing, 28 Sep 2010
– Injunction Granted, Federal Theatre Project Living Newspaper production, staged by Joseph Losey, New York, 1936

Scenario
Kathryn runs to bathroom and Ray sits next to Ryan. Ray gets angry at Ryan for inflaming situation with Kathryn. Clown alternates between the two men, playing each man's thug or mimicking them. At some points Clown tries to mediate or break up the fight and at others she's trying to encourage the men to fight.

Szenario
Ein Mann spricht mit seinem Kumpel über seine neuesten amourösen/sexuellen Erfolge. Sie sind alte Freunde. Einer hält das Popcorn, der andere einen XL-Becher mit einem Softdrink.

RYAN (*schubst ihn mit dem Ellbogen*): Klar, und du dachtest: Da sind die Chancen größer als das Risiko, oder?

RAY (*selbstzufrieden*): Mann, das war es wert. Wir hatten da so viel Blut und Schweiß reingesteckt, da mussten wir einfach zugreifen.[9]

RYAN (*mit anzüglichem Unterton*): Wie war das denn im Lagezentrum. Wie war da die Stimmung?

RAY: Angespannt.

RAY (*spricht im Pluralis Majestatis*): Schon, aber wir haben auch viel zugehört, weil wir die Situation in Echtzeit verfolgen konnten (*bestätigend in den Bildschirm*). Über weite Strecken mussten wir alle einfach nur warten. Das waren die längsten 40 Minuten meines Lebens. (*Steht auf, um sich das Jackett auszuziehen, weil es heiß ist; hängt es über die Rückenlehne.*)

[…]

Akt 2, Szene 3 – Wie habt ihr euch kennengelernt?

Adaptierte Dialoge
– John Boehner im Interview mit Lesley Stahl, 60 Minutes, CBS, 12. Dez 2010[6]
– George W. Bush äußert sich zu Wladimir Putin, BBC News, 16. Jun 2001
– Ronald Reagan äußert sich gegenüber Mike Wallace zu Michail Gorbatschow, 60 Minutes, CBS, 15. Jan 1989

Szenario
Kathryn ist mit Lizzie befreundet, trifft zum ersten Mal deren neuen Lover und stellt Fragen.

KATHRYN: Weißt du, was da drüben los ist (*gestikuliert auf der Leinwand mit Ryan*)?

RYAN: Nein, nein. Meine Nase läuft.

KATHRYN: Nein, das tut sie nicht. Was stört dich denn jetzt schon wieder? Weil sie stolz auf dich ist? Heult der die ganze Zeit?

LIZZIE: Nein, aber er macht grade eine ziemlich emotionale Phase durch. Das ist schließlich, wie du ja selber sagst, kein ganz normaler Job. Wer hätte gedacht, dass er in eine solche Position gelangen würde. Als ich ihn kennengelernt habe, war er noch Hauswart. (*Gelächter*) Das war ein weiter Weg für ihn.

KATHRYN: Jemand der früher die Flure gewischt hat, über die er jetzt regiert.

LIZZIE: Klar, das passiert nicht alle Tage.

RYAN: Das ist Amerika (*schnieft*).

[…]

Akt 4, Szene 2 – Aneinandergeraten

Adaptierte Dialoge
– George W. Bush im Interview mit Candy Crowley, State of the Union, CNN, 14. Nov 2010
– Wortwechsel des Kandidaten für die Gouverneurswahlen

RAY: Yes, I feel terrible about it. I wish we'd have found those weapons.

KATHRYN (*returns. Fuming, having heard it all. Clears throat*): You talk about, I didn't see it coming, but why isn't anyone ever accountable for this?! And so we the American people lose confidence in you because no one ever pays![7]

RYAN (*to Kathryn*): You never said to him, "You're responsible for this, you're out!"

RAY (*to Ryan. Irritated*): Excuse me?! What are you trying to do?!

RYAN (*stands up*): You know you can really be despicable.

RAY (*scoffs. Looks around at rest of audience*): Despicable?! (*Rolling his sleeves up as Clown enters, excited about the fight*) This is about to get a whole lot nastier …

LIZZIE (*tries to quell situation, but ends up offending Kathryn*): Come on, it was just a rhetorical device to lift the spirits of the country (*indicating Kathryn with a nod*).

RAY: A guy that's been in the gutter and spent a good deal of his life in the gutter (*pointing at Ryan*), should think twice about accusing me.

(*Clown bucks toward Ryan like a threatening thug.*)

RYAN (*to clown*): Hey, fingers don't come any closer.

(*Clown changes sides to Ryan's side. Wags finger threateningly at Ray. She continues to shift back and forth, arguing each side.*)

KATHRYN: Hey, guys, take it easy.

RAY (*lunging threateningly toward Ryan*): Ok, that's it!

RYAN: Stay away from me!

RAY (*softly*): Fuck him.

RYAN: That's it!

RAY (*louder*): Fuck him.[12]

[…]

Act 4 Scene 4 – Capitulation

Dialogue adapted from
−Anthony Weiner press conference, 6 Jun 2011
−Congressman Joe Wilson heckling Barack Obama, 9 Sept 2009
−Barack Obama speaking about Michelle Obama during 1996 interview, Le Monde, 11 Jan 2009
−Barack Obama speaking to Hearst Magazine publishers, FoxNews.com, 4 Apr 2011
−Arnold Schwarzenegger interview with Michael Lewis, California and Bust, Vanity Fair, November 2011
−George W. Bush's Speech to the Nation on the Economic Crisis, 24 Sept 2008

Scenario
Married man apologizing to his wife for his infidelities. Led by Rafael and Annie, the other two couples (Ray/Kathryn and Ryan/Lizzie) join in, amplifying or taking over the lines periodically. Clown puts on headset and is directing cameramen throughout scene.

RAY: This was a very dumb thing to do, and it was a destructive thing to do. But it wasn't part of any plan to be hurtful to you.

RYAN: It wasn't part of a plan to be deceitful to you. It wasn't part of a plan to be …

Carl Paladino mit dem Reporter Frederic Dicker in Bolton Landing, 28. Sep 2010
−Injunction Granted (Verfügung erteilt), Die Lebende Zeitung, Federal Theatre Project, unter der Regie von Joseph Losey, New York, 1936

Szenario
Kathryn läuft ins Bad, Ray sitzt neben Ryan. Ray ist wütend auf Ryan wegen der hitzigen Auseinandersetzung mit Kathryn. Der Clown wechselt zwischen den beiden Männern hin und her, mimt bei jedem den Schläger oder äfft ihn nach. Zwischendurch versucht er zu vermitteln oder die Streithähne auseinanderzubringen, dann ermutigt er die beiden zu kämpfen.

RAY: Ja, ich finde das fürchterlich. Mir wäre lieber, wir hätten diese Waffen gefunden.

KATHRYN (*kommt zurück. Sie hat alles mitangehört und ist aufgebracht. Räuspert sich*): Ihr sagt das einfach so daher: „das war nicht absehbar", aber ist eigentlich nie jemand dafür verantwortlich?! Und am Ende verlieren wir, das amerikanische Volk, das Vertrauen in euch, weil dann wieder keiner die Zeche zahlt![7]

RYAN (*zu Kathryn*): Du hast ihm ja nie gesagt: „Dafür bist du verantwortlich, das war's, du bist raus!"

RAY (*zu Ryan, aufgebracht*): Wie bitte?! Was soll das denn?!

RYAN (*steht auf*): Du kannst ganz schön eklig sein, weißt du das?

RAY (*abschätzig. Schaut um sich ins Publikum*): Eklig?! (*Krempelt sich die Ärmel hoch, der Clown tritt ein, begierig auf den Kampf*) Gleich wird's noch ein ganzes Stück ungemütlicher …

LIZZIE (*versucht die Situation zu beruhigen, was aber nur dazu führt, dass sich Kathryn auf den Schlips getreten fühlt*): Mensch, das war doch nur ein rhetorischer Kniff, um die Stimmung im Lande zu heben (*weist mit einem Kopfnicken auf Kathryn*).

RAY: Ein Typ der aus der Gosse kommt und einen Gutteil seines Lebens in der Gosse verbracht hat (*zeigt auf Ryan*), sollte sich genau überlegen, ob er mir mit irgendwelchen Anschuldigungen kommt.

(*Clown provoziert Ryan wie ein Schläger.*)

RYAN (*zum Clown*): He, behalt' deine Pfoten bei dir.

(*Clown wechselt auf Ryans Seite. Rückt Ray mit dem Finger bedrohlich auf den Leib. Er wechselt immer wieder die Seiten, ergreift dabei jeweils Partei für einen der beiden.*)

KATHRYN: He, Jungs, lasst es gut sein.

RAY (*lacht Ryan drohend ins Gesicht*): Okay, jetzt reicht's.

RYAN: Bleib' mir vom Leib!

RAY (*leise*): So ein Arschloch.

RYAN: Jetzt reicht's!

RAY (*lauter*): So ein Arschloch.[12]

[…]

Akt 4, Szene 4 – Kapitulation

Adaptierte Dialoge
−Pressekonferenz von Anthony Weiner, 6. Jun 2011
−Der Kongressabgeordnete Joe Wilson attackiert Barack Obama mit Zwischenrufen, 9. Sept 2009
−Barack Obama spricht in einem Interview von 1996 über Michelle Obama, Le Monde, 11. Jan 2009

RAFAEL, RAY, RYAN: It wasn't part of a plan!

ANNIE: Have you really apologized to the people? Are you gonna run again?

RAFAEL: I told Leno I was running. I just thought, it would freak everyone out. It'll be so funny. And two months later I was elected. What the fuck is that? All these people are asking me, "What's your plan? Who's on your staff?" I didn't have a plan. I didn't have a staff. I wasn't running until I went on Leno.[14]

RAY (*aside to camera*): You have to realize the thing was so much fun! We had a great time!

KATHRYN: When others were caught and had to resign, did that make you stop and think, maybe I shouldn't be doing this because I could be caught next? (*Annie and Lizzie join in unison*) Did that ever go through your mind?

RYAN: If you want to live rather than just exist, you want the drama.

ANNIE, KATHRYN, LIZZIE: How's anything ever gonna change?[13]

[…]

– Barack Obama im Gespräch mit den Herausgebern des Hearst Magazine, FoxNews.com, 4. Apr 2011
– Arnold Schwarzenegger im Interview mit Michael Lewis, California and Bust, Vanity Fair, November 2011
– George W. Bush wendet sich in einer Rede über die Wirtschaftskrise an das amerikanische Volk, 24. Sept 2008

Szenario

Ein Ehemann entschuldigt sich bei seiner Frau für seine Seitensprünge. In der Folge von Rafael und Annie stoßen die anderen beiden Paare (Ray/Kathryn und Ryan/Lizzie) hinzu, verstärken oder übernehmen immer wieder den Text. Der Clown setzt sich ein Headset auf und dirigiert während der gesamten Szene die Kameraleute.

RAY: Dass ich das getan habe, war wirklich dumm und destruktiv. Aber es war nicht meine Absicht, dich zu verletzen.

RYAN: Es ging nicht darum, dich zu betrügen. Es ging nicht darum …

RAFAEL, RAY, RYAN: Das war nicht geplant!

ANNIE: Hast du dich wirklich beim Volk entschuldigt? Kandidierst du nochmal?

RAFAEL: Ich habe Leno gesagt, dass ich nochmal kandidiere. Ich dachte einfach, da flippen alle aus. Das wird wirklich lustig. Und zwei Monate später war ich dann gewählt. Was ist das denn für ein Mist? Alle fragen mich: „Was haben Sie vor? Wer ist in Ihrem Team?" Ich hatte gar keinen Plan. Ich hatte auch kein Team. Ich kandidierte gar nicht, bis ich bei Leno war.[14]

RAY (*zur Seite, in Richtung Kamera*): Man muss sich mal klarmachen, wie witzig das war! Wir hatten einen Riesenspaß!

KATHRYN: Als andere erwischt wurden und zurücktreten mussten, hast du da gestutzt und gedacht, ich sollte das lieber lassen, sonst könnte ich der Nächste sein, den sie erwischen? (*Annie und Lizzie, unisono*) Ist dir das jemals durch den Kopf gegangen?

RYAN: Wenn man wirklich leben will, nicht nur existieren, dann wird's eben auch mal dramatisch.

ANNIE, KATHRYN, LIZZIE: Wie soll sich jemals irgendwas ändern?[13]

[…]

In Camera, 2012
[Excerpts]

Produced by Malmö Konsthall in collaboration with SVT
Script adapted by Liz Magic Laser and Sofia Pontén from Jean
Paul Sartre's H u i s c l o s (No Exit; 1944)

Liz Magic Laser as the news producer VALET
Anders E Larsson as the Anchorman JOSEPH GARCIN
Karin Hallén as the Reporter on the Scene INEZ SERRANO
Maria Lindh as the Interviewee ESTELLE RIGAULT

Scene Description
GARCIN reporting from SVT television news studio in Malmö,
Sweden.
INEZ reporting from Gustav Adolfs torg in Malmö, Sweden.
ESTELLE giving an interview from the living room of
Finn Juhl's House, Ordrupgaard, built in 1942 in Charlottenlund,
Denmark, with blue, red and green furniture elements and a
bronze sculpture.

Costumes
GARCIN in a grey suit, grey button down shirt, and a maroon tie.
INEZ in a peach and olive blazer and skirt combination.
ESTELLE in a yellow top and blue skirt (mimicking a 1946
portrait of Finn's partner Hanne Wilhelm Hansen painted by
Vilhelm Lundstrøm that hangs above the sofa).

General Directions
The camera – is your scene partner/the public/your captor.
Lines are predominantly addressed to the camera.
Gaze – maintain an upward steady gaze above camera
(upward corner of room or sky). Demonstrate an altered state
of consciousness as if viewing a cinema-size surveillance screen
displaying life on earth in your absence.

Scene I – Intro Garcin
Opening Segment (*Garcin enters, looks left, looks right, scans
room. Approaches anchor desk, sits, inserts earpiece.*)

*1. Camera I pans 360 degrees from Garcin's position starting
with control room.*
GARCIN (*sitting at news desk with hands folded,
as if rehearsing his introductory 'Good evening.'
Glances around*): Hmm, so here we are?![15]
VALET (*delivered through a PA system from control room.
Deadpan delivery throughout*): Yes.
GARCIN: And this is what it looks like?[16]
VALET: Yes, this is what it looks like.

2. Opening jingle and graphics
GARCIN: A well-equipped studio, I see … Well, well, I dare say
one gets used to it in time.
VALET: Some do. Some don't.
GARCIN: Are all the other rooms like this one?
VALET: How could they be? We cater for all sorts: the Chinese
and the Saudis, for instance. What use would they have for a
studio like this?

In Camera, 2012
[Auszüge]

Produktion der Malmö Konsthall in Zusammenarbeit mit SVT
Skript von Liz Magic Laser und Sofia Pontén, eine Adaption
von Jean Paul Sartres Stück H u i s c l o s (Geschlossene
Gesellschaft, 1944)

Liz Magic Laser als Nachrichtenredakteurin VALET
Anders E Larsson als Nachrichtensprecher JOSEPH GARCIN
Karin Hallén als Reporterin im Außeneinsatz INEZ SERRANO
Maria Lindh als die Interviewte ESTELLE RIGAULT

Beschreibung der Szene
GARCIN berichtet aus dem Nachrichtenstudio des Senders SVT
im schwedischen Malmö.
INEZ berichtet vom Gustav Adolfs torg in Malmö.
ESTELLE gibt ein Interview im Wohnzimmer des Finn Juhls
hus in Ordrupgaard; das Haus wurde 1942 in Charlottenlund,
Dänemark, errichtet und mit blauen, roten und grünen Möbeln
und einer Bronzestatue ausgestattet.

Kostüme
GARCIN trägt einen grauen Anzug mit grauem Button-Down-
Hemd und rotbrauner Krawatte.
INEZ trägt einen Blazer mit Rock in Pfirsich und Olivgrün.
ESTELLE trägt ein gelbes Oberteil über blauem Rock (in Nach-
ahmung eines 1946 von Vilhelm Lundstrøm gemalten Porträts
von Juhls Lebenspartnerin Hanne Wilhelm Hansen, das über dem
Sofa hängt).

Allgemeine Anweisungen
Die Kamera – ist euer Mitspieler/das Publikum/hält euch im
Bann. Der Text wird vorwiegend zur Kamera gesprochen.
Aufwärts – ständiger Blick über die Kamera hinweg (in die
obere Raumecke oder in den Himmel). Zeigt einen gesteiger-
ten Grad an Bewusstheit, als würdet ihr auf einem Überwachungs-
monitor in Kinogröße das Leben beobachten, das sich in eurer
Abwesenheit auf der Erde vollzieht.

Szene I – Auftritt Garcin
Eingangssegment (*Garcin kommt herein, schaut links,
schaut rechts, schaut sich im Raum um. Er geht zum
Sprechertisch, setzt sich, legt das Headset an.*)

*1. Kamera I 360°-Schwenk aus Garcins Position, beginnend mit
dem Regieraum.*
GARCIN (*sitzt mit gefalteten Händen am Sprechertisch als
wolle er sein einleitendes „Guten Abend" proben. Schaut herum*):
Hm, da sind wir also?![15]
VALET (*über Lautsprecher aus dem Regieraum. Durchweg
ausdruckslos*): Ja.
GARCIN: Und so sieht das aus?[16]
VALET: Ja, so sieht das aus.

2. Eröffnungsjingle und Animation
GARCIN: Aha, ein gut ausgerüstetes Studio … Ich nehme an,
dass man sich auf Dauer daran gewöhnen wird.

GARCIN: And what use do you suppose I have for this one? (*Firm, confident man of knowledge; as if delivering obituary of a well-known figure*) Do you know who I was? … Oh, well, it's no great matter. And, to tell the truth, I had quite a habit of working in scenarios that I didn't relish, and in questionable roles. I'd even come to like it. A bit part on a daily show – you know the type of gig? – well, it had its high points anyhow. "There's no business like show business," as they say.

VALET: And you'll find that working in a studio has its points.

GARCIN: Really? … Yes, yes, I dare say … (*He takes another look around.*) Still, I certainly didn't expect – this! You know what they tell us out there?

VALET: What about?

GARCIN: About (*makes a sweeping gesture*) this – bureau.

VALET: Really, how could you believe such gossip? Unsubstantiated rumors told by people who'd never set foot in here. For, of course, if they had –

GARCIN: Quite so. (*Subtle laugh. Abruptly the laugh dies from Garcin's face.*) But, I say, where are the instruments of torture?

VALET: The what?

GARCIN: The racks and red-hot pincers and all the other paraphernalia?

VALET: Ah, you must have your little joke!

GARCIN (*as if he's James Bond in villain's lair; calm and collected in the face of immanent torture*): My little joke? Oh, I see. No, I wasn't joking. (*A short silence; strolls around the studio examining it.*) No mirrors, I see. No windows. Only to be expected. And nothing breakable. (*Bursts out angrily*) But, damn it all, you might have left me my toothbrush!

VALET: That's good! So you haven't yet got over your – what-do-you-call-it? – sense of human dignity? Excuse my laughing.

GARCIN (*thumping on desk*): I'll ask you to be more polite. I quite realize the position I'm in, but I won't tolerate …

VALET: Sorry. No offense meant. But all our guests ask me the same questions. Silly questions, if you'll pardon my saying so. Where's the torture-chamber? That's the first thing they ask, all of them. They don't bother their heads about the bathroom requisites, that I can assure you. But after a bit, when they've got their nerve back, they start in about their toothbrushes and what-not. Good heavens, Mr. Garcin, can't you use your brains? What, I ask you, would be the point of brushing your teeth in here?

GARCIN (*more calmly; trying to suppress fear and prove that he's unafraid*): Yes, of course you're right. (*He looks around again*) And why should one want to see oneself in a mirror? (*Gesturing to camera*) But that contraption over there, that's another story. I suppose there will be times when I stare my eyes out at it. Stare my eyes out (*Stares into camera; slight undercurrent of fear*) – see what I mean? … Alright, let's put our cards on the table. I assure you I'm quite conscious of my position. Shall I tell you what it feels like?

3. Image changes on studio monitor behind Garcin's anchor desk to show bronze sculpture at Finn Juhl's House.

GARCIN (*emphasizing dissociated reportage-style delivery*): A man's drowning, choking, sinking by inches, till only his eyes are just above water. And what does he see? That eye staring back at him. As in a nightmare. That's their idea, isn't it? … No, I suppose you're under orders not to answer questions; and I won't insist.

VALET: Das kommt ganz auf die Leute an.

GARCIN: Sind alle Räume so?

VALET: Wo denken Sie hin? Zu uns kommen Chinesen und Saudis, zum Beispiel. Was sollen die denn mit so einem Studio anfangen?

GARCIN: Und ich, was soll ich damit anfangen? (*Ein bestimmter, selbstbewusster Mann, der sich auskennt; als würde er den Nachruf auf eine bekannte Persönlichkeit sprechen.*) Wissen Sie, wer ich war? … Na ja, was macht das schon. Schließlich habe ich schon immer in Szenarien gearbeitet, die ich nicht mochte, und in fragwürdigen Rollen. Am Ende hat's mir sogar gefallen. Eine Nebenrolle in einer täglichen Sendung – kennen Sie solche Auftritte? – das hatte allerdings auch seine Höhepunkte. „There's no business like show business", heißt es.

VALET: Und Sie werden sehen: die Arbeit im Studio hat auch was.

GARCIN: So? Gut, würde ich schon sagen … (*Schaut sich noch einmal um*) Trotzdem, das hätte ich nicht erwartet! Sie wissen bestimmt, was man da unten erzählt?

VALET: Worüber?

GARCIN: Na, (*mit einem unbestimmten, weit ausholenden Gebärde*) über dieses – Büro.

VALET: Wirklich? Glauben Sie etwa an diesen Blödsinn? Haltlose Gerüchte, die von Leuten verbreitet werden, die nie ein Fuß hierher gesetzt haben. Denn schließlich, wenn sie hierher gekommen wären …

GARCIN: Richtig. (*Lacht subtil. Plötzlich weicht das Lachen aus Garcins Gesicht.*) Aber wo sind eigentlich die Folterwerkzeuge.

VALET: Was?

GARCIN: Die Roste, die rotglühenden Zangen, die Ausstattung?

VALET: Sie machen wohl Witze?

GARCIN (*wie James Bond, der im Hauptquartier des Bösewichts ruhig und gefasst der drohenden Folter entgegensieht*): Ob ich scherze? Verstehe. Nein, ich mache keine Witze. (*Pause. Er geht im Studio umher.*) Keine Spiegel, keine Fenster, natürlich. Nichts Zerbrechliches. (*Mit plötzlicher Heftigkeit*) Und warum ist mir meine Zahnbürste abgenommen worden?

VALET: Da haben wir es. Die Menschenwürde macht sich wieder bemerkbar. Fantastisch. Entschuldigen Sie, wenn ich lache.

GARCIN (*schlägt wütend auf den Tisch*): Bitte keine Vertraulichkeiten. Ich kenne meine Lage durchaus, aber ich dulde nicht, dass Sie …

VALET: Schon gut! Entschuldigen Sie. Aber das ist einfach so, alle Gäste stellen dieselbe Frage. Wo ist die Folterkammer? In dem Augenblick denken sie, das schwöre ich Ihnen, überhaupt nicht an ihre Toilette. Und dann, wenn man sie beruhigt hat, kommt die Zahnbürste. Aber um Gottes Willen, Herr Garcin, können Sie nicht mal nachdenken? Denn wozu, frage ich Sie, wollen Sie sich denn die Zähne putzen?

GARCIN (*beruhigt; versucht seine Befürchtungen zu unterdrücken und zu zeigen, dass er keine Angst hat*): Ja, richtig, wozu? (*Er sieht sich um*) Und warum sollte man sich im Spiegel sehen? (*Gestikuliert in die Kamera.*) Aber dieser Apparat da drüben, das ist natürlich was ganz anderes. Ich kann mir vorstellen, dass ich den in bestimmten Augenblicken mit aufgerissenen Augen anstarren werde. Mit aufgerissenen Augen, was (*starrt in die Kamera, mit einem leichten Anflug von Angst*) – sehen Sie? … Machen wir uns nichts vor, es gibt nichts zu verbergen; ich sagen Ihnen, dass ich meine Lage durchaus kenne! Soll ich Ihnen sagen, wie sich das anfühlt?

But don't forget, I've a good notion of what's coming to me, so don't you boast about catching me off my guard. (*Gesturing to camera*) I'm facing the situation, facing it. (*Takes a lap around desk, checking out the television studio.*) So that's that; no toothbrush. And no bed, either. One never sleeps here, I take it?

VALET: That's so.

GARCIN: Just as I expected. Why should one sleep? A sort of drowsiness steals on you, tickles you behind the ears, and you feel your eyes closing – but why sleep? You rest your head on your desk and – in a flash, sleep flies away. Miles and miles away. So you rub your eyes, sit down, and it starts all over again. (*Behaves as if it's end of segment. Pause for interlude jingle/graphics.*)

4. Interlude jingle/graphics

VALET: Romantic, that's what you are.

GARCIN: Will you keep quiet, please! … I won't make a scene, I shan't be sorry for myself, I'll face the situation, as I said just now. Face it fairly and squarely. I won't have it springing at me from behind, before I've had time to size it up. And you call that being "romantic"! … So it comes to this; one doesn't need rest. Why bother about sleep if one isn't sleepy? That stands to reason, doesn't it? Wait a minute, there's a snag somewhere; something disagreeable. Why, now, should it be disagreeable? … Ah, I see; it's life without a break.

VALET: What do you mean by that?

GARCIN: What do I mean? (*Eyes camera/Valet suspiciously*) I thought so. That's why there's something so beastly, so damn bad-mannered, in the way you stare at me. They're paralyzed.

VALET: What are you talking about?

GARCIN: Your eyelids. We move ours up and down. Blinking, we call it. It's like a small black shutter that clicks down and makes a break. Everything goes black; one's eyes are moistened. You cannot imagine how restful, refreshing, it is. Four thousand little rests per hour. Four thousand little respites – just think! … So that's the idea. I'm to live without eyelids. Don't act the fool, you know what I mean. No eyelids, no sleep, right? I shall never sleep again. But then – how shall I endure my own company? Try to understand. You see, I'm fond of teasing, it's second nature for me – and I'm used to teasing myself. Plaguing myself, if you prefer; I don't tease nicely. But I cannot go on doing that without a break. Out there I had my nights. I slept. I always had good nights. By way of compensation, I suppose. And happy little dreams. There was a green field. Just an ordinary field. I used to stroll in it … (*Tone shift*) Is it daytime now?

VALET: Can't you see? The lights are on.

GARCIN: Ah yes, I've got it. It's your daytime. And outside?

VALET: Outside?

GARCIN: Damn it, you know what I mean. Beyond that wall.

VALET: There's a passage.

GARCIN: And at the end of the passage?

VALET: There's more rooms, more passages, and stairs.

GARCIN: And what lies beyond them?

VALET: That's all.

GARCIN: But surely you have a day off sometimes. Where do you go?

VALET: To my uncle's place. He's the head producer here. He has an office on the third floor.

GARCIN: I should have guessed as much. Where's the light switch?

3. Auf dem Studiomonitor hinter Garcins Sprechertisch wird ein anderes Bild eingeblendet; es erscheint die Bronzestatue im Finn Juhls hus.

GARCIN (*Betonung des unzusammenhängenden, reportage-artigen Vortrags*): Ein Mann erstickt, er geht unter, ertrinkt, nur die Augen bleiben über dem Wasser, und was sieht er? Dieses Auge, das ihn anstarrt. Was für ein Alptraum! So hatten die sich das gedacht, nicht wahr? … Na ja, man hat Ihnen sicher verboten, mir zu antworten, ich will Sie nicht weiter behelligen. Aber merken Sie sich, dass man mich nicht überrumpeln kann. (*Gestikuliert in die Kamera*) Ich sehe der Situation ins Gesicht, ins Gesicht. (*Dreht eine Runde um den Tisch, schaut sich im Studio um*) Also keine Zahnbürste. Auch kein Bett. Denn man schläft hier natürlich nie?

VALET: Logisch!

GARCIN: Ich hätte wetten können. Wozu sollte man auch schlafen? Der Schlaf packt einen hinter den Ohren. Man merkt, dass einem die Augen zufallen, aber wozu schlafen. Man legt den Kopf auf den Tisch, und ssst … schon ist die Müdigkeit verflogen! Meilenweit weg. Man braucht sich nur die Augen zu reiben und sich wieder hinzusetzen, und schon fängt alles wieder an. (*Verhält sich, als wäre die Sequenz zu Ende. Pause für das Einspielen des Jingles und der Animation.*)

4. Eingespieltes Jingle mit Animation

VALET: Was für eine blühende Fantasie Sie haben!

GARCIN: Halten Sie den Mund. Ich werde nicht schreien, ich werde nicht in Selbstmitleid versinken, ich will der Situation wie gesagt ins Gesicht sehen. Sie aufrecht und umstandslos angehen. Ich will nicht von ihr überfallen werden, ohne dass ich sie hätte erkennen können. Blühende Fantasie? Also man hat nicht einmal das Bedürfnis nach Schlaf. Wozu auch schlafen, wenn man nicht müde ist? Klingt doch vernünftig, oder? Moment mal: Warum ist denn das zwangsläufig quälend? Ich hab's: ein Leben ohne Unterbrechung.

VALET: Wie meinen sie das?

GARCIN: „Wie meinen Sie das?" (*Schielt misstrauisch zur Kamera/Valet*) Ich war sicher! Das erklärt die plumpe, unausstehliche Aufdringlichkeit Ihres Blicks. Tatsächlich, Sie sind gelähmt.

VALET: Wovon sprechen Sie denn?

GARCIN: Von Ihren Augenlidern. Wir nämlich machen die Augenlider auf und zu. Zwinkern nennt man das. Ein kleiner schwarzer Blitz, Vorhang zu, Vorhang auf: Das war die Unterbrechung. Das Auge wird feucht, die Welt verschwindet. Sie können sich gar nicht vorstellen, wie erholsam das ist. Viertausend Pausen in einer Stunde. Viertausend kleine Fluchten. Darum geht es also. Ich werde also ohne Augenlider leben? Sehen Sie mich doch nicht so dämlich an! Ohne Augenlider, ohne Schlaf, das ist doch dasselbe. Ich werde nicht mehr schlafen können … Aber wie kann ich mich dann ertragen? Versuchen Sie mal, sich das vorzustellen, los, strengen Sie sich an: Ich bin ein Widerspruchsgeist, verstehen Sie, und ich … ich provoziere gern. Auch mich selbst. Aber ich kann nicht pausenlos provozieren. Da unten gab es Nächte. Ich schlief. Ich hatte einen sanften Schlaf. Als Ausgleich. Ich gönnte mir einfache Träume. Eine Wiese … Eine Wiese, sonst nichts. Ich träumte, dass ich darüber ging. (*Wechsel im Tonfall*) Ist eigentlich Tag?

VALET: Sie sehen doch, dass die Lampen an sind.

93

VALET: There isn't any.

GARCIN: What? Can't one turn off the light?

VALET: Oh, the producers can cut off the current if they want to. But I can't remember their having done so on this floor. We have all the electricity we want in here.

GARCIN: So one has to live with one's eyes open all the time?

VALET: To live, did you say?

GARCIN: Let's not quibble over words. With one's eyes open. Forever. Always broad daylight in my eyes – and in my head. (*Short silence*) And suppose I took that contraption and threw it at the light – wouldn't it go out?

5. *Camera 1 reveals camera 3 and studio lights.*

VALET: You can't move it. It's too heavy.

GARCIN (*as if seizing the camera and trying to lift it*): You're right? It's too heavy. (*A short silence follows.*)

VALET: Very well, if you don't need me any longer, I'll be off.

GARCIN: What? You're going? (*As if camera/Valet is leaving*) Wait. (*Takes out earpiece*) This is an earpiece, isn't it?

VALET: Yes.

GARCIN: And if I ring, you're bound to respond?

VALET: Well yeah, I suppose. But you can never be too sure about that. There's something wrong with the wiring, and it doesn't always work. (*Tests earpiece.*)

GARCIN: Testing, testing, one, two, three … It seems to work.

VALET: So it does. But I shouldn't count on it too much if I were you. It's – capricious. Well, I really must go now.

Garcin: (*Makes a gesture to detain him*) Wait!

VALET: Yes?

GARCIN: No, never mind. (*He goes to the desk and picks up a pen*) What's this?

VALET: Can't you see? An ordinary ballpoint pen.

GARCIN: Is there any paper here? Are there books?!

VALET: No.

GARCIN: Then what's the use of this? (*Valet scoffs; doesn't answer*) Very well. You can go.

(*'Exit' Valet*)

Scene 2 – Enter Inez
Reference: Morning show fluff piece on "Midsommar"

GARCIN (*goes to the camera and strokes its lens shaft reflectively. He sits down; then gets up, tests earpiece*): Hello …? Hello? … Hello?[17] (*Goes towards green screen, frantically knocks on it*) Hello …! Help! (*Gives up, beats again; suddenly grows calm; at same moment Inez materializes via green screen, gazing slightly downward left.*)[19]

6. *Video feed of Inez appears via green screen.*[20]

VALET: Did you call?

GARCIN (*on the verge of answering 'Yes' – but then he sees Inez on studio monitor*): No.

VALET (*to Inez*): And we're rolling, we'll be going live in five. (*Inez says nothing*) Is there any information you require – ?[18] (*Inez still keeps silent, and the Valet is slightly huffed.*) Most of our guests have quite a lot to ask me. But I won't insist. Anyhow, regarding the toothbrush, and mic, and that contraption over there, this gentleman can tell you anything you want to know as

GARCIN: Natürlich. Das ist Ihr Tag. Und draußen?

VALET: Draußen?

GARCIN: Verdammt noch mal, Sie wissen doch, was ich meine. Hinter diesen Wänden.

VALET: Da ist ein Flur.

GARCIN: Und am Ende des Flurs?

VALET: Da sind andre Zimmer und andre Flure und Treppen.

GARCIN: Und dann?

VALET: Das ist alles.

GARCIN: Sie haben doch sicher mal einen freien Tag. Wo gehen Sie dann hin?

VALET: Zu meinem Onkel, der leitender Redakteur ist. Sein Büro ist im zweiten Stock.

GARCIN: Das hätte ich mir denken können. Wo ist der Lichtschalter?

VALET: Es gibt keinen.

GARCIN: Man kann also das Licht nicht ausmachen?

VALET: Die Produzenten können den Strom abschalten, wenn sie wollen. Aber ich erinnere mich nicht, dass sie es in diesem Stock irgendwann mal getan hätten. Strom ist bei uns umsonst.

GARCIN: Also muss man mit offenen Augen leben?

VALET: Leben, sagten Sie?

GARCIN: Reiten Sie doch nicht auf einem Wort herum. Mit offenen Augen. Immer. Es wird heller Tag in meinen Augen sein. Und in meinem Kopf (*kurze Pause*). Und wenn ich den Apparat nach der elektrischen Lampe schmeiße? Geht sie dann aus?

5. *Kamera 1 zeigt Kamera 3 und die Studiolampen.*

VALET: Den können Sie nicht bewegen, der ist zu schwer.

GARCIN (*tut so, als wolle er die Kamera packen und versuchen, sie hochzuheben*): Sie haben recht? Er ist zu schwer (*kurzes Schweigen*).

VALET: Also wenn Sie mich jetzt nicht mehr brauchen, lasse ich Sie allein.

GARCIN: Was? Sie gehen? (*Als ob die Kamera/Valet ginge*) Warten Sie. (*Nimmt das Headset vom Ohr*) Das ist doch ein Headset?

VALET: Ja.

GARCIN: Und wenn ich klingle, dann müssen Sie antworten?

VALET: Im Prinzip, ja. Aber es hat seine Mucken. Irgendwas stimmt mit den Kabeln nicht, es funktioniert nicht immer. (*Probiert das Headset aus.*)

GARCIN: Test, Test, eins, zwei, drei … Scheint zu funktionieren.

VALET: Es geht. Aber freuen Sie sich nicht zu früh, das wird nicht lange dauern. Also, ich muss jetzt wirklich los.

GARCIN (*macht eine Gebärde, um ihn zurückzuhalten*): Warten Sie!

VALET: Ja?

GARCIN: Nein, nichts. (*Er geht zum Tisch und nimmt einen Stift*) Was ist denn das?

VALET: Das sehen Sie doch, ein gewöhnlicher Kugelschreiber.

GARCIN: Gibt es denn Papier hier? Gibt es Bücher?!

VALET: Nein.

GARCIN: Wozu ist er dann da? (*Valet zuckt mit den Achseln, ohne zu antworten*) Gut. Gehen Sie.

(*Valet ab*)

well as I could. We've had a little chat, him and me.

(*'Exit' Valet*)

(*Garcin retreats to anchor desk and refrains from looking at Inez, who is inspecting the room. Abruptly she turns to Garcin.*)[23]

INEZ: Where's Florence? (*Garcin does not reply*) Didn't you hear me? I asked you about Florence. Where is she?

GARCIN: I haven't an idea.

INEZ (*to Garcin*): Ah, that's the way it works, is it? Torture by separation. Well, as far as I'm concerned, you won't get anywhere. Florence was a tiresome little fool, and I shan't miss her in the least.

GARCIN: I beg your pardon. Who do you suppose I am?

INEZ: You? Why, the torturer, of course.

GARCIN (*looks startled, then bursts out laughing as if he's a reporter engaged in cheerful banter*): Well, that's a good one! Too comic for words. I the torturer! So you came in, had a look at me, and thought I was – er – one of the staff. Of course, it's that silly producer's fault; she should have introduced us. A torturer indeed! I'm Joseph Garcin, journalist and man of letters by profession. And as we're both in the same boat, so to speak, might I ask you, Mrs. – ?

INEZ (*testily*): Not "Mrs." I'm unmarried.

GARCIN: Right. That's a start, anyway. Well, now that we've broken the ice, do you really think I look like a torturer? And, by the way, how does one recognize torturers when one sees them? Evidently you've ideas on the subject.

INEZ: They look frightened.

GARCIN: Frightened! But how ridiculous! Of whom should they be frightened? Of their victims?

INEZ: Laugh away, but I know what I'm talking about. I've often watched my face in the mirror.

GARCIN: In the mirror? (*He looks around him*) How beastly of them! They've removed everything in the least resembling a mirror. (*Short silence*) Anyhow, I can assure you I'm not frightened. Not that I take my position lightly; I realize its gravity only too well. But I'm not afraid.

INEZ (*shrugging her shoulders*): That's your affair. (*Silence*) Must you be in there all the time, or can you take a stroll outside, now and then?

GARCIN: We're stuck here.

INEZ: Oh! … That's too bad.

GARCIN (*sits in anchorman position with hands folded*): I can quite understand that it bores you having me here. And I, too – well, quite frankly, I'd rather be alone. I want to think things out, you know; to set my life in order, and one does that better by oneself. But I'm sure we'll manage to pull along together somehow. I'm no talker, I don't move much; in fact I'm a peaceful sort of fellow. Only, if I may venture on a suggestion, we should make a point of being extremely courteous to each other. That will ease the situation for us both.

INEZ: I'm not polite.

GARCIN: Then I must be polite for two. (*A longish silence. Garcin is staring at camera lens composing his face, while Inez paces up and down.*)

INEZ (*fixing her eyes on him – as if they are off camera for a moment*): Your mouth!

GARCIN (*as if waking from a dream*): I beg your pardon.

INEZ: Can't you keep your mouth still? You keep twisting it about all the time. It's grotesque.

Szene 2 – Auftritt Inez

Bezug: Morgensendung mit einem belanglosen Beitrag über den „Midsommar".

GARCIN (*geht zur Kamera und streichelt sie. Er setzt sich. Er steht wieder auf, testet das Headset*): Hallo …? Hallo …?[17] Hallo …? (*Er geht auf den grünen Hintergrund zu und klopft energisch dagegen.*) Hallo …! Hilfe …! (*Gibt auf, schlägt noch einmal; plötzlich wird er ruhig, in diesem Moment erscheint Inez als Einblendung per Greenscreen, schaut leicht nach unten links.*)[19]

6. *Videoeinspielung von Inez über Greenscreen*[20]

VALET: Sie haben nach mir gerufen?

GARCIN (*will „Ja" antworten, wirft aber einen Blick auf Inez auf dem Studiomonitor*): Nein.

VALET (*zu Inez*): Und, Kamera läuft, wir sind live, in fünf. (*Inez schweigt.*) Wenn Sie noch Fragen haben …[18](*Inez schweigt noch immer, Valet ist leicht eingeschnappt.*) Im Allgemeinen erkundigen sich die Gäste gern … Aber ich will nicht aufdringlich sein. Was übrigens die Zahnbürste, das Mikro und den Apparat dort angeht, ist der Herr hier im Bilde und kann Ihnen ebenso gut Auskunft geben wie ich. Wir beide haben schon ein wenig geplaudert.

(*Valet ab*)

(*Garcin geht zurück zum Sprechertisch und vermeidet es, Inez anzuschauen, die sich im Raum umsieht. Plötzlich wendet sie sich Garcin zu.*)[23]

INEZ: Wo ist Florence? (*Garcin sagt nichts.*) Hören Sie mich? Ich frage Sie, wo Florence ist.

GARCIN: Keine Ahnung.

INEZ (*zu Garcin*): Aha, so funktioniert das also, nicht wahr? Folter durch Trennung. Gut, das zieht bei mir nicht. Florence war eine dumme Gans, und ich traure ihr nicht nach.

GARCIN: Verzeihung! Für wen halten Sie mich?

INEZ: Sie? Sie sind der Folterknecht.

GARCIN (*zuckt zusammen und fängt laut an zu lachen, wie ein Reporter in ausgelassener Runde*): Zu komisch. Der Folterknecht, großartig! Sie kommen rein, Sie sehen mich und denken: Das ist – äh – einer von der Belegschaft. Daran ist natürlich diese dämliche Redakteurin schuld; sie hätte uns vorstellen sollen. Der Folterknecht! Ich bin Joseph Garcin, Journalist und Literat. Die Wahrheit ist, dass wir in derselben Lage sind. Frau –

INEZ (*kühl*): Fräulein. Ich bin unverheiratet.

GARCIN: Gut. Schön. Nun, das Eis ist gebrochen. Also Sie finden, dass ich aussehe wie ein Folterknecht? Und woran erkennt man Folterknechte, bitteschön? Sie haben da offensichtlich bestimmte Vorstellungen.

INEZ: Die sehen aus, als hätten sie Angst.

GARCIN: Angst? Sehr witzig. Und vor wem? Vor ihren Opfern?

INEZ: Lachen Sie nur! Ich weiß, was ich sage. Ich habe mich im Spiegel gesehen.

GARCIN: Im Spiegel? (*Er sieht sich um*) Gemein, man hat alles weggenommen, was nach einem Spiegel aussehen könnte. (*Pause*) Jedenfalls kann ich Ihnen versichern, dass ich keine Angst habe. Ich nehme die Situation nicht leicht, und ich bin mir ihres Ernstes voll bewusst. Aber ich habe keine Angst.

INEZ (*zuckt die Achseln*): Das ist Ihre Sache. (*Pause*) Müssen

GARCIN: So sorry. I wasn't aware of it.

INEZ: That's just what I reproach you with. (*Garcin's mouth twitches*) There you are! You talk about politeness, and you don't even try to control your face. Remember you're not alone; you've no right to inflict the sight of your fear on me.

GARCIN (*getting up and going towards her*): How about you? Aren't you afraid?

INEZ: What would be the use? There was some point in being afraid before; while one still had hope.

GARCIN (*in a low voice*): There's no more hope – but it's still "before." We haven't yet begun to suffer.

INEZ: That's so. (*A short silence. Back on camera.*) Well? What's going to happen?

GARCIN: I don't know. I'm waiting. (*Silence again. Garcin sits down and Inez walks away from camera and back towards it as if introducing a new segment.*)

(*Garcin's mouth twitches; after a glance at Inez he buries his face in his hands.*)

[…]

Scene 14 – No Way Out
Reference: Right-wing Greek politician, Kasidiaris, hits
prominent Communist Party member, Liana Kanelli, on
a mainstream morning talk show.

22. *Video feed of Inez is on studio monitor*

ESTELLE: What are you up to?

GARCIN: I'm going.

INEZ (*to the public/camera*): He won't get far. There's no way out.

GARCIN: I'll make them open it. (*He tries the earpiece, but it doesn't work*) Hello? Hello?!

(*Storms off toward green screen.*)

ESTELLE: Please! Please!

INEZ (*to Estelle*): Don't worry, my pet. The earpiece doesn't work.

GARCIN: I tell you they shall open. (*Bangs on the green screen as if it's a door*) I cannot endure it any longer, I'm through with you both. (*Estelle runs to camera; reacts as if Garcin is pushing her away*) Go away. You're even fouler than she. I won't let myself get bogged in your eyes. You're soft and slimy. Ugh! (*Bangs on 'door' again*) Like an octopus. Like a quagmire.

ESTELLE: I beg you, oh, I beg you not to leave me alone. I promise not to speak again, I won't trouble you in any way – but don't go. Don't leave me alone with her, now that she has shown her claws.

GARCIN: Look after yourself. I never asked you to come here.

ESTELLE: Oh, how mean you are! Yes, it's quite true you're a coward.

INEZ (*to camera/Estelle*): Well, my little sparrow has fallen from the nest, I hope you're satisfied now. You spat in my face – (*to passersby*) – All of you spat in my face – playing up to him, of course – and we had a tiff on his account. But he's going, and good riddance! (*Widely gesturing to crowd on street*) And we, the people, will have this all to ourselves.

(*Garcin starts banging on 'door'/green screen; stomping to make sound effects in tandem with fist thrusts.*)

Sie die ganze Zeit hier sein oder machen Sie ab und an draußen eine Runde?

GARCIN: Wir sitzen hier fest.

INEZ: Oh, schade.

GARCIN (*setzt sich auf den Platz des Sprechers und faltet die Hände*): Ich verstehe sehr gut, dass Sie meine Anwesenheit stört. Und ich persönlich wäre auch lieber allein: Ich muss mein Leben ordnen und will mich sammeln, und das macht man besser allein. Aber ich bin sicher, dass wir uns arrangieren können: Ich rede nicht, ich bewege mich kaum, und ich mache wenig Lärm. Nur, wenn ich mir einen Rat erlauben darf, wir sollten äußerste Höflichkeit zwischen uns bewahren. Das wird unser bester Selbstschutz sein.

INEZ: Ich bin nicht höflich.

GARCIN: Dann muss ich es eben doppelt sein. (*Langes Schweigen. Garcin starrt ins Objektiv der Kamera mit gefasstem Gesicht, während Inez auf und ab geht.*)

INEZ (*schaut ihn an – als wären sie einen Moment nicht vor der Kamera*): Ihr Mund!

GARCIN (*aus seinem Grübeln herausgerissen*): Wie bitte?

INEZ: Können Sie Ihren Mund nicht stillhalten. Er bewegt sich unter Ihrer Nase wie ein Kreisel. Grotesk.

GARCIN: Verzeihung. Ich habe es nicht gemerkt.

INEZ: Das finde ich ja gerade schlimm an Ihnen. (*Garcin zuckt mit dem Mund*) Schon wieder! Sie wollen höflich sein, und Sie haben nicht einmal Ihr Gesicht unter Kontrolle. Sie sind nicht allein, und Sie haben kein Recht, mich mit dem Anblick Ihrer Angst zu belästigen.

GARCIN (*steht auf und geht auf sie zu*): Haben Sie etwa keine Angst?

INEZ: Warum denn? Angst konnte man vorher haben, als wir noch Hoffnung hatten.

GARCIN (*sanft*): Es gibt zwar keine Hoffnung mehr, aber wir sind immer noch vorher. Wir haben noch nicht angefangen zu leiden, mein Fräulein.

INEZ: Ich weiß. (*Pause*) Also? Was wird kommen?

GARCIN: Ich weiß nicht. Ich warte. (*Wieder Schweigen. Garcin setzt sich, Inez entfernt sich von der Kamera und nähert sich ihr wieder, als wolle sie einen neuen Abschnitt einleiten.*)

(*Garcins Mund zuckt; er wirft einen Blick auf Inez und verbirgt dann sein Gesicht in den Händen.*)

[…]

Szene 14 – Kein Ausweg
Bezug: Der rechtsgerichtete griechische Politiker Kasidiaris
schlägt in einer populären Morgensendung des Fernsehens
das prominente Mitglied der Kommunistischen Partei Liana Kanelli.

22. *Videoeinspielung von Inez auf dem Studiomonitor*

ESTELLE: Was machst du?

GARCIN: Ich gehe.

INEZ (*ins Publikum/zur Kamera*): Du wirst nicht weit kommen: Die Tür ist zu.

GARCIN: Sie werden schon aufmachen müssen. (*Er probiert das Headset, doch es funktioniert nicht*) Hallo? Hallo?

(*Stürmt zum grünen Hintergrund.*)

ESTELLE: Bitte! Bitte!

23. Finn Juhl's House photo of closed door appears via green screen.

ESTELLE: You won't gain anything. If that door opens, I'm going, too.

INEZ: Where might that be?

ESTELLE: I don't care where. As far from you as I can.

GARCIN (*as if he's an anchorman who's pissed off at his producer, threatening to quit. Livid yet professional. Banging on 'door'*): Let me out! Open up! I'll endure anything, your red-hot tongs and molten lead, your racks and prongs and garrotes – all your fiendish gadgets, everything that burns and flays and tears – I'll put up with any torture you impose. Anything, anything would be better than this agony of mind, this creeping pain that gnaws and fumbles and caresses one and never hurts quite enough. (*He grips the camera lens and rattles it. Rage erupts.*) Now will you open?

24. Finn Juhl's House photo of open door appears via green screen.

(*Imaginary door flies open and he just avoids falling*) Ah!

(*A long silence*)

INEZ: Well, Garcin? You're free to go.

GARCIN (*knowingly*): Now I wonder why that happened.

INEZ: What are you waiting for? Hurry up and go.

GARCIN: I shall not go.

INEZ (*to camera*): And now what? (*Bursts out laughing*) What do you think? Place your bets – who's gonna go? The barrier's down, what are we all waiting for? … But what a situation! It's a scream! We're – inseparables!

(*Estelle springs at Inez/camera.*)

ESTELLE: Inseparables! Garcin, come and lend a hand. Quickly. We'll push her out and slam the door on her. That'll teach her a lesson.

(*Estelle and Inez struggle; Estelle moves toward camera with left hand appearing to tug Inez.*)

INEZ: Estelle! I beg you, let me stay. I won't go, I won't go! Not into the passage.

GARCIN: Let go of her.

ESTELLE: You're crazy. She hates you.

GARCIN: It's because of her I'm staying here.

(*Estelle releases Inez and stares dumb-foundedly at Garcin.*)

INEZ: Because of me? (*Pause*) All right, shut the door. It's ten times hotter here since it opened. (*Garcin shuts the door*) Because of me, you said?

GARCIN: Yes. You know what it means to be a coward.

INEZ: Yes, I know.

GARCIN (*turns to camera*): And you know what wickedness is, and shame, and fear. There were days when you peered into yourself, into the secret places of your heart, and what you saw there made you faint with horror. And then, the next day, you didn't know what to make of it, you couldn't interpret the horror you had glimpsed the day before. Yes, you know what evil costs. And when you say I'm a coward, you know from experience what that means. Is that so?

INEZ: Yes.

GARCIN: So, it's you whom I have to convince; you are of my kind. Did you suppose I meant to go? No, I couldn't leave you here, gloating over my defeat, with all those thoughts about me running in your head.

INEZ (*zu Estelle*): Keine Angst, mein Liebes, das Headset ist kaputt.

GARCIN: Ich sage euch doch, dass sie aufmachen werden. (*Er trommelt gegen den grünen Hintergrund wie an eine Tür.*) Ich kann euch nicht mehr ausstehen, ich kann nicht mehr. (*Estelle läuft zur Kamera, verhält sich, als würde Garcin sie von sich stoßen.*) Geh weg! Du widerst mich noch mehr an als die da. Ich will nicht in deinen Augen versacken. Du bist klebrig! Du bist wabblig. Bah! (*Er schlägt wieder gegen die 'Tür'.*) Du bist ein Krake, du bist ein Sumpf.

ESTELLE: Garcin, ich flehe dich an, geh nicht weg, ich werde nicht mehr mit dir sprechen, ich werde dich völlig in Ruhe lassen, aber geh nicht weg. Inez hat ihre Krallen gezeigt, ich will nicht mehr mit ihr allein bleiben.

GARCIN: Das ist deine Sache. Ich habe dich nicht gebeten zu kommen.

ESTELLE: Wie gemein du bist! Ja, es stimmt, dass du feige bist.

INEZ (*zur Kamera/Estelle*): Nun ist mein kleiner Spatz aus dem Nest gefallen, ich hoffe, jetzt bist du zufrieden. Du hast mir ins Gesicht gespuckt, um ihm zu gefallen, und wir haben uns seinetwegen verkracht. Aber jetzt geht er, den sind wir los! (*Gestikuliert mit ausladender Geste zur Menschenmenge auf der Straße*) Und wir, das Volk, werden es ganz für uns haben.

(*Garcin beginnt gegen die Tür/den grünen Hintergrund zu trommeln; stampft auf, um Geräusch zu seinen Schlägen zu machen.*)

23. Das Foto einer verschlossenen 'Tür' aus dem Finn Juhls hus wird per Greenscreen eingeblendet.

ESTELLE: Davon wirst Du nichts haben; wenn diese Tür aufgeht, laufe ich weg.

INEZ: Wohin?

ESTELLE: Irgendwohin. Möglichst weit weg von dir.

GARCIN (*wie ein Nachrichtenmoderator, der sich über seinen Redakteur ärgert, der droht, aufzuhören. Aufgebracht aber professionell. Schlägt gegen die 'Tür'*): Lasst mich raus! Aufmachen! Ich nehme alles hin: Beinschrauben, Zangen, flüssiges Blei, Halseisen, alles, was brennt, alles, was quält, ich will richtig leiden. Lieber hundert Stiche, lieber Peitsche, Vitriol als dieses abstrakte Leiden, dieses Schattenleiden, das einen streift, das einen streichelt und das niemals richtig weh tut. (*Er fasst die Kamera am Objektiv und rüttelt sie. Wutausbruch*) Wollen Sie wohl aufmachen?

24. Das Foto einer offenen Tür aus dem Finn Juhls hus wird per Greenscreen eingeblendet.

(*Die imaginäre Tür geht plötzlich auf, und er fällt fast hin.*) Ha!

(*Lange Stille*)

INEZ: Nun, Garcin? Gehen Sie doch.

GARCIN (*bedächtig*): Ich frage mich, warum diese Tür aufgegangen ist.

INEZ: Worauf warten Sie denn? Gehen Sie, schnell!

GARCIN: Ich gehe nicht weg.

INEZ (*in die Kamera*): Und nun? (*Platzt lachend heraus*) Also? Wer? Wer von uns dreien? Der Weg ist frei, wer hält uns zurück? Ha! Das ist ja zum Totlachen! Wir sind unzertrennlich.

(*Estelle springt Inez/die Kamera an.*)

ESTELLE: Unzertrennlich! Garcin! Hilf mir, hilf mir schnell. Wir ziehen sie nach draußen und schließen die Tür hinter ihr; dann wird sie schon sehen.

INEZ: Do you really wish to convince me?

GARCIN: That's the one and only thing I wish for now. (*Gesturing to camera/public*) I cannot hear them any longer, you know. Probably that means they're through with me, for good. The curtain's down, nothing of me is left on earth – not even the name of coward. So, we're alone. Only you remain to think of me. She – she doesn't count. It's you who matter; you who hate me. If you'll have faith in me I'm saved.

INEZ: It won't be easy. Have a look at me. I'm a hard-headed woman.

GARCIN: I'll give you all the time that's needed.

INEZ: Yes, we've lots of time in hand. All the time in the world.

GARCIN (*approaches Inez/video feed of her on monitor behind anchor desk, putting his hand on Inez/monitor*): Listen! Each man has an aim in life, a leading motive; that's so, isn't it? Well, I didn't give a damn for wealth, or for love. I aimed at being a real man. A tough man. I staked everything on the same horse … Can one possibly be a coward when one's deliberately courted danger at every turn? And can one judge a life by a single action?

INEZ: Why not? For thirty years he dreamt he was a hero, and condoned a thousand petty lapses – because a hero, of course, can do no wrong. An easy method, obviously. Then a day came when he was up against it, the red light of real danger – and he took the train to Mexico.

GARCIN: I "dreamt," you say. It was no dream. When I chose the hardest path, I made my choice deliberately. A man is what he wills himself to be.

INEZ (*to Garcin*): Prove it. Prove it was no dream. It's what one does, and nothing else, that shows the stuff one's made of.

GARCIN: I died too soon. I wasn't allowed time to – to do my deeds.

INEZ (*direct gaze into camera*): One always dies too soon – or too late. And yet one's whole life is complete at that moment, with a line drawn neatly under it, ready for summing up. You are – your life, and nothing else.

GARCIN: What a poisonous woman you are! With an answer for everything. (*Sits down.*)

INEZ (*to camera/public/humanity at large*): Now then! Don't lose heart. It shouldn't be so hard, convincing me. (*Needling him*) Pull yourself together, man, rake up some arguments. (*Garcin shrugs his shoulders*) I was right, wasn't I, when I said you were vulnerable? Now you're going to pay the price, and what a price! You're a coward, because I wish it. I wish it – do you hear? – I wish it. And yet, just look at me, see how weak I am, a mere breath on the air, (*emphasis*) a gaze observing you, a formless thought that thinks you. (*Garcin walks towards studio monitor showing live feed of Inez, raises right hand tensely to hit it; Inez shifts gaze up and left as if seeing his threatening palm*) Ah, they're open now, those big hands, those coarse, man hands! But what do you hope to do? You cannot throttle thoughts with hands. So you've no choice, you must convince me. You're at my mercy.

Scene 15 – Acceptance
Reference: The results are in. Romney/Putin/Sverige Demokraterna wins election by a landslide.

ESTELLE: Garcin!

GARCIN: What?

(*Estelle und Inez kämpfen; Estelle nähert sich mit der Linken der Kamera als würde sie an Inez zerren.*)

INEZ: Estelle! Estelle! Ich flehe dich an, behalte mich. Nicht in den Flur, wirf mich nicht in den Flur!

GARCIN: Lass sie los!

ESTELLE: Du bist verrückt. Sie hasst dich.

GARCIN: Ihretwegen bin ich geblieben.

(*Estelle lässt Inez los und sieht Garcin erstarrt an.*)

INEZ: Meinetwegen? (*Pause*) Gut, mach die Tür wieder zu. Es ist zehnmal heißer, seit sie offen ist. (*Garcin macht die Tür wieder zu.*) Meinetwegen, sagst Du?

GARCIN: Ja, du weißt, was ein Feigling ist.

INEZ: Ja, das weiß ich.

GARCIN (*wendet sich der Kamera zu*): Und Du weißt, was das Böse ist, die Schande, die Angst. Es hat Tage gegeben, wo du dir tief ins Herz gesehen hast – und das hat dich plötzlich fertiggemacht. Und am nächsten Tag wusstest du nicht mehr, was du davon halten solltest, es gelang dir nicht mehr, die Enthüllung des vergangenen Tages zu entziffern. Ja, du kennst den Preis des Bösen. Und wenn du sagst, dass ich ein Feigling bin, dann weißt du, wovon du sprichst, nicht?

INEZ: Ja.

GARCIN: Dich muss ich also überzeugen: Du bist von meiner Art. Konntest du dir vorstellen, dass ich weggehen würde? Ich konnte dich nicht hierlassen triumphierend, mit all diesen Gedanken im Kopf; all diesen Gedanken, die mich betreffen.

INEZ: Du willst mich wirklich überzeugen?

GARCIN: Was bleibt mir sonst übrig? Ich höre sie nicht mehr, weißt du. Sie sind sicher fertig mit mir. Fertig. Die Angelegenheit ist abgeschlossen, ich bin nichts mehr auf der Erde, nicht einmal mehr ein Feigling. Wir sind jetzt allein: Nur noch ihr beide könnt an mich denken. Sie zählt nicht. Aber du, du, die mich hasst, wenn du mir glaubst, rettest du mich.

INEZ: Das wird nicht leicht sein. Sieh mich an: Ich bin hartnäckig.

GARCIN: Ich werde dir die nötige Zeit geben.

INEZ: Ja, wir haben viel Zeit. Alle Zeit der Welt.

GARCIN (*nähert sich Inez/ihrem eingeblendeten Bild auf dem Monitor hinter dem Sprechertisch, legt seine Hand auf Inez/den Monitor*): Hör zu, jeder hat sein Ziel im Leben, mir waren Geld und Liebe egal. Ich wollte ein Mann sein. Ein harter. Ich habe alles auf dasselbe Pferd gesetzt. Kann man denn ein Feigling sein, wenn man die gefährlichsten Wege gewählt hat? Lässt sich ein Leben nach einer einzelnen Tat beurteilen?

INEZ: Warum nicht? Er hat dreißig Jahre geträumt, er hätte Mut, und ließ sich selbst tausend kleine Schwächen durchgehen, weil dem Helden alles erlaubt ist. Wie bequem das war! Und dann, in der Stunde der Gefahr, hat man ihm die Pistole auf die Brust gesetzt und … er ist nach Mexiko gefahren.

GARCIN: Ich „träumte", sagst du. Von einem solchen Heldentum habe ich nicht geträumt. Ich habe es gewählt: Man ist, was man will.

INEZ (*zu Garcin*): Beweis es. Beweis, dass es kein Traum war. Nur Taten entscheiden über das, was man gewollt hat.

GARCIN: Ich bin zu früh gestorben. Man hat mir nicht die Zeit gelassen, meine Taten auszuführen.

INEZ (*blickt direkt in die Kamera*): Man stirbt immer zu früh – oder zu spät. Und nun liegt das Leben da, abgeschlossen; der Strich ist gezogen, fehlt nur noch die Summe. Du bist nichts andres als dein Leben.

ESTELLE: Revenge yourself.

GARCIN: How?

ESTELLE: Kiss me, darling – then you'll hear her squeal.

GARCIN: That's true. I'm at your mercy, (*approaches camera*) but you're at mine as well. (*He approaches green screen; bends over image of Estelle. Inez gives a little cry.*)

25. *Video of Estelle for make-out session appears via green screen.*[21]

INEZ: Oh, you coward, you weakling, running to women to console you!

ESTELLE: That's right, Inez. Squeal away. (*Engages camera/ Garcin in make-out session.*)

INEZ (*to public; as if describing the wedding of Prince William and Kate Middleton*): What a lovely pair they make! If you could see his big paw splayed out on her back, rucking up her skin and creasing the silk. Be careful, though! His sweaty hands will leave a blue stain on her dress.

ESTELLE: Squeal away, Inez, squeal away! … Hug me tight, darling; tighter still – that'll finish her off!

INEZ: Yes, Garcin, she's right. Carry on with it, press her to you till you feel your bodies melting into each other; a lump of warm, throbbing flesh … (*To passersby*) Love's a grand solace, isn't it, my friends? Deep and dark as sleep. (*To camera*) But I'll see you don't sleep.

ESTELLE: Don't listen to her. Press your lips to my mouth. Oh, I'm yours, yours, yours.

INEZ: Well, what are you waiting for? Do as you're told. What a lovely scene we're witnessing: coward Garcin holding baby-killer Estelle in his manly arms! Make your bets, everyone. Will coward Garcin kiss the lady, or won't he dare? What's the betting? I'm watching you, everybody's watching, I'm a crowd all by myself. (*Like a freak show MC saying, 'step right up!'*) Do you hear the crowd? Do you hear them muttering, Garcin? Mumbling and muttering. "Coward! Coward! Coward! Coward!" – that's what they're saying … It's no use trying to escape, I'll never let you go. What do you hope to get from her silly lips? Forgetfulness? (*To public/camera; Big brother style*) But I shan't forget you, not I! "It's I you must convince." So come to me. I'm waiting. (*Garcin goes toward Inez/studio monitor.*)

26. *Image on studio monitor switches from Estelle back to Inez.*

INEZ: … Come along, now. (*To a passerby*) Look how obedient he is, like a well-trained dog who comes when his mistress calls. Sit! (*Garcin sits*) You cannot hold him, and you never will.

GARCIN (*as if saying 'thousands have perished'*): Will night ever come?

INEZ: Never.

GARCIN: You will always see me?

INEZ: Always. (*Garcin rises, moves toward right-hand camera.*)

GARCIN: This camera.[29][30] (*Grazes lens shaft thoughtfully. 'Our fallen hero' tone.*) Yes, now's the moment; I look at this thing and I understand that I'm in hell. I tell you, everything's been thought out beforehand. You knew I'd be sitting at my desk, your eyes intent on me. Devouring me. (*Pause. Realization*) What? Is it only you? I thought there were more; many more. (*Laughs*) So this is hell. I'd never have believed it. You remember all we were told about the torture-chambers, the fire and brimstone. Old wives' tales! (*Directly to center camera*) There's no need for

GARCIN: Schlange! Du hast für alles eine Antwort. (*Garcin setzt sich.*)

INEZ (*zur Kamera/zum Publikum/zur ganzen Menschheit*): Komm! Verlier nicht den Mut. Es sollte dir leichtfallen, mich zu überzeugen. (*Stichelt ihn*) Such nach Argumenten, streng dich an! (*Garcin zuckt die Achseln.*) Na? Ich hatte dir gesagt, dass du verletzbar bist. Oh! – wie du jetzt büßen wirst. Du bist ein Feigling, Garcin, ein Feigling, weil ich es so will. Ich will es so, hörst du, ich will es! Und trotzdem, sieh doch, wie schwach ich bin, ein Hauch; ich bin nichts als (*betont*) der Blick, der dich sieht, als dieses farblose Denken, das dich denkt. (*Garcin geht zum Studiomonitor, auf dem die Livebilder von Inez laufen, hebt die rechte Hand im Begriff, auf ihn einzuschlagen; Inez wendet den Blick nach links oben, als sähe sie die bedrohliche offene Hand.*) Ha! Sie öffnen sich, diese großen Männerhände. Aber was erhoffst du denn? Gedanken lassen sich mit Händen nicht fangen. Komm, du hast keine Wahl. Du musst mich überzeugen. Ich halte dich gefangen.

Szene 15 – Einwilligung
Bezug: Die Ergebnisse liegen vor. Romney/Putin/Sverige Demokraterna fahren einen Erdrutschsieg ein.

ESTELLE: Garcin!

GARCIN: Was?

ESTELLE: Räche dich!

GARCIN: Wie?

ESTELLE: Küss mich, du wirst sie jaulen hören.

GARCIN: Das stimmt tatsächlich. Du hältst mich gefangen (*nähert sich der Kamera*), aber ich dich auch. (*Er geht zum Greenscreen, beugt sich über das Bild von Estelle. Inez stößt einen kleinen Schrei aus.*)

25. *Video von Estelle erscheint für die Knutschszene per Greenscreen.*[21]

INEZ: Ha! Feigling! Feigling! Lässt dich von Frauen trösten.

ESTELLE: Jaul nur, Inez, jaul nur! (*Wendet sich der Kamera/ Garcin zum Knutschen zu*).

INEZ (*zum Publikum, als würde sie die Hochzeit von Prinz William und Kate Middelton beschreiben*): Was für ein schönes Paar! Wenn du seine große Flosse auf ihrem Rücken sehen könntest, die das Fleisch und den Stoff knetet. Er hat feuchte Hände; er schwitzt. Er wird einen blauen Abdruck auf ihrem Kleid hinterlassen.

ESTELLE: Jaul nur, Inez, jaul nur! Drück mich stärker an dich. Das wird ihr den Rest geben!

INEZ: Aber ja, drück sie stärker, drück sie, bis ihr spürt, wie eure Körper miteinander verschmelzen; ein Batzen warmes, pochendes Fleisch … (*Zu einem Passanten*) Die Liebe ist doch ein schöner Trost, ihr Lieben. Das ist mild und tief wie der Schlaf. (*Zur Kamera*) Aber ich werde dich am Schlafen hindern.

ESTELLE: Hör nicht auf sie! Nimm meinen Mund; ich gehöre ganz dir.

INEZ: Na los, worauf wartest du? Tu, was man dir sagt. Was für eine hübsche Szene: Garcin, der Feigling, umarmt Estelle, die Kindesmörderin. Worum wollen wir wetten? Wird Garcin, der Feigling, sie küssen? Ich sehe euch, ich sehe euch; ich bin ganz allein eine Menge, die Menge, Garcin, die Menge, hörst du? (*Wie der Impressario einer Freakshow, der ruft: „Treten Sie*

red-hot pokers. Hell is – other people![28]

ESTELLE: My darling! Please –

GARCIN (*thrusts camera/Estelle away*)

27. *Center camera suddenly zooms out when Garcin 'thrusts' Estelle away.*

GARCIN: No, let me be. She is between us. I cannot love you when she's watching.

ESTELLE: Right! In that case, I'll stop her watching. (*Picks up the pen from the table, rushes at camera/Inez and stabs her several times. Inez stabs herself with mic as if Estelle/cameraman is stabbing her.*)

INEZ (*struggling and laughing*): But, you crazy creature, what do you think you're doing? You know quite well I'm dead.

ESTELLE: Dead? (*She drops the pen. Pause.*)

INEZ (*picks up the mic and jabs herself with it mockingly*): Dead! Dead! Dead! Knives, poison, ropes – all useless. It has happened already, do you understand? Once and for all. So here we are, forever. (*Laughs*) Over and out.

ESTELLE (*laughing*): Forever. My God, how funny! Forever.

GARCIN (*looks at the two women, and joins in the laughter*): Forever, and ever, and ever.

(*All three slump into laughter that continues for thirty seconds. Their laughter dies away and they gaze at each other via their respective cameras.*)

GARCIN (*sits down, folds hands; like an anchorman saying, 'goodnight'*): Well, well, let's get on with it …

28. *Closing jingle and graphics*

nur näher!") Hörst du die Menge? Hörst du sie raunen, Garcin? Murmeln und raunen. „Feigling! Feigling! Feigling! Feigling!" – das sagen sie. Du fliehst umsonst vor mir, ich lasse dich nicht los. Was suchst du auf ihren Lippen? Das Vergessen? (*Zum Publikum/ in die Kamera im Stil von Big Brother*) Aber ich werde dich nicht vergessen! „Mich musst du überzeugen." Komm her, komm! Ich warte auf dich. (*Garcin geht zu Inez/dem Studiomonitor.*)

26. *Das Bild auf dem Studiomonitor wechselt von Estelle zu Inez.*

INEZ: … nun komm mit. (*Zu einem Passanten*) Schau, er gehorcht wie ein wohlerzogener Hund, der kommt, wenn sein Frauchen ruft.

Sitz! (*Garcin setzt sich.*) Du wirst ihn nicht kriegen, niemals.

GARCIN (*als wollte er sagen „Tausende sind gestorben"*): Wird es denn nie Nacht?

INEZ: Nie.

GARCIN: Du wirst mich immer sehen?

INEZ: Immer. (*Garcin steht auf, nähert sich der Kamera rechts.*)

GARCIN: Diese Kamera.[29][30] (*Streicht bedächtig über das Objektiv. In der Tonlage „Unser gefallener Held"*) Tja, das ist der Moment. Ich schaue mir dieses Ding an und begreife, dass ich in der Hölle bin. Ich sage euch, alles war vorgesehen. Sie haben vorgesehen, dass ich an meinem Tisch sitze, eure Augen auf mich gerichtet. Blicke, die mich auffressen. (*Pause. Ihm wird etwas klar.*) Was? Ihr seid alle? Ich dachte ihr wärt mehr, viel mehr. (*Lacht*) Also das ist die Hölle. Ich hätte es nie geglaubt … Wisst ihr noch: Folterkammern, Scheiterhaufen und Schwefel … Was für Albernheiten. (*Direkt mitten in die Kamera*) Rotglühende Schürhaken sind gar nicht nötig. Die Hölle, das sind die anderen.[28]

ESTELLE: Liebster! Bitte –

GARCIN (*stößt Kamera/Estelle zurück*):

27. *Die mittlere Kamera zoomt in dem Moment, als Garcin Estelle wegstößt, plötzlich heraus.*

GARCIN: Lass mich. Sie ist zwischen uns. Ich kann dich nicht lieben, wenn sie mich sieht.

ESTELLE: Ha! Dann wird sie uns eben nicht mehr sehen (*Nimmt den Stift vom Tisch, stürzt auf die Kamera/Inez zu und sticht auf sie ein. Inez sticht sich mit dem Mikrofon, als würde Estelle/der Kameramann auf sie einstechen.*)

INEZ (*wehrt sich lachend*): Was machst du, was machst du, bist du verrückt? Du weißt doch, dass ich tot bin.

ESTELLE: Tot? (*Sie lässt den Stift fallen. Pause.*)

INEZ (*hebt das Mikrofon auf und äfft nach, dass man auf sie einsticht*): Tot! Tot! Tot! Weder Messer noch Gift, noch Strick – alles nutzlos. Es ist schon geschehen, verstehst du? Und wir sind für immer zusammen. (*Lacht*) Over and out.

ESTELLE (*lacht schallend*): Für immer, mein Gott, ist das komisch! Für immer!

GARCIN (*sieht beide an und lacht mit*): Für immer und ewig.

(*Alle drei lachen 30 Sekunden lauthals. Dann hören sie auf zu lachen und schauen einander durch die jeweiligen Kameras an.*)

GARCIN (*setzt sich, faltet die Hände wie ein Nachrichten- sprecher vor dem „Gute Nacht"*): Also, machen wir weiter …

28. *Schlussjingle und Animation*

Scenario / Szenario

REPORTER ON THE SCENE is set on the streets of Münster, conducting man-on-the-street interviews / ist in den Straßen von Münster unterwegs, führt Interviews mit Passanten.

DER KLEINE MANN is sitting in a café stage set with a cup of coffee, reading his newspaper / sitzt in einem Café-Bühnenbild mit einer Tasse Kaffee, liest seine Zeitung.

Ext – Ludgeristraße

REPORTER ON THE SCENE (*to cameraman / zu Kameramann*): First. Fast. Accurate.

Int – Café

DER KLEINE MANN (*reading the newspaper, imitates the reporter / liest Zeitung, macht Reporterin nach*): Zuerst. Schnell. Genau.

REPORTER ON THE SCENE (*to passerby / zu Passanten*): 'Tschuldigung, eine kurze Frage … Sagen Sie, kennen wir uns nicht?

PASSERBY / PASSANT 1: Ja, irgendwoher. Ich weiß nicht, woher.

REPORTER ON THE SCENE (*to cameraman / zu Kameramann*): Hold on a second, I think I know that guy. I don't think we can continue … [73]

DER KLEINE MANN (*lowers newspaper, turns to camera / lässt seine Zeitung herabsinken, dreht sich zur Kamera*): Really, have we met? Not that I know of.

PASSERBY / PASSANT 1: Kommen Sie aus Münster? [69]

REPORTER ON THE SCENE: Manchmal. (*To passerby / zu Passanten*): Ich bin mir ziemlich sicher, dass wir uns schon mal irgendwo gesehen haben.

DER KLEINE MANN (*to café crowd / zu Café-Besuchern*): Ich merk' mir doch nicht alle Frauen, die ich hier treffe.

(*To camera / Zur Kamera*) Anyway, how can I be of service?

(*To café crowd / Zu Café-Besuchern*) Ich glaub, die Dame möchte was von mir.

Ext – Ludgeristraße

REPORTER ON THE SCENE (*to camera / zur Kamera*): We want to know what you think about journalism these days. No chit-chat, we're bringing you news that hits home: today we'll be asking the people of Münster what they think of the news.

(*To passerby / Zu Passanten*) 'Tschuldigung, eine kurze Frage … Was halten Sie eigentlich vom Journalismus heutzutage?

PASSERBY / PASSANT 2: Vom Journalismus? Wir haben vielleicht zuviel davon.

PASSERBY / PASSANT 3: Vom Journalismus halte ich sehr viel, wenn er gerecht und authentisch ist.

DER KLEINE MANN (*to camera / zur Kamera*): What a question. Well, if all journalists look like you, I think journalism is in great shape.

(*To café crowd / Zu Café-Besuchern*) Was für eine Frage. Ich weiß nicht, Journalismus, sag's uns, wie geht's Dir heute?

REPORTER ON THE SCENE (*to camera / zur Kamera*): I'm reporting live from Domplatz and the popular weekly market. We're everywhere, asking people: "Do you watch television news and how important is it to you?"

DER KLEINE MANN (*shrugs shoulders; scoffs / zuckt die Schultern; spottet*): Ok, Hände hoch: Wer schaut Nachrichten im Fernsehen? (*To camera / Zur Kamera*) Three people.

REPORTER ON THE SCENE (*to passerby / zu Passanten*): Schauen Sie Nachrichten im Fernsehen an?

PASSERBY / PASSANT 4: Ja, regelmäßig abends. Immer gerne die Sendung … wie heißt es … die L o k a l s e i t e (sic) M ü n s t e r l a n d, nicht? Um zu gucken, was im Münsterland so passiert, und in der Stadt.

REPORTER ON THE SCENE (*to passerby / zu Passanten*): Was halten Sie von den neuen Rundfunkgebühren?

PASSERBY / PASSANT 3: Keine Ahnung. Das interessiert mich nicht. Weiß ich wirklich nicht. Gibt's da neue Rundfunkgebühren?

PASSERBY / PASSANT 5: Gibt's neue Rundfunkgebühren? Gibt's neue? Ach ja, die sind jetzt anders gestaffelt.

DER KLEINE MANN (*to camera / zur Kamera*): I bet you like the tax.

(*To café crowd / Zu Café-Besuchern*) Da staubt sie doch bestimmt 'nen guten Bonus ab, oder?!

REPORTER ON THE SCENE (*to passerby / zu Passanten*): Welche Bedeutung, welchen Wert hat Journalismus für Sie?

PASSERBY / PASSANT 6: Ich finde es sehr, sehr wichtig – nach wie vor. Es gibt sehr, sehr viele wichtige Dinge, die in der Welt passieren, und auch natürlich vor der Haustür. Und ich finde es einen sehr, sehr wichtigen Beruf.

REPORTER ON THE SCENE (*to passerby / zu Passanten*): Was bin ich Ihnen wert? Als Reporter. Als Journalist. [80]

PASSERBY / PASSANT 7: Sehr viel. Kann ich auch mehr zu nicht sagen, weil so als Mensch kenne ich Sie nicht, aber als Reporter würde ich sagen, ist es gut, wenn Sie einen guten Job machen.

REPORTER ON THE SCENE (*to passerby / zu Passanten*): Überlegen Sie ruhig noch einmal, mit dem Zweiten sieht man schließlich besser. Was denken Sie wirklich?

PASSERBY / PASSANT 3: Das ist Quatsch, ich seh nur mit beiden Augen gut!

DER KLEINE MANN (*to camera / zur Kamera*): Do you want to know what I really think?

(*To café crowd / Zu Café-Besuchern*) Ich sag Euch, was ich wirklich denke! Die da oben sind alle Gauner. Die haben keine Ahnung vom echten Leben. Die interessieren sich nicht für die Probleme unseres Landes, außer es betrifft sie persönlich. [76]

(*Reads from newspaper with corresponding article. / Nimmt die Zeitung mit dem entsprechenden Artikel.*) Hier zum Beispiel: „Gesundheitsminister Daniel Bahr sucht einen Kita-Platz für seine Tochter – Gesundheitsminister Daniel Bahr, 36, wird nach der Geburt seiner Tochter Carlotta Philippa Amelie mit den alltäglichen Problemen von Eltern konfrontiert. [78] Zitat: ‚Ich konnte mir gar nicht vorstellen, dass man sich schon vor der Geburt des Kindes bei der Kita anmelden muss', vertraute der FDP-Politiker, der B i l d a m S o n n t a g an …" Da hat der offensichtlich zum ersten Mal in seinem Leben vom schleppenden Ausbau der Kita-Plätze in Ballungszentren gehört.

(*To café crowd / Zu Café-Besuchern*) Ich mein', warum lässt

sie uns nicht in Ruhe und quetscht die feinen Herren da oben
aus!? Das sind Gauner!

Ext – Domplatz/Samstagsmarkt

REPORTER ON THE SCENE (*to camera / zur Kamera*): We do
question those "fine gentlemen" on your behalf, but don't
just watch us work for you, we need you to take part in the
conversation. We need to know where you stand. We broadcast
your opinion to keep those politicians in check. Health Minister
Daniel Bahr exposes his ignorance about the dire lack of
schools while searching for a kindergarten for his unborn child.
We're here for you: dedicated, determined, dependable.

(*To passerby / Zu Passanten*) Glauben Sie, dass Nachrichtensendungen darauf Einfluss haben, wie Politiker entscheiden?

PASSERBY / PASSANT 7: Nein, das glaube ich nicht.

PASSERBY / PASSANT 8: Ich würde sagen ja. Wenn die Meinung
der Menschen, also die Masse, im Fernsehen kommt, dann denke
ich doch, dass die Politiker, die Politikerinnen, sich darauf ein-
stellen müssen. Sonst kommen sie nicht wieder, da … an die Macht.

Ext – Prinzipalmarkt

REPORTER ON THE SCENE (*to camera / zur Kamera*): Today we
are talking to people about man-on-the-street interviews. Can
the news media effect what politicians do by broadcasting your
opinions?

DER KLEINE MANN (*to café crowd / zu Café-Besuchern*):
Politiker lügen doch, sobald sie den Mund aufmachen. Immer
dasselbe Gelaber. Alle korrupt!

(*To camera, sarcastic / Zur Kamera, sarkastisch*) And when
you get them in the hot seat, you really sock it to them, right?

REPORTER ON THE SCENE (*to camera / zur Kamera*): We're
here for you. (*Anchor-style delivery / Im Stil eines Nachrichtensprechers*) Politicians always get off easy with the same empty
phrases: how can we really sock it to them? We're on your side.

DER KLEINE MANN (*to café crowd / zu Café-Besuchern*): Ey,
das hab ich doch gerade gesagt! Habt ihr das gehört?

REPORTER ON THE SCENE (*to passerby / zu Passanten*): Was
halten Sie von Journalisten?

PASSERBY / PASSANT 9: Ja, gut, die muss es wohl geben, ja.
Aber manchmal sind sie mir ein bisschen zu aufdringlich.

DER KLEINE MANN (*to camera / zur Kamera*): You just stole
my line!

Ext – Domplatz/Samstagsmarkt

REPORTER ON THE SCENE (*to passerby / zu Passanten*): What
concerns you, concerns us. You can count on us, we're working
for you.

PASSERBY / PASSANT 10: Heißt jetzt?

REPORTER ON THE SCENE (*to passerby / zu Passanten*):
Welche Themen interessieren dich gerade am meisten? Worüber
sollen wir berichten?

PASSERBY / PASSANT 11: Ach, ganz schrecklich finde ich die
EU-Flüchtlingspolitik. Die ist doof.

PASSERBY / PASSANT 12: Mich interessiert ja das Snowden-
Thema total. Also das finde ich sehr interessant. Weil, darüber
hat man sonst irgendwie nie was gehört … das ist wirklich so –
Datenschutz … ja, gerade jetzt so im Facebook-Zeitalter … fand
ich das sehr interessant. Also das ist absolut so mein Favorite-
Thema gerade in der Politik. Ja.

REPORTER ON THE SCENE (*to passerby / zu Passanten*): Wie
informieren Sie sich? Woher nehmen Sie Ihre Nachrichten?

PASSERBY / PASSANT 13: Politischer Art, oder welcher Art
meinen Sie das jetzt? Also ansonsten lese ich Zeitungen. Oder
T a g e s s c h a u, Fernsehen, wie auch immer.

PASSERBY / PASSANT 14: Aus der WN [W e s t f ä l i s c h e
N a c h r i c h t e n]. Schon seit über 30 Jahren.

REPORTER ON THE SCENE (*to passerby / zu Passanten*): Schauen
Sie auch Fernsehen oder gehen Sie online?

PASSERBY / PASSANT 14: Mmmh. Ich schau fern. T a g e s s c h a u.
Danach wird ausgeschaltet.

(*To passerby / Zu Passanten*) Und was davon benutzen Sie
am meisten?

PASSERBY / PASSANT: Zeitungen und äh … Google News.

REPORTER ON THE SCENE (*to passerby / zu Passanten*): Und
posten Sie manchmal auch Kommentare unter Artikel oder auf
Blogs, wenn Sie online sind?

PASSERBY / PASSANT 15: Nö, nicht so.

PASSERBY / PASSANT 16 (*lacht*): Nein, nein.

PASSERBY / PASSANT 17: Ja, das mache ich auch manchmal.

REPORTER ON THE SCENE (*to passerby / zu Passanten*): Sind
die eher positiv oder negativ?

PASSERBY / PASSANT 17: Mal so mal so. Ich bin ja kein Miese-
peter, dass ich immer nur schlechte Nachrichten verbreite. Nee,
ich schreib auch mal was Nettes.[74][83][85]

REPORTER ON THE SCENE (*to passerby / zu Passanten*):
Wann habt ihr das letzte Mal etwas Berichtenswertes getan?

PASSERBY / PASSANT 12: Wir sind keine Superhelden,
also sowas ist uns noch nicht passiert.

REPORTER ON THE SCENE (*to passerby / zu Passanten*): It's
up to you to make a difference: get out there and report back to
us. Give us some good news to report on.

PASSERBY / PASSANT 18: Good news by you? Only today
or about newspapers, or, something like this.

REPORTER ON THE SCENE (*to passerby / zu Passanten*): Always.

PASSERBY / PASSANT 18: The weather, the weather is great.

DER KLEINE MANN (*to café crowd / zu Café-Besuchern*): Diese
blöde Kuh! Die sucht doch nur jemanden, dem sie die Schuld
für alle Probleme der Welt in die Schuhe schieben kann. Macht
mir ein schlechtes Gewissen, und wofür, was hab ich denn damit
zu tun?

(*Gestures aggressively, knocking his coffee over. / Gestikuliert
aggressiv, schmeißt seinen Kaffee um.*)

Ext – Prinzipalmarkt

REPORTER ON THE SCENE (*to camera / zur Kamera*): The time
is right. Put down your coffee and listen. We must go beyond the
headlines. It's about all of us. It's about real people who care.
We bring the world to you.

DER KLEINE MANN (*to café crowd / zu Café-Besuchern*):
Da will man einmal in Ruhe seinen Kaffee trinken … (*lights

cigarette / zündet Zigarette an).

(*To camera, scoffs / Zur Kamera, spottet*) What do you want from me?

(*To camera / Zur Kamera*) Come on now, you're not bringing the world to me, all you're telling me is what I think of you!

(*To café crowd / Zu Café-Besuchern*) Hat die nichts Wichtigeres zu berichten?

(*To camera / Zur Kamera*) I think you may be a bit preoccupied with me.

(*To café crowd / Zu Café-Besuchern*) Die soll das aufdecken, was hinter verschlossenen Türen vor sich geht, aber sie berichtet uns nichts! Das ist doch nicht unsere Schuld, dass ihre Bosse sich ihre Ärsche mit der Dritten Welt abwischen.

Ext – Prinzipalmarkt

Reporter on the scene (*to passerby / zu Passanten*): Haben Sie das Gefühl, dass wir in Ihrem Interesse arbeiten?

Passerby / Passant 19: Au weia.

Reporter on the scene (*to passerby / zu Passanten*): Ist unsere Arbeit gut für Sie?

Passerby / Passant 19: Ja, auf jeden Fall.

Reporter on the scene (*to camera / zur Kamera*): Why do you turn on the news? What are you looking for?[82]

Der kleine Mann (*to camera / zur Kamera*): Don't worry, honey, I'd be happy to turn you on anytime.

Reporter on the scene (*to passerby / zu Passanten*): Was kann ich für Sie tun? Was würden Sie sich wünschen?

Passerby / Passant 20: Also, wenn z.B. irgendwelche Skandale da sind oder so, würde ich wohl auch gerne das Ende mitkriegen.

Der kleine Mann (*to café crowd / zu Café-Besuchern*): Echt jetzt? Hier so, vor allen?

(*To camera / Zur Kamera*) Why not try standing up for us for a change?

(*To café crowd / Zu Café-Besuchern*) Einer für alle, alle für einen! Die fühlt wohl den Druck von der Straße, was?

Ext – Prinzipalmarkt

Reporter on the scene (*to camera / zur Kamera*): Our focus is on you, just watch.

Der kleine Mann (*sings to camera / singt zur Kamera*): Start spreading the news … Do you want to know my opinion or sell them to me?

(*To café crowd / Zu Café-Besuchern*) Will sie wirklich unsere Meinung hören oder will sie uns eine unterjubeln?

(*To camera / Zur Kamera*) Look around you, we are living in a world where Snowden reveals this abuse of power on a blog and what do you do about it?! All you report on is what we think of it all. You're the one who should be doing the exposing!

(*To café crowd / Zu Café-Besuchern*) Auf welcher Seite steht die jetzt eigentlich? Sieht fast so aus, als würde sie mit den Politikern und den Wirtschaftsbossen unter einer Decke stecken und wir müssen uns alleine durchschlagen.

(*To camera / Zur Kamera*) You could be rough on them if you wanted to.

(*To café crowd / Zu Café-Besuchern*) Sie macht es aber nicht. Deswegen müssen wir jetzt eben mal sie hart ran nehmen. Ich fühle mich ja sehr geehrt, dass sie uns eingeladen hat, ihre ‚Tagesschau' mitzugestalten, aber findet Ihr es nicht auch ein bisschen seltsam, dass ausgerechnet sie den „Kleinen Mann" einlädt mehr Verantwortung zu übernehmen? Das soll sie mal schön selber machen.

(*To camera / Zur Kamera*) You're talking a great game about holding politicians' feet to the fire. But we all know you're full of shit and then you have the nerve to blame me for not liking you.[74]

Ext – Prinzipalmarkt

Reporter on the scene (*to camera / zur Kamera*): We're listening to you.

Der kleine Mann (*to camera / zur Kamera*): Well then, try a little harder. I need your help, but all you seem to do is put on a show. You're doing theater, when you should be doing journalism. I mean look at what you've done in Egypt!

Ext – Ludgeristraße

Reporter on the scene (*to camera / zur Kamera*): Many say the media did not behave responsibly with Egypt. First off we didn't emphasize the atrocities of Mubarak's regime, we failed to criticize our politicians for working with him. Then we tried to support the revolution even though we were skeptical of Morsi, but everybody wants a happy ending and we gave it to the viewers at the expense of the Egyptian people who had to oust him themselves.[71]

(*To passerby / Zu Passanten*) Glauben Sie wir machen die Nachrichten für Sie?

Passerby / Passant 21: Nicht unbedingt.

Passerby / Passant 22: Also, das wird ja schon so ein bisschen gefiltert das alles, die Informationen, die man so kriegt. Je nach dem. Ich weiß nicht, unter was für einer Aufsicht das alles steht, aber ich denke schon, dass da viel unterschlagen wird, auch.

Passerby / Passant 21: Wenn man nur anstellt: Ägypten, Ägypten, Ägypten. Was in Deutschland passiert, da hören sie wenig von. Das find' ich nicht so gut.

Passerby / Passant 23: Ja, die Medien. Ich meine immer, die tun immer mehr. Das Fernsehen geht dorthin, dass diese Parteien grundsätzlich wieder gewählt werden, die die Menschen unterdrücken, bevormunden, diskriminieren und ausbeuten.

Reporter on the scene (*to passerby / zu Passanten*): Glauben Sie, wir bringen die Nachrichten, die tatsächlich da draußen sind und die berichtenswert sind, oder die Nachrichten, die Sie hören wollen?

Passerby / Passant 24: Ich hab' manchmal den Eindruck, dass … dass das also nicht wirklich so transparent ist, wie … wie's passiert. Also, dass es schon so ein bisschen forciert wird oder nicht … nicht weitergegeben wird. Aber gut, das ist so 'ne Meinung, und … das betrifft nicht alle Medien.

Passerby / Passant 23: Aber, die machen ja nur das, was die hören wollen, und nicht, was sie nicht hören wollen. Das ist ja der Haken.[75]

REPORTER ON THE SCENE (*to passerby* / *zu Passanten*): Am Anfang war die Berichterstattung über den Arabischen Frühling sehr vereinfacht. Ist das die Schuld der Reporter oder die Schuld des Zuschauers und Lesers, der gerne einfache Wahrheiten haben möchte?

PASSERBY / PASSANT 25: Das weiß ich jetzt nicht, warum. Das ist, glaube ich, nicht die Schuld der Zuschauer. Ich glaub' nicht, dass die das vereinfacht haben möchten. Ich glaub', die Reporter waren im Moment 'n bisschen überfordert mit der Situation. Die ergab sich ja peu à peu. Also ich glaube, das war nicht die Schuld der Zuschauer. Also glaub' ich nicht.[70]

REPORTER ON THE SCENE (*to passerby* / *zu Passanten*): It's our job to make you see things differently.

PASSERBY / PASSANT 24 (*laughing* / *lacht*): Das wär schön, wenn das so … so wäre, ja.

REPORTER ON THE SCENE (*to passerby* / *zu Passanten*): What concerns you, concerns us.

PASSERBY / PASSANT 26: Versteh' ich nicht.

DER KLEINE MANN (*to camera* / *zur Kamera*): No, what concerns you, concerns you!

Ext – Domplatz/Samstagsmarkt

REPORTER ON THE SCENE (*to camera* / *zur Kamera*): Reaching out to you, right here, right now.

(*To passerby* / *Zu Passanten*) Glauben Sie, dass Medien und Öffentlichkeit sich wirklich gegenseitig auch beeinflussen können?

PASSERBY / PASSANT 27: Ja, da glaube ich fest dran, dass Medien und Öffentlichkeit sich gegenseitig beeinflussen, wobei ich der Meinung bin, dass die Medien die Öffentlichkeit mehr beeinflussen, als umgekehrt.

DER KLEINE MANN (*to camera* / *zur Kamera*): Show me that we're in this together, that we're not just using each other.[65]

REPORTER ON THE SCENE (*to passerby* / *zu Passanten*): Glauben Sie an die Medien?

PASSERBY / PASSANT 28: Ja!

PASSERBY / PASSANT 29: Äh, ja.

REPORTER ON THE SCENE (*to passerby* / *zu Passanten*): Vertraust Du mir?

PASSERBY / PASSANT 30: Ja? Doch, ja.

REPORTER ON THE SCENE (*to passerby* / *zu Passanten*): Will you stay with us?

PASSERBY / PASSANT 30: Where?

REPORTER ON THE SCENE (*to passerby* / *zu Passanten*): Will you stay with us?

PASSERBY / PASSANT 31: Ehm … How do you mean, if I want to stay with you all … about what … now you mean, or to go somewhere, or … what do you mean?

DER KLEINE MANN (*to café crowd* / *zu Café-Besuchern*): Sie kann jederzeit dazustoßen, oder? Ich bin jedenfalls bereit. Was ist mit euch?

REPORTER ON THE SCENE (*to passerby* / *zu Passanten*): Ich sehe, dahinter steckt ein kluger Kopf.

PASSERBY / PASSANT 31: Ich denke so, ja.

DER KLEINE MANN (*to café crowd* / *zu Café-Besuchern*): Das hier ist es doch, was uns immer noch trennt. Was werden wir machen? Werden wir uns wehren? Werden wir uns verteidigen?

REPORTER ON THE SCENE (*to passerby* / *zu Passanten*): Versprich mir, dass du nie aufhörst mich anzuschauen.

PASSERBY / PASSANT 32: Äh. Das kann ich nicht.

DER KLEINE MANN (*to camera* / *zur Kamera*): Woher kennt die mich so gut?

(*To camera* / *Zur Kamera*) Without you I don't even know what to think about myself. I know nothing. I need you.

Ext – Ludgeristraße

REPORTER ON THE SCENE (*to camera* / *zur Kamera*): Without you watching me I cease to exist.

Absolute Event, 2013

Synopsis

In Absolute Event, two actors (who are former
congressional staffers) perform a dialogue in which a political
strategist coaches a politician from behind the scenes of a
situation room. The script combines material from Edmond
Rostand's 1897 play Cyrano de Bergerac with current
American political rhetoric and interviews conducted by Laser
with political and public relations strategists. The gallery
was transformed into a control room and a situation room,
incorporating elements from a disco nightclub. During the
performances, a live-feed video was produced, edited and
projected. Select audience members were invited to register
moment-to-moment approval ratings using Audience Response
System keypads. This data is reflected in graphs that appear
in the video.

Cameras

1. Leader at table: Medium; head on with green screen
backdrop; needs operator for zooming in and out when Leader
stands
2. Leader at table: Wide; three-quarter with green screen/rain
curtain backdrop; on c-stand
3. Leader at table: Medium; profile with green screen backdrop
4. Computer feed: ARS computer graphics against black
5. Roving Camera
6. Daniel Camera: Medium and high until start of Act II when
it lowers and zooms to three-quarter
7. Security Camera: Control Room from back. Wide; next to
projector

General directions Gary, Leader

Your purpose is to convince the audience that you are a real
solid person, you're honest and practical. You want to make
them confident that you can lead, that you will do what's best
for them.

General directions Daniel, Strategist

Your purpose is to give Gary the tools to succeed. You're
the big brother, you know what's best for him and for the people
he has to win over.

Act I – Preparation
Strategist and Leader in Control Room standing around desk;
neither are amplified, both must project voice.

STRATEGIST: There's a world of people waiting for you. Get
out there![86]
LEADER: Oh, no! It's impossible.
STRATEGIST: Take it easy. I believe in you.
LEADER: Fuck, I'm not ready for this. (*Looks around; looks
at himself / his clothes*) I feel like a fool.
STRATEGIST: None is a fool who knows himself a fool. You
got this, you're in control, own it.
LEADER: I have a simple military wit, I know how to hold a
gun, not a microphone! Before an audience I get tongue-tied.
When the camera is on me and everyone's watching I just freeze

---

Absolute Event, 2013

Synopse

In Absolute Event spielen zwei Darsteller (die ehemalige
Kongress-Mitarbeiter sind) einen Dialog, in dem ein politischer
Strategieberater aus dem Hintergrund einen Politiker im
Nachrichtenstudio coacht. Das Skript kombiniert Material aus
dem Stück Cyrano de Bergerac von Edmond Rostand mit
der aktuellen Rhetorik der amerikanischen Politik und
Interviews, die Laser mit Beratern aus den Bereichen Politik
und Public Relations geführt hat. Der Galerieraum wurde in
einen Regieraum und ein Nachrichtenstudio verwandelt, ergänzt
um Elemente einer Disko. Während der Performances wurde
in Echtzeit ein Video gedreht, geschnitten und projiziert.
Ausgewählte Personen aus dem Publikum wurden aufgefordert,
über ein System zur Erfassung von Zuschauerreaktionen
begleitend Zustimmungsraten aufzuzeichnen. Diese Daten
wurden zu Grafiken verarbeitet, die im Video gezeigt werden.

Kameras

1. Politiker am Tisch: halb gezoomt, frontal vor Greenscreen-
Hintergrund; es wird ein Kameramann zum Zoomen benötigt,
wenn der Politiker steht
2. Politiker am Tisch: Weitwinkel; Dreiviertelansicht mit
Greenscreen/Fadenvorhang als Hintergrund; auf C-Stand
3. Politiker am Tisch: halb gezoomt; Profil vor Greenscreen
4. Computeranimation: Grafiken des ARS vor Schwarz
5. Bewegliche Kamera
6. Daniels Kamera: halb gezoomt und hoch bis Anfang
Akt 2, dann schwenkt sie für den Rest der Aufnahme nach unten
und zoomt dreiviertel heran
7. Überwachungskamera: Regieraum von hinten; Weitwinkel;
neben dem Projektor

Regieanweisungen Gary, Politiker

Deine Aufgabe ist es, das Publikum davon zu überzeugen, dass
du eine grundsolide Persönlichkeit bist, ehrlich und pragmatisch.
Du willst ihnen die Gewissheit geben, dass du Führungsqualitäten
hast, dass du tun wirst, was am besten für sie ist.

Regieanweisungen Daniel, Stratege

Deine Aufgabe ist es, Gary die Mittel an die Hand zu geben,
um erfolgreich sein zu können. Du bist der große Bruder, du
weißt, was am besten für ihn ist und für die Menschen, die er für
sich einnehmen muss.

Akt I – Vorbereitung
Stratege und Politiker stehen im Regieraum um einen Tisch; beide
unverstärkt, beide müssen laut und deutlich sprechen.

STRATEGE: Draußen wartet ein ganzes Volk auf dich. Geh
da raus![86]
POLITIKER: Oh, nein! Unmöglich!
STRATEGE: Keine Bange. Ich glaub' an dich.
POLITIKER: Scheiße, das bring ich nicht. (*Schaut sich um; schaut
sich selbst an, seine Kleider.*) Ich komme mir vor wie ein Idiot.
STRATEGE: Wer sich selbst für einen Narren hält, ist keiner. Du
hast das erreicht, du hast es unter Kontrolle, nimm es dir.

up. I can't utter a word: my tongue thickens to a lump, my eyes go blind, my ears fill with humming, and sweat streams down my body.

STRATEGIST: I'm here for you, don't worry, I'll make that handsome face speak with facile grace. Forget all that gun business, real power comes when you master this (*referring to the script*), the camera, the twitter feed … You know the first thing you do in a coup? You take over the radio and the TV cause you want to control what people hear.

LEADER: The people out there seem suspicious, they're growing weary, I don't want to disappoint them.

STRATEGIST (*aside*): Physically you're looking good. With the right words you can command. They'll love you. Just stay on message.

LEADER (*in despair*): Eloquence! Where to find it?

STRATEGIST (*abruptly*): That I lend, if you lend me your charms. Blended we can make a true hero and win hearts and minds!

LEADER: How do we start? I haven't prepped much … (*rolls shoulders, preening*).

STRATEGIST: Do you think you can repeat the lines I feed you?

LEADER: I guess.

STRATEGIST: They won't catch on, we can woo them double-handed, my phrases on your lips, it will be soul-inspiring![94]

LEADER: You're getting pretty revved up, does it give you such pleasure?

STRATEGIST (*excited*): Yes! (*Then calmly, business-like*) It is an enterprise to tempt a poet. (*Sarcastically erotic; touching his face*) Will you complete me, and let me complete you? You march victorious, I follow in your shadow …

LEADER (*peeks into situation room*): Shit, they're waiting for me already! The speech, let me see it!

STRATEGIST (*taking out the speech*): Here it is – your speech monsieur! Take it! It wants but your delivery.

LEADER: It's a bit long …

STRATEGIST: Fear nothing. It will suit.

LEADER: But have you …?

STRATEGIST: Oh, come on, take it, and change feigned love-words into true; I breathed my heart and soul into these lettered lines. Now, get out there: call all these wandering love-birds home to nest.

LEADER: Can I change some words to fit their mood?

STRATEGIST: No need, 'twill fit like a glove!

LEADER: But, but …

STRATEGIST: Shut off the voice in your brain, cause the voice in your brain is the problem. If you don't know what you're getting at, just stop, don't elaborate. Now, let's hear a "rubber, baby, buggy, bumpers"!

LEADER: Rubber, baby, buggy bumpers (*repeating a few times; they get jazzed up*) My friend! (*They hug; pal around; then bravado suddenly fades from his face*) … I'm uneasy …

STRATEGIST: We'll kindle their hearts yet. I know all that is needed. This is an occasion for you to deck yourself with glory. Come, lose no time; put away those sulky looks.[92]

LEADER: I don't know … I gotta say I'm weary of these borrowed words – borrowed love-makings! I don't want to just act a part.[93] 'Twas well enough at the beginning! – But now I want them to love me for me, I don't want to fear any longer! – I will speak for myself.

POLITIKER: Ich habe einen schlichten militärischen Verstand, ich weiß wie man ein Gewehr hält, kein Mikrofon! Vor Publikum werde ich einsilbig. Wenn die Kamera auf mich gerichtet ist und alle mich anschauen, erstarre ich einfach nur. Ich bekomm kein einziges Wort mehr heraus: Meine Zunge wird dick wie ein Klumpen, meine Augen werden blind, in meinen Ohren ist ein Brummen, und mir rinnt der Schweiß.

STRATEGE: Mach dir keine Sorgen, ich bin für dich da. Ich schaffe es, dass gutaussehende Gesichter mit eleganter Leichtigkeit sprechen. Vergiss den ganzen Waffenkram, echte Macht kommt erst, wenn du das beherrschst (*deutet auf das Manuskript*), die Kamera, den Twitter-Feed … Weißt du, was man bei einem Staatsstreich als erstes macht? Man besetzt Radio- und Fernsehsender, weil man bestimmen will, was die Leute zu hören bekommen.

POLITIKER: Die Menschen da draußen wirken misstrauisch, denen wird langsam langweilig, ich will die nicht enttäuschen.

STRATEGE (*beiseite*): Körperlich siehst du gut aus. Mit den richtigen Worten kannst du bestimmen. Sie werden dich lieben. Bleib einfach bei deiner Botschaft.

POLITIKER (*verzweifelt*): Redetalent! Wo soll das herkommen?

STRATEGE (*abrupt*): Das borg ich dir, wenn du mir deinen Charme borgst. Mit beidem zusammen können wir ein echter Held sein, die Herzen und Köpfe gewinnen!

POLITIKER: Wie sollen wir anfangen? Ich hab' kaum geprobt … (*rollt die Schultern, wirft sich in die Brust*).

STRATEGE: Schaffst du es, den Text zu wiederholen, den ich dir vorlege?

POLITIKER: Denke schon.

STRATEGE: Die merken das gar nicht, wir wickeln die zu zweit um den Finger, meine Sätze auf deinen Lippen, das wird richtig ergreifend![94]

POLITIKER: Du bist ja ganz aus dem Häuschen, macht dir das solchen Spaß?

STRATEGE (*aufgeregt*): Ja! (*Dann ruhig, geschäftsmäßig*) Das ist ein Unterfangen, das einen Dichter reizen könnte. (*Sarkastisch lasziv; berührt sein Gesicht*) Wirst Du mich zur Vollendung bringen und mich dich zur Vollendung bringen lassen? Du schreitest siegreich einher, ich folge in deinem Schatten …

POLITIKER (*flüchtiger Blick in die Nachrichtenredaktion*): Mist, die warten schon auf mich! Die Rede, zeig mal!

STRATEGE (*holt das Manuskript heraus*): Da ist sie – Ihre Rede, Monsieur! Nimm! Du musst sie nur noch vortragen.

POLITIKER: Ein bisschen lang …

STRATEGE: Mach dir keine Sorgen. Das passt schon.

POLITIKER: Aber hast du …?

STRATEGE: Jetzt komm schon, nimm, und mach aus falschen Liebesbekundungen echte. Ich habe Herz und Seele in diese Zeilen gelegt. Nun geh hinaus: Ruf all die umherirrenden Turteltäubchen in ihr Nest.

POLITIKER: Kann ich mal was ändern, um auf ihre Stimmung einzugehen?

STRATEGE: Nicht nötig, das passt wie angegossen.

POLITIKER: Wie, aber …

STRATEGE: Bring diese Stimme in deinem Kopf zum Schweigen, denn die Stimme in deinem Kopf ist das Problem. Wenn du nicht mehr weißt wo du bist, hör einfach auf, führ das nicht weiter aus. So jetzt will ich mal ein schönes „rubber, baby, buggy, bumper" hören!

POLITIKER: Rubber, baby, buggy, bumpers (*wiederholt es einige Male, kommt in Schwung*) Mein Freund! (*Sie umarmen sich;*

STRATEGIST: Mercy!

LEADER: Don't you think I can speak for myself? I am not such a fool when all is said! I've learned your lessons. You'll see I can hold their attention!

STRATEGIST (*with disdain*): Suit yourself, get out there and "speak for yourself"! You're going live in five, four, three …

(*Strategist puts on headset and Leader puts in IFB earpiece.*)

Act 2 – Meet and Greet
Strategist in control room and Leader in situation room;
Leader is amplified, Strategist is not.

(*Strategist sits down and stays seated; Leader enters front room; greets a few audience members; mills about and continues speaking to Strategist under his breath via earpiece.*)

LEADER (*walking into situation room*): Don't leave me! Testing, testing, one, two, three?

STRATEGIST (*huffs*): I'm not going anywhere. Count to three, breathe, regain your composure. I want to hear something that makes my ears smile …[95] (*Leader starts shaking hands with audience members.*)
(*Leader's amplification begins.*)

LEADER: Hello everybody![97] (*Addressing individual audience members*) Thanks for coming out tonight. Your hair looks great. I'm so happy you're here. I appreciate that. I love your shoes. I'm so pleased to be here with you …

STRATEGIST: Ay, speak to them of love.

LEADER: You can't imagine how pleased I am to meet you.

STRATEGIST: That's the theme! But vary it.

LEADER: Very happy you're here tonight.

STRATEGIST: Vary it!

LEADER: I'm so happy to meet you …

STRATEGIST: Oh! without doubt! (*Under his breath; making eye contact with audience member*) No shit – and then …?

LEADER: I am – oh! – so glad – so very glad …[99]

STRATEGIST (*grimaces*): I hoped for cream, – you give me gruel! Say how passion for the public good possesses you.

LEADER: Oh utterly!

STRATEGIST: C'mon, c'mon! … unknot those tangled sentiments!

LEADER: Means a lot that you came out tonight …

STRATEGIST: More specific.

LEADER: Very grateful.

STRATEGIST (*half-rising*): Where's the panache?

LEADER: However, I am also disappointed …

STRATEGIST (*reseating himself*): I can see that you're thinking, "how does this look?" Don't go there, don't let it pull you down.

LEADER: But I have faith in us …

STRATEGIST (*rising, and going further off*): Oh!

LEADER (*nose scratch; whispering to Strategist*): I am grown stupid!

STRATEGIST (*dryly*): And that displeases me almost as much as it would displease me if you grew ill-favored by them.

LEADER: But …

STRATEGIST (*scoffs*): Call me when you regain your eloquence!

LEADER: I …

STRATEGIST: A great success, bravo! You're on your own (*takes off headset, briefly puts it on the table, counts visibly to five, puts it back on*).

machen Späßchen; dann weicht die Entschlossenheit plötzlich aus seinem Gesicht.*) … Ich hab kein gutes Gefühl …

STRATEGE: Wir werden ihre Herzen entflammen. Ich weiß alles, was es dazu braucht. Für dich ist das eine Gelegenheit, dich mit Ruhm zu bekleckern. Komm, verlier keine Zeit, guck nicht so griesgrämig.[92]

POLITIKER: Ich weiß nicht … Mensch, ich bin diese geborgten Sätze leid – geborgte Liebeshändel! Ich will nicht nur eine Rolle spielen.[93] Das habe ich am Anfang gemacht, jetzt reicht es mir – jetzt will ich, dass sie mich um meiner selbst willen lieben, ich will keine Angst mehr haben! Ich werde für mich selbst sprechen.

STRATEGE: Um Himmels Willen!

POLITIKER: Glaubst du, ich könnte nicht für mich selbst sprechen? Am Ende bin ich gar nicht ein solcher Idiot! Ich habe deine Lektionen gelernt. Du wirst schon sehen, dass ich ihre Aufmerksamkeit fesseln kann!

STRATEGE (*verächtlich*): Mach doch, was du willst, geht da raus und „rede für dich selbst"! In fünf Sekunden bist du auf Sendung, vier, drei …

(*Der Stratege setzt sein Headset auf und der Politiker steckt sich seinen Ohrhörer ein.*)

Akt 2 – Begrüßung
Stratege im Kontrollraum und Politiker im Nachrichtenstudio;
Politiker wird verstärkt, Stratege nicht.

(*Stratege setzt sich und bleibt sitzen; Politiker betritt den vorderen Raum; grüßt einige im Publikum; läuft umher und spricht über sein Headset weiter mit dem Strategen, flüsternd.*)

POLITIKER (*geht ins Nachrichtenstudio*): Lass mich nicht allein! Test, Test, eins, zwei, drei?

STRATEGE (*schnauft*): Ich bin hier. Zähl bis drei, atme, sammle dich. Ich will etwas hören, was meine Ohren lächeln lässt …[95] (*Politiker beginnt, Menschen aus dem Publikum die Hand zu schütteln.*)
(*Politiker wird ab jetzt verstärkt.*)

POLITIKER: Hallo, allerseits![97] (*Wendet sich an einzelne im Publikum.*) Danke, dass sie heute Abend gekommen sind. Ihre Haare sehen fantastisch aus. Ich freue mich unheimlich, dass Sie hier sind. Ich weiß das wirklich zu schätzen. Ich mag Ihre Schuhe. Ich freue mich so, heute Abend bei Ihnen sein zu können …

STRATEGE: Prima, sprich mit ihnen über Liebe.

POLITIKER: Sie können sich nicht vorstellen, wie sehr ich mich freue, Sie hier zu treffen.

STRATEGE: Das ist genau das Thema! Aber variiere ein wenig.

POLITIKER: Ich bin sehr froh, dass Sie alle gekommen sind.

STRATEGE: Variiere!

POLITIKER: Ich bin so froh, Sie hier zu treffen …

STRATEGE: Ja! Klar! (*Mit gedämpfter Stimme; Blickkontakt mit jemandem aus dem Publikum*) Nein, verdammt noch mal – und weiter …?

POLITIKER: Ich bin – Mann – so froh – so ausgesprochen froh …[99]

STRATEGE (*verzieht das Gesicht*): Du bietest saure Milch, und ich will Sahne! Sag, wie dich die Leidenschaft für das öffentliche Wohl erfüllt.

POLITIKER: In höchstem Maße!

STRATEGE: Nun komm schon! … entfalte diese verworrenen Gefühle!

LEADER: Oh, please don't go, not yet!

STRATEGIST (*peeking into the situation room*): Aww, what is it? Now you need me? I've heard you grovel before – Forget it!

LEADER (*to Strategist*): Shit, please stay. (*To audience member*) Tonight I want to talk to you about something of grave concern to all of us … (*to Strategist*) Come to my aid! I'll say anything you want …

STRATEGIST (*sarcastically*): Hmm … No.

LEADER (*retreats to Strategist in control room; leans on Strategist's desk*): But I shall die here and now if I find no way to make them love me.

STRATEGIST: Damn it, I'm here to put words in your mouth, not to babysit you.

LEADER (*to Strategist*): Please, I'm dying out here.

STRATEGIST: To reinstate you may not be easy, but I'll stay if you can manage to let me do my job.[100] Now will you just say what I tell you to say?

LEADER (*to Strategist*): Yes, anything! Please, they are waiting for me to say something …

STRATEGIST (*squeezes his shoulders*): Just get back out there.[101]

LEADER (*enters front room again; addressing individual audience members*): Good evening everyone, thank you for being here, thank you for your patience … (*Mutters to Strategist*) Oh! I shall die!

STRATEGIST: Speak lower!

LEADER (*to Strategist; in a whisper*): It's clear that they love me no longer.

STRATEGIST: All can be repaired, I'll prompt your words. Don't worry, let's get this party started … Go get 'em![98] (*Music: Donna Summer's Love To Love You Baby*)

LEADER (*prompted by Strategist, dances up to audience member*): Hi, do I know you? I really like this song.

STRATEGIST (*improvising to find the right participant*): Ask her to dance.

LEADER: Would you like to dance? (*Gets an audience member to dance with him; brings her to dance floor under discoball globe.*)

STRATEGIST (*picks up paper, crumples it and throws it at the screen showing live-feed of Leader*): Tell her who you are!

LEADER: Do you remember me?

STRATEGIST: Who are you?!

LEADER: I'm Gary, the change you've been waiting for.

STRATEGIST: Good. Speak soft and slow.

LEADER (*prompted by Strategist; continues dancing with audience member; turning in circle*): Do people really dance in bars any more? … You know before disco this country was a social wasteland … It's hard to make space in our lives for socializing and when we do I think it's really important that we have great places where we can spend time together as a group … Some people don't even consider this music disco (*referring to the music playing*) … What do you think? (*Extracts answers.*)

Act 3 – Come To The Table.
Strategist in control room and Leader in situation room.

STRATEGIST: Nice warm up, now onto the main course. Let's get them to the table, then we get intimate …

LEADER (*prompted by Strategist*): Listen, this isn't just politics

POLITIKER: Es bedeutet mir eine Menge, dass Sie heute Abend gekommen sind …

STRATEGE: Konkreter.

POLITIKER: Dafür meinen Dank.

STRATEGE (*erhebt sich leicht*): Wo bleibt der Schwung?

POLITIKER: Ich bin aber auch enttäuscht …

STRATEGE (*setzt sich wieder hin*): Ich sehe genau, wie du jetzt denkst: „Wie sieht das denn aus?" Nicht weiter in diese Richtung, lass dich nicht runterziehen.

POLITIKER: Aber ich vertraue auf uns …

STRATEGE (*steht auf und entfernt sich etwas*): Oh!

POLITIKER (*kratzt sich an der Nase; flüstert zum Strategen*): Bin ich blöd!

STRATEGE (*trocken*): Und das missfällt mir fast genau so sehr, als kämst du bei denen nicht gut an.

POLITIKER: Aber …

STRATEGE (*ironisch*): Ruf mich, wenn du deine Eloquenz wiedergefunden hast!

POLITIKER: Ich …

STRATEGE: Ein großer Erfolg, bravo! Jetzt bist du auf dich allein gestellt (*nimmt sein Headset ab, legt es kurz auf den Tisch, zählt sichtbar auf fünf, setzt es wieder auf*).

POLITIKER: Oh nein, geh nicht, jetzt noch nicht!

STRATEGE (*lugt ins Nachrichtenstudio*): Na, was ist das denn? Du brauchst mich? Ich hab gehört, wie du zu Kreuze gekrochen bist … Vergiss es!

POLITIKER (*zum Strategen*): Mist, bitte bleib. (*Zu jemandem im Publikum*) Heute Abend möchte ich zu Ihnen über etwas sprechen, das für uns alle von großer Bedeutung ist … (*Zum Strategen*) Hilf mir doch! Ich sag auch alles, was du willst …

STRATEGE (*sarkastisch*): Hm … Nein.

POLITIKER (*geht zurück zum Strategen in den Regieraum; lehnt sich über den Schreibtisch des Strategen*): Aber ich sterbe hier auf der Stelle, wenn ich sie nicht dazu bringen kann, mich zu lieben.

STRATEGE: Verdammt noch mal, ich bin hier, um dir Worte in den Mund zu legen, nicht als dein Babysitter.

POLITIKER (*zum Strategen*): Bitte, das bringt mich um da draußen.

STRATEGE: Wird nicht ganz leicht, dich wieder ins Spiel zu bringen, aber ich bleibe, wenn du es schaffst, mich meine Arbeit machen zu lassen.[100] Also wirst du jetzt einfach sagen, was ich dir vorgebe?

POLITIKER (*zum Strategen*): Ja, alles! Bitte, sie warten schon darauf, dass ich was sage …

STRATEGE (*drückt ihm die Schultern*): Geh wieder raus.[101]

POLITIKER (*betritt erneut den vorderen Raum; wendet sich an einzelne im Publikum*): Guten Abend allerseits, danke, dass Sie gekommen sind, danke für Ihre Geduld … (*Murmelnd zum Strategen*) Mann, das bringt mich um!

STRATEGE: Sprich leiser!

POLITIKER (*zum Strategen, flüsternd*): Es ist offenkundig, dass sie mich nicht mehr lieben.

STRATEGE: Das lässt sich alles reparieren, ich souffliere dir den Text vor. Mach dir keine Sorgen, fangen wir endlich an mit der Party … Los, hol sie dir![98] (*Musik ab: Donna Summers Love To Love You Baby*)

POLITIKER (*souffliert vom Strategen, tänzelt zu jemandem im Publikum*): Hallo, kenne ich Sie? Ich mag diesen Song total gerne.

STRATEGE (*improvisiert, um den richtigen Teilnehmer zu finden*): Fordere die da zum Tanzen auf.

POLITIKER: Möchten Sie tanzen? (*Bringt eine Frau aus dem*

as usual, there's something I need to speak with you about. Let's go somewhere quiet where we can talk (*leads first person to a seat at the table*).

STRATEGIST: Get another one over, fill those seats.

LEADER (*prompted by Strategist; approaches individual audience members until all seats at table are full*): Excuse me, can I borrow your friend for a second? (*Brings two more people to the table.*)

STRATEGIST: Good, good, reel 'em in, nice and easy.

LEADER (*prompted by Strategist; to another audience member*): We need to have a serious talk about the things that are driving us apart. (*To fill the last seats*) C'mon, let's talk. Won't you join me at the table?

STRATEGIST: Seal the deal.

(*Leader places the ten audience participants around table.*)

STRATEGIST (*amplified; instructing audience participants*): Thank you for agreeing to participate. The session will last approximately twenty minutes. In a moment we'll be distributing Audience Response System keypads to the ten of you selected (*production assistants distribute ARS keypads to audience participants*). If you are unable to remain for the duration please let us know now and we will select an alternate. You should be seeing the first of five questions on your keypad screens right now. (*Green screening of ARS graphics begins.*) Please enter your gender (*pause*). We will need everyone to answer in order to move on. Next question: please identify your age group (*pause*). Please enter your political party (*pause*). Is everyone with us? Please enter your marital status (*pause*). And finally please give us your employment status (*amplification ends*). (*To Gary*) Get your ass back here.

LEADER (*mumbling to Strategist via earpiece; reacts to being summoned*): Please excuse me, I'll be back in a moment (*goes back to control room*). (*To ARS technician*) How's it going? Give me something I can work with.

STRATEGIST: Leave them alone they're processing the data.

LEADER (*to audience in control room*): How am I doing out there? Do you think they like me? Are they going to support me?

(*ARS technician cues Strategist that graphs are ready to go.*)

STRATEGIST (*to Leader*): We're good to go, get back out there!

LEADER: Great, let's do this (*goes back to situation room and sits at table*).

STRATEGIST (*amplified; to participants*): Now you should see a slider graphic on your touch screen. Please use it to indicate whether you agree or disagree with what you're about to hear. "100" means you strongly agree, "0" means you strongly disagree and "50" means you're neutral. Please keep your finger moving on the touch screen to register your feedback. Slide to the left to indicate negative and slide to the right to indicate positive. It is imperative that you keep your fingers moving on the keypad slider.[105] We want to know what you really think and how we can better serve you, but please let your fingers do the talking (*amplification ends*).

LEADER (*prompted by Strategist*): Now that you're all here, let me begin by saying a big thank you. Thank you so much for all the energy you're bringing here tonight. You're wonderful, and you should give yourself a big hand. How about a big round of applause for everybody that came out tonight!? (*Gets everyone to applaud.*) You might be wondering why we're all here. Well, I'm really here to listen to all of you. There's no boundaries here.

Publikum dazu, mit ihm zu tanzen; führt sie zur Tanzfläche unter einer Discokugel.)

STRATEGE (*nimmt sich ein Blatt Papier, zerknüllt es und wirft es auf den Bildschirm, auf dem der Politiker live übertragen wird*): Sag ihr, wer du bist!

POLITIKER: Erinnern Sie sich an mich?

STRATEGE: Wer sind Sie?!

POLITIKER: Ich bin Gary, der Wandel, auf den Sie gewartet haben.

STRATEGE: Gut. Sprich sanft und langsam.

POLITIKER (*souffliert vom Strategen; tanzt weiterhin mit der Frau aus dem Publikum; dreht Kreise*): Wird in Bars heute wirklich noch getanzt? … Wissen Sie, in der Zeit vor Disco war dieses Land eine soziale Wüste … Es ist gar nicht so leicht, in unserem Leben Platz zu finden für das gesellige Beieinander, und wenn, dann ist es wichtig, dass wir einen schönen Ort haben, wo wir als Gruppe gemeinsam Zeit verbringen können … Manche halten diese Musik gar nicht für Disco (*bezieht sich auf die Musik, die gerade läuft*) … Was meinen Sie? (*Ermuntert zu antworten.*)

Akt 3 – Kommen Sie an den Tisch.
Der Stratege im Regieraum und Politiker im Nachrichtenstudio.

STRATEGE: Nette Aufwärmübung, nun zum Hauptgang. Bitten wir sie an den Tisch, dann werden wir intimer …

POLITIKER (*souffliert vom Strategen*): Hören Sie, hier geht es nicht einfach nur um Politik, ich muss was mit Ihnen besprechen. Lassen Sie uns irgendwo hingehen, wo es ruhig ist und wo wir reden können (*führt die erste Person zum Tisch und bittet sie, Platz zu nehmen*).

STRATEGE: Hol noch jemanden, besetze alle Stühle.

POLITIKER (*souffliert vom Strategen; spricht einzelne Personen im Publikum an, bis alle Plätze am Tisch besetzt sind*): Entschuldigung, darf ich mir Ihren Freund mal einen Augenblick borgen? (*Führt zwei weitere Zuschauer zum Tisch.*)

STRATEGE: Gut, wunderbar, zieh sie an Land, immer schön sachte.

POLITIKER (*souffliert vom Strategen; zu einer anderen Person im Publikum*): Wir müssen mal ernsthaft über die Dinge sprechen, die uns entzweien. (*Um die letzten Plätze zu besetzen*) Kommen Sie, reden wir miteinander. Wollen Sie nicht zu uns an den Tisch kommen?

STRATEGE: Mach den Sack zu.

(*Politiker platziert die zehn Zuschauer um den Tisch.*)

STRATEGE (*verstärkt; erteilt den Teilnehmern aus dem Publikum Anweisungen*): Danke, dass Sie bereit sind, mitzumachen. Die Sitzung wird etwa 20 Minuten dauern. […] (*Zu Gary*) Beweg deinen Hintern hierüber.

POLITIKER (*murmelt über das Headset zum Strategen. Reagiert auf das Kommando*): Bitte entschuldigen Sie, ich bin gleich wieder da (*geht zurück in den Regieraum*). (*Zum Techniker, der die Zuschauerreaktionen erfasst*) Wie läuft's? Gib mir was, mit dem ich was anfangen kann.

STRATEGE: Lass sie in Ruhe, die verarbeiten gerade die Daten.

POLITIKER (*zum Publikum im Regieraum*): Na, wie schlage ich mich da draußen? Meint ihr, die mögen mich? Werden sie mich unterstützen?

(*Der Techniker gibt dem Strategen ein Zeichen, dass die Diagramme fertig sind.*)

There's nothing on the table, nothing off the table.

STRATEGIST: Good, pause, inhale, and go.

LEADER (*prompted by Strategist*): As you all know, some of my opponents have accused me of brinksmanship, but the reality is we are here tonight … because more than mere words … must bear the burden of love … I believe deeply that in the face of impossible odds … those who love this country can change it.[104] (*To audience member*) How about you, do you want to see change? … (*To another*) Are you happy with the status quo? … (*To another*) Do you feel that your voice is being heard? (*Eyes darting, trying to make eye contact with each one*) … Because you know, there is a difference between being listened to and being heard. (*Pause; change tone*) Change is the law of life. And those who look only to the past or present are certain to miss the future. But change will not come if we wait for some other person or some other time. We are the ones we've been waiting for. We are the change that we seek. Are you with me?

STRATEGIST: 'Tis a trifle better! But remember everyone is watching your eyes. Control your eyes and your voice will follow.

LEADER (*prompted by Strategist*): Some folks in the press have said – great heavens – that I'm not willing to talk? – When every day I talk to you, more and more! All I want is to sit down and have a reasonable conversation with everyone. I know all of you have questions, and I'm here to answer them.

STRATEGIST: Pick up the pace, but careful – (*emphasis*) enunciation.

LEADER (*solo; flustered by Strategist's comment*): Please don't mind my hesitation, I'm rocked by an anxious beating heart …

STRATEGIST (*emphasis*): Gary, don't mention doubt when your words come so haltingly out! Why dilute your message? We want your message to be nice and concentrated.

LEADER (*prompted by Strategist; stilted delivery*): If we cannot trust our government to protect and promote the public good … all else is lost. We stand … on the precipice … of potential catastrophe … It took a lot of blood, sweat and tears to get to here, but we have just begun. We must strive to make a world for our children that is at least a little better than the one we inhabit today. We're working hard to reach out … my words grope in the darkness … looking for … your ear …

STRATEGIST (*frustrated*): Gary, we've been over this before, extraneous emotion dissipates your energy.

LEADER (*prompted by Strategist*): I'm sorry if I speak passionately, but I just feel so strongly about this … (*Leader's eyes dart around the table*).

STRATEGIST: Why so faltering? Has mental palsy seized on your imaginative faculties? Calm your eye movement, no wandering eye.

LEADER (*prompted by Strategist*): Till now I spoke haphazard … I was in a sort of haze caused by this vertigo, this drunkenness that afflicts all those who tremble in the presence of a crowd. But this one night I feel I can address your hearts for the first time.

STRATEGIST: You're nice and solid, lean forward, engage them. Full voice, assertive.

LEADER (*prompted by Strategist; leaning nearer to an audience member; passionate delivery*): In these trying times, I can't mince words, I have to speak what's on my mind, and if that gets me in trouble, so be it (*drinks water*).

STRATEGIST: Engage, straighten up, tilt your body. Yeah, – to

STRATEGE (*zum Politiker*): Wir sind soweit, geh wieder raus!

POLITIKER: Prima, dann machen wir das (*geht zurück in das Nachrichtenstudio und setzt sich an den Tisch*).

STRATEGE (*verstärkt; zu den Teilnehmern*): So, Sie sollten jetzt auf ihren Touchscreens Schieberegler sehen. Nutzen Sie diese bitte, um anzugeben, ob Sie mit dem, was Sie gleich hören werden, einverstanden sind oder nicht. „100" bedeutet starke Zustimmung, „0" starke Ablehnung und „50", dass Sie neutral sind. Bitte behalten Sie den Finger auf dem Touchscreen, um Ihre Reaktion aufzuzeichnen. Schieben Sie den Regler nach links, um negativ, und nach rechts um positiv zu signalisieren. Es ist unbedingt erforderlich, dass Sie Ihren Finger auf dem Schieber lassen.[105] Wir möchten wissen, was Sie wirklich denken und wie wir Ihnen besser gerecht werden können, aber überlassen Sie bitte Ihrem Finger, dies mitzuteilen (*Ende Verstärkung*).

POLITIKER (*souffliert vom Strategen*): Wo Sie nun alle hier sind, möchte ich zunächst mit einem herzlichen Dankeschön beginnen. Herzlichen Dank für die Energie, die Sie heute Abend mitgebracht haben. Sie sind großartig und sollten sich selbst beglückwünschen. Wie wäre es mit einem großen Applaus für alle, die heute Abend gekommen sind!? (*Bringt alle dazu, zu klatschen.*) Sie wundern sich vielleicht, warum wir alle hier sind. Also ich bin jedenfalls hier, um Ihnen allen zuzuhören. Da gibt es keine Einschränkungen. Es liegt nichts auf dem Tisch, es ist nichts vom Tisch.

STRATEGE: Gut, mach eine Pause, atme tief ein und geh.

POLITIKER (*souffliert vom Strategen*): Wie Sie alle wissen, haben einige meiner Gegner mir vorgeworfen, ich spiele mit dem Feuer, aber wahr ist, dass wir heute Abend hier sind … weil mehr als bloße Worte … die Last der Liebe tragen muss … Ich bin der festen Überzeugung, dass angesichts von scheinbar unüberwindlichen Schwierigkeiten … diejenigen, die dieses Land lieben, es auch ändern können.[104] (*Zu jemandem im Publikum*) Wie ist das bei Ihnen, wollen Sie einen Wandel? … (*Zu jemand anderem*) Sind Sie glücklich mit dem Status quo? … (*Zu wieder jemand anderem*) Haben Sie den Eindruck, dass Ihre Stimme Gehör findet? (*Stechender Blick, versucht mit jedem einzelnen Augenkontakt herzustellen*) … Weil, Sie wissen ja, dass das ein Unterschied ist, ob man Ihnen zuhört oder sie nur hört. (*Pause, wechselt den Tonfall*) Wandel, das ist das Gesetz des Lebens. Und wer nur in die Vergangenheit schaut oder auf die Gegenwart, verpasst gewiss die Zukunft. Aber der Wandel kommt nicht, wenn wir nur auf eine andere Person oder eine andere Zeit warten. Wir sind es, auf die wir gewartet haben. Wir sind der Wandel, nach dem wir suchen. Stimmen wir da überein?

STRATEGE: Das ist schon eine Spur besser! Aber denk dran: Alle schauen auf deine Augen. Kontrolliere deine Augen, und die Stimme wird folgen.

POLITIKER (*souffliert vom Strategen*): Mancher von der Presse hat gesagt – meine Güte – ich sei nicht gesprächsbereit? – Wo ich doch jeden Tag mit Ihnen spreche, immer mehr! Ich will gar nichts anderes als mich hinzusetzen und mich mit allen Leuten vernünftig zu unterhalten. Ich weiß wohl, dass Sie alle Fragen haben, und ich bin hier, um sie zu beantworten.

STRATEGE: Zieh das Tempo an, aber vorsichtig – (*betont*) in der Artikulation.

POLITIKER (*solo; nervös geworden durch den Kommentar des Strategen*): Verzeihen Sie mein Zögern, mich schüttelt ein ängstlich pochend Herz …

STRATEGE (*mit Nachdruck*): Gary, keine Rede von Zweifeln, wenn deine Worte so stockend rauskommen! Warum verwässerst

be at last sincere: smile, bring honesty. We like that. Arch your back. Feed them your passion.

LEADER (*prompted by Strategist; weighty delivery*): Every day we get closer to the point beyond which we have never been and some of my colleagues act like it's all a game: words, poetry, rhymes … They're too busy finger pointing to remember that it's not about words; it's about real people. Do you hear that drum beat of blame? We cannot get distracted by party politics. We cannot yield to the 24-hour news cycle with its panic perfumes.

STRATEGIST: Now stand up, shift your weight.

LEADER (*prompted by Strategist; stands*; *shifts weight side-to-side*): We have to make good on our commitment to peace, love, and freedom. We need to know when to fight and I'm taking that fight to Washington. It's three agencies of government that will be gone once I get there: the lobbyists, the Strategists and the –

STRATEGIST: … press corp.

LEADER (*solo*): … um … I forgot the third, but the point is this is our moment!

STRATEGIST: Control the message. Stay focused. But not too much! That becomes suspicious.

LEADER (*prompted by Strategist*): We are living in an age of semantics; the rich and powerful manipulate words in order to achieve a desired effect on their target audience. Their language is designed to make lies sound truthful. They speak fine words to garnish vain love-letters! It is a crime, in love, to play this pantomime. My heart too has cloaked itself in art, in witty words.

STRATEGIST: Ok, sit back down.

LEADER (*prompted by Strategist; sits; addresses audience members around the table*): But do carefully crafted words really serve you? … Do you really want a leader who just tells you what you want to hear? … Don't you think you deserve transparency? … Can we shake off the shackles of contrivance and speak plainly to one another? My friends, we must ease our hearts of all things artificial lest truth of sentiment dissolve and vanish. Let us declare, right here and now, that we are not going to take it anymore. (*Gets audience riled up*) Say it with me: I'm not going to take it! Let's hear some noise! (*Claps*) Let's hear it! (*Solo; shakes head*) I tremble to think that even the sweetest word may be manipulated …

STRATEGIST: Stay on point. Remember no side-to-side, makes you look wobbly, gestures need to be dynamic, toward the camera.

LEADER (*solo*): Where was I? I don't know … all this … Forgive my emotion … (*pause*)

STRATEGIST: This is getting difficult. Stand, turn away, I'll take it from here …

(*Leader stands up, turns to face wall; Strategist is amplified and speaks for Leader; leader is lip synching and gesticulating.*)

LEADER/STRATEGIST: Have my words the power to make you tremble? The words I spoke just now! – my words – my words! Ah, "art." How I hate art in love![107] Turning frank loving into subtle fencing! Each well-weighed word is futile and soul-saddening![103] If only it were that words still had meaning, I would bring you all the words that ever were, or weren't, or could, or couldn't be. (*Leader turns back toward audience ventriloquized by Strategist*) But this is not a game! I love you. Don't you want a leader who loves?[106]

LEADER (*solo*): This is not normal …

STRATEGIST: Shh, keep it genuine. Smile a few times.

du deine Botschaft? Wir wollen deine Botschaft hübsch konzentriert.

POLITIKER (*souffliert vom Strategen; hochtrabend*): Wenn wir nicht darauf vertrauen können, dass unsere Regierung das öffentliche Wohl schützt und mehrt … dann ist alles andere vergebens. Wir stehen … am Abgrund … einer möglichen Katastrophe … Um an diesen Punkt zu gelangen, brauchte es viel Blut, Schweiß und Tränen, aber wir stehen noch ganz am Anfang. Wir müssen danach trachten, unseren Kindern eine Welt zu hinterlassen, die zumindest ein kleines Stück besser ist als die, in der wir heute leben. Wir arbeiten hart, um andere zu erreichen … Ich taste mit meinen Worten im Dunkeln … auf der Suche nach … Ihrem Ohr …

STRATEGE (*frustriert*): Gary, das hatten wir doch schon abgehakt: Mit belangloser Emotionalität verzettelst du dich nur.

POLITIKER (*souffliert vom Strategen*): Verzeihen Sie, wenn ich so leidenschaftlich spreche, aber mir geht das emotional wirklich nahe … (*Politiker blickt intensiv in die Runde.*)

STRATEGE: Warum so zögerlich? Hat deine Vorstellungsgabe plötzlich eine Lähmung ergriffen? Beruhige deine Augenbewegungen, schau nicht in der Gegend herum.

POLITIKER (*souffliert vom Strategen*): Bisher habe ich ganz planlos gesprochen … war ich wie im Nebel durch den Schwindel, die Trunkenheit, die all jene erfasst, die vor einer Menschenmenge anfangen zu zittern. Doch nun spüre ich, dass es mir heute Abend erstmals gelingen kann, zu Ihren Herzen zu sprechen.

STRATEGE: Du bist hübsch solide, beug dich vor, suche den Kontakt. Volle Stimme, sei bestimmt.

POLITIKER (*souffliert vom Strategen; beugt sich zu einem Zuschauer; leidenschaftlicher Vortrag*): In diesen schweren Zeiten kann ich kein Blatt vor den Mund nehmen, ich muss aussprechen, was ich denke, und wenn mir das Ärger einhandelt, sei's drum (*trinkt einen Schluck Wasser*).

STRATEGE: Geh ran, richte dich auf, neige deinen Körper. Jawohl, – am Ende ganz aufrichtig sein: lächeln, sei ehrlich. Das mögen wir. Spanne den Rücken. Gib ihnen deine Leidenschaft.

POLITIKER (*souffliert vom Strategen*): Wir rücken jeden Tag ein Stückchen weiter auf den Punkt zu, den wir noch nie überschritten haben, und einige meiner Kollegen tun so, als sei das alles nur ein Spiel: Worte, Dichtung, Reime … Sie sind so damit beschäftigt, mit den Fingern auf andere zu zeigen, dass sie gar nicht mehr merken, dass es hier nicht um Worte geht; es geht um die Menschen. Dieses Dröhnen der Schuldzuweisungen, hören Sie das? Wir dürfen uns nicht durch parteipolitisches Gezänk ablenken lassen. Wir dürfen uns nicht dem 24-Stunden-Rhythmus der Nachrichten mit ihrer Panikmache ergeben.

STRATEGE: Jetzt steh auf, verlagere dein Gewicht.

POLITIKER (*souffliert vom Strategen; steht auf, verlagert sein Gewicht vom einen Bein auf das andere*) Wir müssen unserem Engagement für Frieden, Liebe und Freiheit gerecht werden. Wir müssen wissen, wann es gilt zu kämpfen, und ich trage diesen Kampf nach Washington. Wenn ich dort angekommen bin, werden drei Akteure aus dem Regierungsgeschäft verschwinden: die Lobbyisten, die Politstrategen und die –

STRATEGE: … Medienkonzerne.

POLITIKER (*solo*): … ähm …Ich komm gerade nicht auf den dritten, aber der Punkt ist: das ist unser Moment!

STRATEGE: Kontrollierte Botschaften. Bleib konzentriert. Aber nicht übertreiben! Dann werden sie misstrauisch.

POLITIKER (*souffliert vom Strategen*): Wir leben in einer Zeit der Bedeutungen; die Reichen und die Mächtigen manipulieren

LEADER (*prompted by Strategist*): No, this is not normal! We must remember that politics is a battle of ideas, but we advance those ideas through elections and legislation – not extortion. This is not normal … And yet, love, strangely, is not a selfish passion! I for your joy would gladly lay mine own down. My happiness is here to augment yours – to put you first. I ask only one thing that this night you speak and I listen. (*Pause – solo*) Can I count on your support?

STRATEGIST: Fool! You go too quick!

LEADER (*solo; whispering to Strategist*): Since they are moved thus, why shouldn't I reap some benefit?!

STRATEGIST: Be silent! Patience! Let me be the agent of their yes.

LEADER (*prompted by Strategist*): Please excuse my audacity, but I refuse to negotiate our children's future. It seems my opponents have forgotten that it is an honor to be a public servant, not a career. (*Solo; whispering to Strategist via earpiece*) You'd better get me this district …

STRATEGIST: Sit down.

LEADER (*sits down and is prompted again by Strategist*): However the questions remain: how do we restore faith in our social contract? How do we define our bond, the sacrament of a vow, a promissory note on the bank of love and compassion?

STRATEGIST: Keep your gaze locked at the top of the lens. Don't restrict your breathing.

LEADER (*prompted by Strategist*): Hope is the bedrock of this nation. The belief that our destiny will not be written for us, but by us, by all of you who are not content to settle for the world as it is. You have the courage to remake the world as it should be …

STRATEGIST: They're yours for the taking, go for it!

LEADER (*nods head*): Yes we can.

STRATEGIST: What the hell are you waiting for?

LEADER (*solo; whispering to Strategist*): I'm not sure really that this is the right time … I feel now, as though it were ill conceived!

STRATEGIST: Do it now!

LEADER (*prompted by Strategist*): A vote of support, when all is said and done – what is it? An opinion performed, an oath ratified, a promise sealed, a heart's avowal?

STRATEGIST: They love you!

LEADER (*prompted by Strategist*): "I-love-you" does not belong in the realm of language, it is the point of departure for speech, it is the occasion of music. It is a call to action. We will fight. We will win! Together we will achieve our destiny! Will you stand with me?! (*Stands up clapping and gets participants to stand up and clap.*)

STRATEGIST: Let's dance! (*Music: The Hustle*)

LEADER (*to audience member*): Let's dance?! (*Clapping transitions to The Hustle dance; encourages participants to join him on the dance floor to learn the dance throughout song.*)[102]

STRATEGIST (*turns to camera as if it's a mirror; speaking to himself*): A strange pain wrings my heart. Love's feast, so near, won by the words he spoke just now! – my words – my love! He takes the kiss of glory. Yet to me falls only a crumb or two. The shadow for me, for others the applause, the fame (*sighs*). You see, a man fights for far more than the mere hope of winning. Better, far better to know that the fight is totally irreparably incorrigibly in vain. All my old enemies – Falsehood, Compromise, Prejudice, Cowardice. You ask for my Surrender? Oh no, never, no, never.

Wörter, um damit bei ihrem Zielpublikum die gewünschten Wirkungen hervorzurufen. Ihre Sprache wurde geschaffen, damit ihre Lügen wahr klingen. Sie brauchen fünf Worte, um ihre eitlen Liebesbotschaften aufzuhübschen! Es ist eine Untat, in der Liebe ein solches Schauspiel abzuliefern. Auch mein Herz hat sich in Künstelei gehüllt, in kluge Sprüche.

STRATEGE: Okay, setz dich wieder.

POLITIKER (*souffliert vom Strategen; setzt sich; wendet sich an die Zuschauer am Tisch*): Aber bringen Ihnen all diese sorgfältig zurechtgelegten Worte eigentlich etwas? … Wollen Sie wirklich einen politischen Führer, der Ihnen sagt, was Sie hören möchten? … Meinen Sie nicht, Sie hätten mehr Transparenz verdient? … Können wir diesen ganzen Apparat nicht loswerden und offen miteinander sprechen? Liebe Freunde, wir müssen alle Künstlichkeit aus unseren Herzen verbannen, weil sich sonst das wahre Gefühl verflüchtigt, weil es sonst verschwindet. Erklären wir doch hier und heute, dass wir nicht bereit sind, das länger hinzunehmen. (*Stachelt das Publikum auf*) Sagen Sie mit mir: Ich nehme das nicht länger hin! Jetzt will ich was hören! (*Klatscht*) Lasst es hören! (*Solo; schüttelt mit dem Kopf*) Mich schüttelt es bei dem Gedanken, dass selbst die zartesten Worte manipuliert sein könnten …

STRATEGE: Bleib auf der Stelle. Denk dran: kein Hin und Her, dann siehst du wackelig aus, die Gestik muss dynamisch wirken, in die Kamera.

POLITIKER (*solo*): Wo war ich stehengeblieben? Ich weiß nicht … das alles … Verzeihung, dass ich so emotional werde … (*Pause*)

STRATEGE: Jetzt wird's schwierig. Steh, dreh dich weg, ich übernehme das von hier aus …

(*Politiker steht auf, dreht sich zur Wand; Stratege wird verstärkt und spricht für den Politiker; Politiker bewegt die Lippen dazu und gestikuliert.*)

POLITIKER/STRATEGE: Haben meine Worte die Kraft, Sie erschauern zu lassen? Die Worte, die ich gerade gesprochen habe! – meine Worte – meine Worte! „Kunstvoll" – Oh, in der Liebe hasse ich die Kunst![107] Sie macht die ehrliche Liebe zu einer Spiegelfechterei! Jedes der wohl überlegten Worte ist eitel und betrübt die Seele![103] Und wenn die Worte wenigstens noch eine Bedeutung hätten, ich brächte Ihnen alle Worte, die es jemals gab, oder auch nicht, oder die es geben könnte, oder auch nicht. (*Politiker wendet sich wieder dem Publikum zu, als Bauchredner des Strategen.*) Aber das hier ist kein Spiel! Ich liebe Sie. Sie wollen doch einen Führer, der Sie liebt?[106]

POLITIKER (*solo*): Das ist doch nicht normal …

STRATEGE: Pssst, bleib authentisch. Lächle immer mal wieder.

POLITIKER (*souffliert vom Strategen*): Nein, normal ist das nicht! Wir müssen uns wieder klar machen, dass die Politik ein Kampf der Ideen ist, aber wir bringen diese Ideen durch Wahlen und die Gesetzgebung voran – nicht durch Zwang. Das ist nicht normal … Und doch ist die Liebe sonderbarerweise keine egoistische Leidenschaft! Für Ihr Wohlergehen würde ich meines nur allzu gerne aufgeben. Mein Glück ist dazu da, Ihres zu mehren – Sie an erste Stelle zu rücken. Ich will nur eines: dass Sie heute Abend sprechen und ich höre zu. (*Pause – solo*) Kann ich auf Ihre Unterstützung zählen?

STRATEGE: Idiot! Du bist zu schnell!

POLITIKER (*solo; flüstert zum Strategen*): Die sind doch gerührt, warum soll ich mir das nicht zunutze machen?

STRATEGE: Sei still! Geduld! Ich bring sie schon zu einem Ja.

Are you there too, Stupidity? You above all others perhaps were predestined to get me in the end. But no, I'll fight on, fight on, fight.[108] (*He exits control room to join the party*) Hi, I'm Daniel.

(*David Bowie, Let's Dance; credits roll on screen.*)

POLITIKER (*souffliert vom Strategen*): Verzeihen Sie bitte meine Kühnheit, aber die Zukunft unserer Kinder ist für mich keine Verhandlungsmasse. Mir kommt es vor, als hätten meine Gegner vergessen, dass es eine Ehre ist, der Gesellschaft zu dienen, nicht einer Karriere. (*Solo; flüstert über sein Headset mit dem Strategen.*) Verschaff mir bloß diesen Wahlkreis …
STRATEGE: Setz dich.
POLITIKER (*Politiker setzt sich, wieder souffliert vom Strategen*): Jedenfalls bleiben die Fragen: Wie schaffen wir es, dass die Menschen wieder an unseren Gesellschaftsvertrag glauben? Wie definieren wir unsere Verpflichtung, einen Schwur, einen verbindlichen Wechsel auf unser Guthaben an Liebe und Mitgefühl?
STRATEGE: Halte den Blick auf den oberen Rand des Objektivs. Behindere deine Atmung nicht.
POLITIKER (*souffliert vom Strategen*): Hoffnung ist eine der Grundfesten des Landes. Die Überzeugung, dass unser Schicksal nicht für uns bestimmt wird, sondern von uns, von Ihnen allen, die sich nicht damit zufrieden geben, wie die Welt heute ist. Sie haben den Mut, die Welt neu zu gestalten, wie sie sein soll …
STRATEGE: Die hast du in der Tasche, leg los!
POLITIKER (*nickt*): Yes we can – ja, das schaffen wir.
STRATEGE: Mensch, worauf wartest du denn noch?
POLITIKER (*solo; flüstert mit dem Strategen*): Ich weiß nicht so recht, ob das der richtige Zeitpunkt ist … Ich hab so ein Gefühl, das ist nicht richtig durchdacht!
STRATEGE: Mach es – jetzt!
POLITIKER (*souffliert vom Strategen*): Eine Stimme, die Sie zur Unterstützung eines Kandidaten abgeben, was ist das am Ende eigentlich? Ist sie Ausdruck einer Meinung, die Bekräftigung eines Schwurs, die Besiegelung eines Versprechens, ein Bekenntnis von Herzen?
STRATEGE: Sie lieben dich!
POLITIKER (*souffliert vom Strategen*): „Ich-liebe-dich", das fällt nicht in den Bereich der Sprache, das ist der Ausgangspunkt für eine Rede, das ist Anlass für Musik. Das ist eine Aufforderung zum Handeln. Wir werden kämpfen. Wir werden gewinnen! Gemeinsam werden wir unser Schicksal in die Hand nehmen! Stehen Sie mir zur Seite?! (*Steht auf, klatscht, bringt die Teilnehmer dazu, aufzustehen und zu klatschen.*)
STRATEGE: Tanzen wir! (*Gibt Einsatz für Musik: The Hustle.*)
POLITIKER (*zu jemandem im Publikum*): Tanzen wir?! (*Klatschen zum Tanz zu The Hustle, ermuntert Teilnehmer, zu ihm auf die Tanzfläche zu kommen und den Tanz bei diesem Song zu lernen.*)[102]
STRATEGE (*schaut in die Kamera wie in einen Spiegel; spricht zu sich selbst*): Ein sonderbarer Schmerz ergreift mein Herz. Der Liebe Fest so nah, errungen durch Worte, die er gesprochen! – meine Worte – meine Liebe! Des Ruhmes Kuss gilt ihm. Für mich fallen nur Brosamen ab. Für mich der Schatten, den andern der Applaus, der Ruhm (*seufzt*). Ein Mann kämpft, wie man sieht, für mehr als nur die Hoffnung auf den Sieg. Besser, so viel besser, zu wissen, dass der Kampf unweigerlich, unrettbar vergeblich ist. All meine alten Feinde – Falschheit, Kompromiss, Vorurteil, Feigheit. Ich soll kapitulieren? Oh nein, nie und nimmer. Und Dummheit, bist auch du zugegen? Dir war es vielleicht vor allen anderen vorherbestimmt, mich am Ende dranzukriegen. Aber nein, ich kämpfe weiter, werde kämpfen.[108] (*Verlässt den Regieraum und geht zu den anderen*) Hallo, ich bin Daniel.

(*David Bowie, Let's Dance, Abspann läuft über den Bildschirm.*)

Essays

The Factographic Gesture
Jordan Troeller

Since 2011, Liz Magic Laser's videos and performances have cast a critical gaze on the rhetorical strategies of contemporary American – and, more recently, European – politicians and pundits. This emerging theme marks a consolidation of Laser's long-standing interest in considering the mechanics of media culture from unlikely perspectives. The aria in her operatic film I Have You (2009) draws on television commercials for residential security alarm systems, and Flight (2010) recreates staircase chase scenes from well-known films, including Battleship Potemkin and American Psycho, on the steps of MoMA PS1 in 2010 and in New York's Times Square in 2011. Whereas Laser's previous works drew on explicitly theatrical sources, her recent projects, focused on reportage, illuminate the unrecognized dramatic dimensions of a genre typically regarded as objective.

The pivotal work in this development is I Feel Your Pain, an eighty-minute piece commissioned by Performa and performed in New York in November 2011. The script for I Feel Your Pain was the first in which Laser relied on actual dialogue from television interviews and newspaper articles. In preparing the script, she gathered excerpts from interviews with significant American political figures from the 2008 presidential election and the following years. She rearranged the dialogue and stitched it back together with word changes, omissions, and additions, in order to create a series of scenes with two or three characters. Intertitles on screen and a playbill program identify the source material for each scene. The characters are generic, even at times archetypal. The first scene, for instance, is modeled on a first date and begins with a male (Rafael Jordan) and female (Annie Fox) coyly flirting with one another:

RAFAEL (*pulls away from embrace*): Hey, can I read you what I wrote last night in my journal, (*he pulls out journal*) it's about you. (*Reading from journal*) Tomorrow, I meet her for the first time. I'm actually a little nervous – as she is one of the only people that I can see that can possibly lead us out of where we are. I don't know yet if she's strong enough, if she's well enough

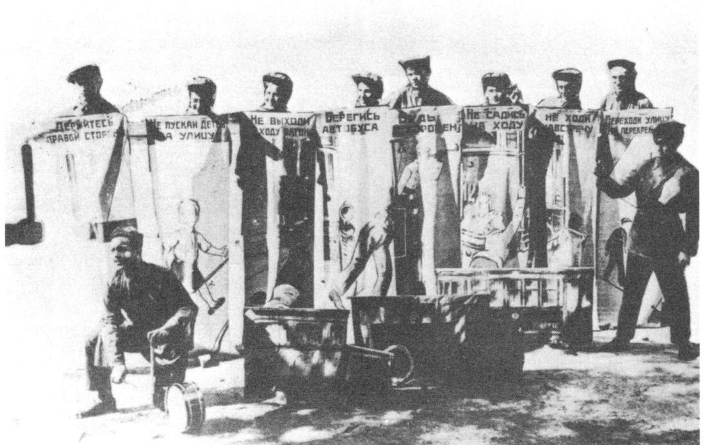

Living Newspaper, Blue Blouse (workers' theater group), Russia, 1920s / Lebende Zeitung, Blaue Bluse (Arbeitertheatergruppe), Russland, 1920er Jahre

Der faktografische Gestus
Jordan Troeller

Mit ihren Videos und Performances hat Liz Magic Laser seit 2011 die rhetorischen Strategien aktueller amerikanischer – und jüngst auch europäischer – Politiker und Meinungsführer in den Blick genommen. Die zunehmende Beschäftigung mit dieser Thematik ist Ausdruck eines schon lange ausgeprägten Interesses der Künstlerin für die Funktionsmechanismen der Medienkultur, die sie aus ungewöhnlichen Perspektiven betrachtet. Die Arie in ihrem opernhaften Film I Have You (2009) macht Anleihen bei Werbespots für häusliche Alarmanlagen, und in Flight (2010) wurden 2010 auf der Treppe zum MoMA PS 1 und 2011 auf dem New Yorker Times Square Verfolgungsszenen auf Treppen aus berühmten Filmen wie Panzerkreuzer Potemkin oder American Psycho nachgespielt. Während Lasers frühere Arbeiten sich dezidiert auf theatrale Vorlagen bezogen, konzentrieren sich die jüngeren Projekte auf das Medium Reportage und beleuchten dabei die unbeachteten dramatischen Dimensionen eines Genres, das eigentlich als besonders objektiv gilt.

Das Schlüsselwerk für diese Entwicklung in Lasers Œuvre ist I Feel Your Pain, eine 80-Minuten-Performance, die als Auftragsarbeit für Performa entstand und im November 2011 in New York stattfand. Beim Skript von I Feel Your Pain setzte Laser erstmals auf echte Dialoge aus Fernsehinterviews und Zeitungsartikeln. Bei der Vorbereitung sammelte sie Ausschnitte aus Interviews, die wichtige Persönlichkeiten der amerikanischen Politik im Präsidentschaftswahlkampf 2008 und in den nachfolgenden Jahren gegeben hatten. Sie arrangierte die Dialoge neu und setzte sie mit Änderungen im Wortlaut, Auslassungen und Hinzufügungen zusammen. So entstand eine Folge von Szenen mit zwei oder drei Figuren. Zwischentitel auf der Leinwand und ein Programmplakat benennen die Quellen, aus denen das in jeder Szene verarbeitete Material stammt. Die Figuren wirken stereotyp, manchmal sogar archetypisch. Die erste Szene zeigt ein Paar, das zum ersten Mal zusammen ausgeht, und sie beginnt damit, dass ein Mann (Rafael Jordan) und eine Frau (Annie Fox) verhalten miteinander turteln:

RAFAEL (*löst sich aus der Umarmung*): Darf ich dir mal vorlesen, was ich gestern Abend in mein Tagebuch geschrieben habe, (*er holt sein Tagebuch hervor*) da geht's um dich. (*Liest aus dem Tagebuch*) Morgen treffe ich sie zum ersten Mal. Ich bin schon ein bisschen nervös – schließlich zählt sie zu den wenigen Leuten, von denen ich mir vorstellen kann, uns da wieder herausführen zu können. Ich weiß noch nicht, ob sie stark genug ist, ob sie gut genug beraten wird oder ob sie weiß, dass sie nun keinem mehr trauen kann. Ich weiß nicht, ob sie uns führen kann, ohne dabei ihre Seele aufzugeben (*betont*).

ANNIE: Ja. Das mit dem Vertrauen, weißt du, da hast du den Nagel auf den Kopf getroffen. Wir sind von vertrauenswürdigen Menschen umgeben, sie zeigen uns den Weg, wir müssen ihnen *vertrauen* können. Aber jemandem zu vertrauen, das ist sehr, sehr gefährlich.

Indem sie die Worte bekannter Persönlichkeiten und Ereignisse aus ihrem ursprünglichen Zusammenhang löst und verlagert, lenkt Laser die Aufmerksamkeit der Zuschauer auf den emotionalen

advised, or if she knows she can no longer trust anyone. I don't know if she can lead us and not lose her soul (*emphasis*).

ANNIE: Yes. That trust thing, you nailed it, you know? Trustworthy people surrounding us, leading us, we've got to be able to *trust*. But it's very, very dangerous to trust anybody.

By displacing the words of well-known figures and events from their original context, Laser concentrates the audience's attention on the emotional subtext of this exchange, on the nervousness, doubt, and vulnerability familiar to anyone who has experienced a first date. The audience must reconcile this empathetic appeal with their knowledge that the dialogue derives from an interview between Glenn Beck and Sarah Palin on Fox News in 2010. Beck speaks to Palin as if he were a longtime secret admirer just now revealing his fears and anticipation. The disjunction between the generic scene before us and the original context of the dialogue generates a range of emotions on the part of the audience, including amusement and discomfort, but the discomfort is instructive: in contemplating the exchange, we recognize that a crucial task of the American political system, for reporters and politicians alike, is to choreograph the emotions of the viewing public. Vignette after vignette in I Feel Your Pain reveals that dynamic. Anxiety and anticipation fuel a decision-making process that is, nevertheless, founded on the principle of rationality.

Laser's strategy of defamiliarization draws on early twentieth-century Russian theater and Soviet agitation propaganda. Each vignette, for instance, unfolds in the theater seats. This spatial dislocation disrupts the separation between actors and audience, thus collapsing the distinction between the fictional temporality of the drama and the actual temporality of spectatorship. Audience members become aware of their own physical proximity to and potential implication in the unfolding action, rendering disengagement nearly impossible. This collapse between actors and audience – and the effective activation of the spectator – was an innovation of the Russian dramaturge and theater director Vsevolod Meyerhold. As early as 1907, Meyerhold opposed the idea set out by Constantin Stanislavsky that the actor must exclude the audience from her consciousness. Instead, Meyerhold's plays intensify the relationship between performer and spectator through spatial dislocations between audience and stage and through direct address.[1] For Meyerhold, it was only the participation of the spectator that completed the production, whose role was to draw conclusions from the manner in which the performance was structured.

What distinguishes Laser's interpretation of the Soviet avant-garde's strategy of participation from any number of contemporary fetishizations of "experience" is her commitment to the history and technology of theater as a discrete form of audience engagement. According to Meyerhold, to give just one definition, the theater is defined by at least three dimensions: the playwright, the director, and the actors, with the audience functioning as a crucial fourth dimension. I Feel Your Pain intensified these structural aspects of theater by incorporating a fifth element: live-feed video. During the performance, three cinematographers filmed the actors as they performed from the theater seats. Laser acted as a real-time editor, choosing which shots would appear on the movie theater's screen facing the audience. In this way, the play situated the audience in two positions simultaneously: as participants in the actual activity unfolding around them and as spectators of the recorded image before them.

Subtext dieser Wortwechsel, auf die Nervosität, die Zweifel, die Verletzlichkeit, die jeder kennt, der ein erstes Date erlebt hat. Das Publikum muss nun seine empathische Anteilnahme in Einklang bringen mit dem Wissen darum, dass der Dialog aus einem Interview stammt, das Glenn Beck 2010 auf Fox News mit Sarah Palin führte. Beck spricht mit Palin, als sei er seit langem ein heimlicher Verehrer, der erst jetzt seine Befürchtungen, seine freudige Erwartung zu erkennen gibt. Der Bruch zwischen der Alltagsszene, die wir sehen, und dem ursprünglichen Kontext des Dialogs ruft beim Publikum eine Reihe von Emotionen hervor, Amüsiertheit oder Unbehagen, doch das Unbehagen ist durchaus instruktiv: Wenn wir uns diesen Wortwechsel in Ruhe anschauen, wird uns bewusst, dass in Amerika die entscheidende Aufgabe des politischen Systems – das gilt für Journalisten ebenso wie für Politiker – darin besteht, die Emotionen der Zuschauer zu choreografieren. Mit jeder Spielszene von I Feel Your Pain kommt diese Dynamik deutlicher zum Vorschein. Angst und gespannte Erwartung befeuern einen Prozess der Entscheidungsfindung, dem gleichwohl rationale Prinzipien zugrunde liegen.

Lasers Strategie der Verfremdung vertrauter Muster geht auf Vorbilder aus dem frühen 20. Jahrhundert zurück, auf das russische Theater und die sowjetische Propaganda. So spielt jede der kleinen Szenen in den Zuschauerrängen eines Filmtheaters. Diese räumliche Verlagerung hebt die Trennung zwischen Schauspielern und Publikum auf, eliminiert den Unterschied zwischen der fiktionalen Zeitlichkeit des Dramas und der realen Zeit der Zuschauer. Die im Publikum sitzen, werden sich ihrer körperlichen Nähe zur Handlung des Stücks und der Möglichkeit ihrer Einbeziehung bewusst, was es fast unmöglich macht, sich aus dem Geschehen herauszuhalten. Dieses Zusammenfallen von Darstellern und Publikum – und die wirksame Aktivierung des Zuschauers – zählt zu den Innovationen des russischen Dramaturgen und Theaterleiters Wsewolod Meyerhold. Schon 1907 sprach sich Meyerhold gegen die von Konstantin Stanislawski vertretene Auffassung aus, der Schauspieler müsse das Publikum aus seinem Bewusstsein verbannen. Meyerholds Stücke verstärken hingegen die Beziehung zwischen Darsteller und Zuschauer durch die räumliche Verlagerung von Bühne und Zuschauerraum sowie durch eine direkte Publikumsansprache.[1] Für Meyerhold kam die Aufführung erst durch die Teilnahme des Zuschauers zur Vollendung, der aus der Struktur der Darbietung seine eigenen Schlüsse zu ziehen hatte.

Lasers Interpretation der partizipativen Strategien der sowjetischen Avantgardisten unterscheidet sich insofern von all den anderen zeitgenössischen Theorien, die das „Erlebnis" zum Fetisch erheben, als sie sich zu Geschichte und Technik des Theaters als einer eigenständigen Form der Publikumsbeteiligung bekennt. Für Meyerhold ist das Theater, um nur eine seiner Definitionen zu zitieren, durch mindestens drei Dimensionen bestimmt: den Dramatiker, den Regisseur und die Schauspieler, wobei das Publikum als entscheidende vierte Dimension fungiert. I Feel Your Pain verstärkte diese strukturellen Aspekte des Theaters, indem ein fünftes Element mit einbezogen wurde: die Videoprojektion in Echtzeit. Während der Aufführung filmten drei Kameraleute die Schauspieler bei ihrem Spiel in den Zuschauerrängen. Laser übernahm in Echtzeit die Bildregie, entschied, welche Aufnahmen auf der Leinwand des Kinos vor den

In addition to the six characters whose dialogue draws on news media clips, the cast includes two character types that were also prominent within Soviet theater: a Chaplinesque silent clown and a disembodied announcer. Laser's announcer was derived from a type of theater that became known as the "Living Newspaper". The Living Newspaper first emerged in the Soviet Union in the early 1920s and later migrated to the Federal Theatre Project of the Works Progress Administration in the United States. The function of the Living Newspaper was to translate the news into performances in order to inform the largely illiterate masses of the young socialist state.[2]

Robert Leach locates the origins of the Living Newspaper in the work of Mikhail Pustynin, a poet and playwright who served as the Vitebsk director of the Soviet telegraph agency (ROSTA), and in 1919 established the first Theater of Revolutionary Satire (TEREVSAT).[3] A typical program not only dramatized news items and letters to the editor, it often included a short talk by a professional agitator, one-act agit-plays illustrating the victories of the Red Army, parodies of poetry and novels, educational content (on land cultivation or disease prevention), and a mass singing of The Internationale. Props were minimal due to the massive material shortages in the post-revolutionary country. Crucial to the Living Newspaper was the rejection of theatrical illusionism and the embrace of early forms of nascent abstraction (some of the backdrops and costumes were designed and painted by the painter Marc Chagall). Sets often included large posters of life-sized geometric drawings with areas cut out of them so that the actor could stand behind and insert her own head and arms in order to animate the drawing.[4]

One strategy of TEREVSAT's Living Newspaper was the substitution of character development based on psychological interiority for the interplay between various types such as the Hero, Lover, Clown, or Mischief Maker in a revision of the traditional *commedia dell'arte* to suit the revolutionary context. This strategy was part of a larger program to infuse the project of mass education, initiated by the Commissariat of Education, Anatoly Lunacharsky, with familiar forms of humor derived from Russian folk traditions such as the *chastushka* (a simple rhyme similar to a limerick) and the *lubok* (popular print and predecessor of the comic strip).[5] In I Feel Your Pain, the role of the Clown (Audrey Crabtree) employs a similar strategy. The Clown and the Announcer (Lynn Berg) exist outside the performance's fictive construct. The Clown often reacts in ways that conflict with expected responses to the dramatic action, thus distancing the audience from that action. The Clown's exaggerated slapstick gestures serve as a foil for the six main characters' appeals for empathy.

The Living Newspaper emerged in the context of a broader artistic movement, which Soviet artists termed "factography." A designation that first emerged in the mid-1920s, "factography" refers to a type of Soviet literature, photography, and theater that defined the work of art as the inscription of facts. Unlike similar impulses in Europe and the United States that evolved into the more familiar documentary mode, factography defined a fact not as the objective recording of reality, but as the active transformation of it in accordance with the emerging socialist society. Sergei Tret'iakov, one of the most famous factographers and coeditor with Aleksandr Rodchenko of the avant-garde journal Novyi LEF, defined the *fact* as a process, an action,

Zuschauern erscheinen sollten. Auf diese Weise versetzte das Stück das Publikum in eine doppelte Position: Die Besucher waren Teilnehmer der Handlung, die sich um sie herum abspielte, und zugleich Zuschauer der aufgenommen Bilder auf der Leinwand vor ihnen.

Neben den sechs Figuren, deren Dialoge aus Nachrichtensendungen stammten, gehörten zur Besetzung zwei Charaktere, die auch im sowjetischen Theater eine wichtige Rolle spielten: ein stummer, an Charlie Chaplin erinnernder Clown und ein körperloser Ansager. Lasers Ansager ist aus einer Spielart des Theaters abgeleitet, das unter der Bezeichnung „Living Newspaper" (Lebende Zeitung) bekannt wurde. Das Format der Lebenden Zeitung entwickelte sich zuerst in der Sowjetunion der frühen 1920er Jahre; später wurde es in den USA vom Federal Theatre Project der Works Progress Administration übernommen. Die Funktion der Lebenden Zeitung war es, Nachrichten in gespielten Szenen zu verbreiten, um so die weitgehend analphabetischen Massen des jungen Sowjetstaates zu informieren.[2]

Robert Leach sieht die Ursprünge der Lebenden Zeitung im Werk von Michail Pustynin, einem Dichter und Dramatiker, der in Witebsk als Direktor des sowjetischen Telegrafenamts (ROSTA) tätig war und 1919 das erste Theater der revolutionären Satire (TEREVSAT) gründete.[3] Bei einer solchen Aufführung wurden typischerweise nicht nur Nachrichten und Leserbriefe dramaturgisch umgesetzt, sie umfasste oft auch die kurze Ansprache eines professionellen Agitators, einaktige Agitprop-Stücke, in denen die Siege der Roten Armee geschildert wurden, Parodien zu Gedichten und Romanen, Elemente der Volksbildung (über Landwirtschaft und Gesundheitsfürsorge) und das gemeinsame Absingen der Internationalen. Aufgrund der massiven Versorgungsengpässe in dem nachrevolutionären Land beschränkten sich die Requisiten auf ein Minimum. Entscheidend für das Format der Lebenden Zeitung war der Verzicht auf theatralen Illusionismus und die Übernahme von Frühformen der Abstraktion (einige der Kulissen und Kostüme wurden von Marc Chagall entworfen und ausgeführt). Für das Bühnenbild wurden häufig Plakate mit lebensgroßen geometrischen Zeichnungen verwendet, mit Ausschnitten, aus denen der Schauspieler oder die Schauspielerin Kopf und Arme stecken und so die Zeichnung verlebendigen konnte.[4]

Eine Strategie der Lebenden Zeitung des TEREVSAT-Theaters bestand darin, die Entwicklung der Figuren nach psychologischen Kategorien der Innerlichkeit zu ersetzen durch bestimmte festgelegte Typen wie Held, Liebhaber, Clown oder Quatschmacher, eine Neuauflage der traditionellen *Commedia dell'arte* unter den Bedingungen der revolutionären Umstände. Diese Strategie war Teil eines umfassenderen Programms der Volkserziehung, das der Volkskommissar für das Bildungswesen Anatoli Lunatscharski auf den Weg gebracht hatte. Es arbeitete mit ähnlichen, aus der volkstümlichen Tradition Russlands abgeleiteten humoristischen Formen wie der *Tschastuschka* (ein einfaches Gedicht, etwa wie ein Limerick) oder dem *Lubok* (ein Volksbilderbogen und Vorläufer der Comics).[5] In I Feel Your Pain folgt die Rolle des Clowns (Audrey Crabtree) einer ähnlichen Strategie. Der Clown und der Ansager (Lynn Berg) existieren außerhalb der fiktiven Konstruktion des Stücks. Die Reaktionen des Clowns stehen oft in Widerspruch zu den erwarteten Antworten auf die Handlung, was zu einer Distan-

and an operation. Factographic strategies included substituting the monolithic voice of the nineteenth-century novel for the polyphonic voice of the newspaper that was produced collectively and renewed on a daily basis. Similarly, the singular portrait gave way to the snapshot and the oblique view, disrupting the conventionally passive relationship between spectator and object. In this respect, as Devin Fore points out in a recent essay on the term's evolution, Soviet factography followed the word's etymology from the Latin *facere*, "to make" or "to do." A phrase from his essay stands as a useful summation of factography's seemingly paradoxical nature: far from objectively given, "the fact is quite literally *made*."[6]

Laser's recent performances not only mine strategies first developed in the context of factographic photography, poetry, and theater; they situate themselves within a lineage that recognized modern media – at first radio and the newspaper, and today television and the Internet – as crucial sites of political formation. Factography argued that sites of reception mold the emotional tenor of everyday life and shape the nature of political engagement, which is in large part why post-revolutionary Russia was the first to exploit their potential. Laser's commitment to the theatrical, rather than the documentary – or, rather, the documentary as *already* theatrical – contains a significant political dimension, which the comparison with the historical project of factography begins to illuminate.

In 2012, Laser began an ongoing series of performances titled Living Newspaper in a direct reference to the Soviet and American precedents. Laser's Living Newspaper has been performed in art galleries, in theaters, in newspaper kiosks, and on the street using willing volunteers as well as actors. These performances take various forms. In gallery settings, participants engage with the day's newspaper, reflecting on its contents and sometimes acting out specific photographs. On the street, actors interview participants regarding their opinions about the effect of the media on the election process or pose personal questions intended to provoke identification with the key players in news items. The actors work with a script that has been prepared beforehand, appropriate the demeanor and gestures of a news reporter, use props, and are filmed, mimicking an actual "man on the street" interview.

Public Relations / Öffentlichkeitsarbeit, one of Laser's most recent project in this vein, resulted in a two-channel video installation exhibited at the Westfälischer Kunstverein in Münster. Much of Laser's work involves actors, but in this case an actual vox pop reporter plays the female protagonist questioning passersby on the street. Opposite the projected video of the reporter an actor appears on a television monitor installed on a set that mimics a news anchor's desk. He is the antagonist, the "kleine" man sitting in a café reading the paper and watching the reporter on television. The reporter poses questions like: "Do you watch news on television; How important is journalism to you?" "Do you think the news can have an impact on politicians making decisions?" The answers, given largely by a local German public, are refreshingly candid, and range from skepticism ("We have too much journalism") to sincerity ("I think it's a very, very important job"; "As a reporter […] it is good if you do a good job").

As the film progresses, the reporter expresses familiar platitudes found in the media – "We bring the world to you" or "Tell us

zierung des Publikums führt. Die überzeichneten Slapstick-Einlagen des Clowns dienen den sechs an das emphatische Einfühlungsvermögen der Zuschauer appellierenden Hauptdarstellern gleichsam als Kontrastfolie.

Die Lebende Zeitung entstand im Kontext einer breiter angelegten künstlerischen Bewegung, für die sowjetische Künstler den Begriff Faktografie prägten. Diese Bezeichnung tauchte erstmals Mitte der 1920er Jahre auf. Sie bezieht sich auf einen Typus der sowjetischen Literatur und Fotografie sowie des sowjetischen Theaters, bei dem Kunst als Aufzeichnung von Fakten verstanden wird. Im Unterschied zu ähnlichen Bestrebungen in Europa und den Vereinigten Staaten, aus denen die bekannten dokumentarischen Formate hervorgingen, definiert die Faktografie ein Faktum nicht als objektive Erfassung der Wirklichkeit, sondern als ihre aktive Transformation in Übereinstimmung mit der im Entstehen begriffenen sozialistischen Gesellschaft. Sergei Tretjakow, einer der bekanntesten Faktografen und gemeinsam mit Aleksandr Rodtschenko Herausgeber der Avantgarde-Zeitschrift Nowy LEF, definierte den *Fakt* als Prozess, als Aktion und Operation. Eine der faktografischen Strategien war es, die monolithische Erzählstimme des Romans des 19. Jahrhunderts durch die polyphone Stimme einer Zeitung zu ersetzen, die jeden Tag von neuem im Kollektiv erstellt wird. Entsprechend traten an die Stelle des Einzelporträts der Schnappschuss und der schräge Blick, wodurch das herkömmliche, durch Passivität geprägte Verhältnis zwischen Betrachter und Gegenstand aufgebrochen wurde. In dieser Hinsicht folgte die sowjetische Faktografie, wie Devin Fore jüngst in einem Essay über die Entwicklung dieses Begriffs gezeigt hat, der Etymologie des Wortes, das sich vom lateinischen *facere* (machen, tun) ableitet. Ein Satz aus diesem Artikel bringt die vermeintlich paradoxe Natur der Faktografie sehr schön auf den Punkt: Der Fakt ist alles andere als objektiv gegeben, er „ist ganz im Wortsinne *gemacht*".[6]

Die jüngsten Performances von Laser greifen nicht nur Strategien auf, die im Kontext von Fotografie, Dichtung und Theater der Faktografen entwickelt wurden, sie ordnen sich in die Traditionslinie einer Theorie ein, die moderne Medien – der frühe Rundfunk und die Zeitung sowie heute das Fernsehen und das Internet – als entscheidende Orte politischer Prägungen anerkennen. Die Vertreter der Faktografie waren der Auffassung, die Orte der Rezeption formten die emotionale Grundstimmung des Alltagslebens und konturierten die Art des politischen Engagements, was ein wesentlicher Grund dafür sei, dass das nachrevolutionäre Russland als erstes in der Lage war, die Potenziale dieser Medien auszuschöpfen. Dass Laser auf das Theatrale, weniger auf das Dokumentarische setzt – genauer: auf das Dokumentarische als etwas bereits an sich Theatrales –, hat auch eine eminent politische Dimension, wie schon durch den Vergleich mit dem historischen Projekt der Faktografie deutlich wird.

Laser hat 2012 eine noch nicht abgeschlossene Serie von Performances begonnen, die in direkter Anlehnung an sowjetische und amerikanische Vorbilder den Titel Living Newspaper (Lebende Zeitung) trägt. Ihr Living Newspaper wurde in Galerien, Theatern, an Zeitungskiosken und auf der Straße mit Freiwilligen und professionellen Schauspielern durchgeführt. Die Performances können verschiedene Formen annehmen. In Galerieräumen setzen sich die Teilnehmer mit der Zeitung des jeweiligen Tages auseinander, reflektieren über die Inhalte und stellen manchmal bestimmte Fotos nach. Auf der Straße befragen

what matters to you" – and asks her interviewees what they think about the media's increasing emphasis on viewer-generated content. This new phenomenon, the fetishization of opinion as news, quickly emerges as a major theme of the film and of twenty-first-century journalism. Several interviewees in the film express their dissatisfaction with the replacement of investigative journalism with opinion polls in the guise of democratic accessibility. The antagonist of the film embodies this position. Sitting in a staged café, complete with a rack of newspapers, several wall clocks showing the times of major world cities, and a painting by Sanya Kantarovsky depicting a café scene reminiscent of Otto Dix's Bildnis der Journalistin Sylvia von Harden (1926), the actor performs the role of the disillusioned Everyman. His monologue consists of skeptical comments in response to the reporter and critiques of articles in the newspaper that he reads.

Laser's hybrid theatrical reportage derives from a second form of the Living Newspaper. This lineage emerged from the Moscow Institute of Journalism and was first performed in October 1923 by a group under the directorship of Boris Yuzhanin. Known as the Blue Blouse, the agitprop troupe created performances predicated on actual events and audience accessibility. The group deployed many of the same theatrical strategies as TEREVSAT. Costumes were made of a simple blue shirt, black pants or long skirt, and red headscarf (Laser has devised similar one-piece jumpsuit costumes, marked by a long zipper in the back). Actors had to be able to perform numerous tasks, including acrobatics, storytelling, dancing, singing, and puppetry, often in spaces not designed for theatrical performances, such as clubrooms, street corners, pubs, and factory halls.[7] The group became quite well known due to its international visibility. One of its most famous tours was in Germany in 1927, when the troupe gave nearly a hundred performances and caught the attention of Bertolt Brecht, whose archives include an annotated clipping of an article on the Blue Blouse published at that time in the German press.[8]

Though Laser's reinterpretation of the Living Newspaper limits the dramatic action to the interview and to reenactments of the news using audience members, her ongoing series nonetheless carries forward a tradition of versatile and nonprofessional theater that developed with the Blue Blouse in Russia and migrated to the United States under the auspices of the Federal Theatre Project. Established in 1935 by the playwright Elmer Rice, the Federal Theatre Project broke away from commercial theater and developed an audience for socially conscious, affordable plays, while also employing out-of-work actors, playwrights, and directors. Rice conceived of the Living Newspaper in collaboration with journalists and with the sponsorship of the Newspaper Guild.[9] One of the original members of the Federal Theatre Project described the Living Newspaper in terms that could be applied to Laser's own use of the genre to investigate the affective dimension of political rhetoric: the Living Newspaper was less the dramatization of a particular event than that of a problem that was itself "composed in greater or lesser extent of many news events, all bearing on the one subject and interlarded with typical but non-factual representations of the effect of these news events on the people to whom the problem is of great importance."[10] Whereas the Russian Living Newspaper appropriated the montage aesthetic of the newsreel and variety show, the American Living Newspaper limited itself to single subjects that investigated specific topical issues. For instance, one of the first such theme-based performances,

Schauspieler die Teilnehmer zu ihren Ansichten über die Auswirkungen der Medien auf die Wahlen, oder sie stellen ganz persönliche Fragen, die zur Identifikation mit den Hauptakteuren aus den Zeitungsberichten führen sollen. Die Schauspieler arbeiten mit einem vorbereiteten Skript, nehmen dabei das Auftreten und die Gestik von Reportern an, verwenden Requisiten und werden gefilmt, ahmen eine Befragung von Passanten, vom „kleinen Mann von der Straße" nach.

Am Ende eines von Lasers jüngsten Projekten dieser Art, Public Relations / Öffentlichkeitsarbeit, stand eine Zweikanal-Videoinstallation im Westfälischen Kunstverein in Münster. An vielen von Lasers Arbeiten sind Schauspieler beteiligt, in diesem Fall spielt jedoch eine echte, auf O-Töne von Bürgern spezialisierte Reporterin die weibliche Hauptrolle, indem sie Passanten auf der Straße befragt. Dem Video mit der Reporterin gegenüber erscheint auf einem Fernsehbildschirm ein Schauspieler, wobei der Bildschirm in einer Kulisse steht, die dem Pult eines Nachrichtensprechers nachempfunden ist. Er ist der Gegenspieler der Reporterin. Der „kleine Mann" sitzt zeitungslesend in einem Café und schaut sich die Sendung der Reporterin im Fernsehen an. Die Journalistin stellt Fragen wie: „Schauen Sie Nachrichten auch im Fernsehen an?", „Welche Bedeutung, welchen Wert hat Journalismus für Sie?", „Glauben Sie, dass Nachrichtensendungen darauf Einfluss haben, wie Politiker entscheiden?" Die Antworten, die großenteils von lokalen Passanten gegeben werden, sind erfrischend unverblümt, das Spektrum reicht von skeptisch („Wir haben vielleicht zu viel davon") bis ernsthaft („Ein sehr, sehr wichtiger Beruf", „Als Reporter […] ist es gut, wenn Sie einen guten Job machen").

Im Verlauf des Films sagt die Reporterin vertraute Plattitüden, wie man sie aus den Medien kennt – „We bring the world to you!" (Wir bringen ihnen die Welt nach Hause!) oder „Tell us what matters to you!" (Sagen Sie uns, was Ihnen wichtig ist!) –, und sie fragt die Interviewten, was sie davon halten, dass die Medien zunehmend auf zuschauergenerierte Inhalte setzen. Dieses neue Phänomen, die Überhöhung von Meinungen zu Nachrichten, kristallisiert sich bald schon als ein entscheidendes Thema des Films und des Journalismus im 21. Jahrhundert heraus. Einige der Befragten bringen ihre Unzufriedenheit zum Ausdruck, dass investigativer Journalismus unter dem Vorwand der Bürgerbeteiligung durch Meinungsumfragen ersetzt wird. Der Gegenspieler des Films verkörpert diese Position. Er sitzt in einer Kaffeehauskulisse mit Zeitungsständer und Weltzeituhren, an der Wand ein Gemälde von Sanya Kantarovsky mit einer Szene in einem Café, das an das Bildnis der Journalistin Sylvia von Harden (1926) von Otto Dix erinnert, und spielt die Rolle des desillusionierten Normalbürgers. Sein Monolog besteht aus skeptischen Kommentaren auf die Äußerungen der Reporterin und kritischen Anmerkungen zu den Artikeln, die er in einer Zeitung liest.

Das von Laser verwendete hybride Format einer theatral inszenierten Reportage geht auf eine weitere Form der Lebenden Zeitung zurück. Dieser Traditionsstrang nahm seinen Anfang am Moskauer Institut für Journalismus und wurde erstmals im Oktober 1923 von einer Gruppe unter der Leitung von Boris Juzhanin aufgeführt. Die unter dem Namen Blaue Bluse auftretende Agitprop-Truppe veranstaltete Aufführungen, die auf aktuellen Ereignissen und einer Beteiligung des Publikums

Ethiopia, took up the Italian invasion of Abyssinia (and was later censored for its negative portrayal of Mussolini). As with its Soviet precedents, this play, too, employed a Loudspeaker character, who relayed important dates and background information and relied on the use of direct quote – both of which Laser repurposes in I Feel Your Pain.

More recently, Laser has extended this preoccupation with the nature of political language and gesture into nonverbal performances that approximate dance. In the ten-minute performance The Digital Face (2012), two dancers in gray unitards, one male and one female, stand on pedestals facing one another across a room. They replicate the oratorical gestures from State of the Union speeches, President Barack Obama's in 2012 and President George H.W. Bush's in 1990, which Laser claims was the first televised State of the Union to include gesticulating hands. During the performance, no sound is heard except that of a metronomic camera shutter snapping closed at one-second intervals. The audience, meanwhile, observing between and around the two performers, must split its attention between the two opposite sides of the room. The regularity of the metronomic beat, the silence that accrues during its duration, and the nondescript dress of the two professional Merce Cunningham dancers denaturalize political speech. Intended to subliminally generate empathy on the part of their audience, these gestures become evident as a premeditated score that has been masterfully choreographed for a television audience.

The work's title references the vocabulary of the French nineteenth-century musician and teacher François Delsarte, who analyzed everyday patterns of speech and gesture for the podium and stage. In his schema, "digital" refers to the digits of the hand, whose various positions correspond to emotional states. Delsarte's theory of acting attempted to restore motivation to bodily gesture, which had become overly melodramatic in the contemporary theater of his day. Delsarte's ideas were later deployed both for silent film and modern dance, two areas of performance that embraced a conception of the body as fragmentary and mechanical (as seen in Chaplin's films). Isadora Duncan, for instance, who arrived in Moscow in 1921 to found a school of modern dance, was deeply influenced by the work of Delsarte.

The Blue Blouse relied on Delsarte's conception of the body as they developed a form of theatrical dance based on what they called "'industrial' movements".[11] These were dances in which performers mimicked the components of a machine as a strategy by which to purge characters of psychological interiority. This form of dance was developed by Nikolai Foregger, who emerged from the TEREVSAT studio in the early 1920s to form his own workshop, MastFor (MASTerskaya FOReggera), which quickly earned the approval of luminaries such as the poet Vladimir Mayakovsky with its theatrical parodies (including of Living Newspapers), cabaret-style dramas, and acrobatics. Foregger's most original contribution was what became known as "the machine dance," first performed in 1923. Dressed in black-and-white leotards, his actors would form a configuration of bodies that mimicked that of a fantastic machine complete with gears, pistons, and a transmission belt. Movement was thus systematized into strictly geometric patterns that no longer served to portray convincing emotional expression, as it had for Delsarte, but now sought to adapt the individual movements of the body to the universal functions of the machine.[12]

basierten. Dabei kamen vielfach die gleichen dramaturgischen Strategien zum Einsatz wie beim TEREVSAT. Die Kostüme bestanden aus einfachen blauen Hemden, schwarzen Hosen oder langen Röcken und roten Kopftüchern (Laser hat ähnliche Kostüme als durchgehende Overalls entworfen, mit einem Reißverschluss auf der Rückseite). Die Schauspieler mussten in der Lage sein, ganz unterschiedliche Aufgaben zu erfüllen, darunter akrobatische Einlagen, Geschichtenerzählen, Tanzen, Singen und Puppenspiel, und dies oft an Orten, die nicht für Theateraufführungen geschaffen waren, etwa in Klubs, an Straßenecken, in Kneipen und Fabrikhallen.[7] Die Truppe erlangte dank ihrer internationalen Sichtbarkeit einige Bekanntheit. Eine ihrer Aufsehen erregendsten Tourneen fand 1927 in Deutschland statt, wo die Truppe fast 100 Aufführungen hatte und wo Bertolt Brecht auf sie aufmerksam wurde; in seinem Archiv findet sich ein mit Anmerkungen versehener Ausschnitt eines in einer deutschen Zeitschrift erschienenen Artikels über die Blaue Bluse.[8]

In ihrer Neuinterpretation der Lebenden Zeitung beschränkt Laser die dramatische Handlung zwar auf das Interview und das Nachspielen der Nachrichten unter Einbeziehung von Zuschauern, und doch führt ihre noch nicht abgeschlossene Serie die Tradition eines vielseitigen Laientheaters fort, die mit der Blauen Bluse in Russland entstanden war und später unter der Ägide des Federal Theatre Project in die USA wanderte. Das 1935 von dem Theaterautor Elmer Rice gegründete Federal Theatre Project hatte sich vom kommerziellen Theater losgesagt und sich ein Publikum für sozial engagierte Stücke zu bezahlbaren Preisen herangezogen, wobei auch arbeitslose Schauspieler, Autoren und Regisseure beschäftigt wurden. Das Format Lebende Zeitung (Living Newspaper) entwickelte Rice in Kooperation mit Journalisten und mit Unterstützung der Journalistengewerkschaft Newspaper Guild.[9] Die Beschreibung der Lebenden Zeitung, die von einem der Gründungsmitglieder des Federal Theatre Project überliefert ist, ließe sich auch auf Lasers Verwendung dieses Formats zur Erkundung der emotionalen Dimension der politischen Rhetorik übertragen: Die Lebende Zeitung war weniger die theatrale Inszenierung eines bestimmten Ereignisses als vielmehr die eines Problems, das seinerseits „zu einem bestimmten Maße aus vielen Ereignissen in den Nachrichten bestand, die alle ein Thema betrafen, durchsetzt mit charakteristischen, aber fiktionalen Darstellungen der Auswirkungen, die diese Ereignisse auf die Menschen haben, für die das Problem von großer Bedeutung ist".[10] Während die russische Lebende Zeitung den Montagestil von Wochenschauen oder Varietéaufführungen übernommen hatte, beschränkte sich die amerikanische Living Newspaper auf Einzelthemen zu bestimmten typischen Problemlagen. So griff etwa die erste dieser themenorientierten Aufführungen, Ethiopia, den italienischen Einmarsch in Abessinien auf. (Sie wurde später wegen der negativen Darstellung Mussolinis zensiert.) Wie bei den sowjetischen Vorläufern gab es in diesem Stück die Figur eines Ansagers, der wichtige Daten und Hintergrundinformationen verkündete und dabei mit direkten Zitaten arbeitete – beides Elemente, die Laser in I Feel Your Pain wiederverwendet hat.

Später hat Laser diese Beschäftigung mit dem Charakter politischer Sprache und politischer Gestik auf nonverbale Performances ausgedehnt, die sich dem Tanz annähern. In der 10-minütigen Performance The Digital Face (2012) stehen sich ein Tänzer und eine Tänzerin in grauen Trikots auf Podesten an zwei Seiten eines Raums gegenüber. Sie reproduzieren die

The difference between these theatrical experiments of interwar Europe and Laser's adaptation goes beyond historical context. Whereas the revolutionary context of Tret'iakov and Meyerhold promulgated a certain faith in the effectiveness of such agitprop interventions, the audience of the current era in which Laser works exhibits little tolerance for such idealism. Laser has adapted to these conditions by mining the legacy of factography for its pedagogical potential. In watching her performances, the audience learns how to dissect the rhetoric of contemporary oration – how a certain argument gains legitimacy through a series of gestures and emotional tactics in order to generate public allegiance. The politician no longer relies on melodramatic rhetoric in order to generate sympathy; she or he now performs in a way that belies any performance at all. Gestures become subtle differences in chin height and wrist angle, as the politician strives to appear as natural as possible within an environment that is now subjected to the constant presence of a camera. By way of humor, irony, and montage, Laser's work equips her audience with a rhetorical literacy that enables one to analyze the bodily mechanics and patterns of speech attending messages that increasingly mimic those of the lowest denominator. If Soviet factography and the Living Newspaper are remembered as the first instances in which the media became a site of artistic production, Laser's recent performances not only keep that project alive; they retool its tactics for the digital age.

Endnotes

1 Robert Leach, V s e v o l o d M e y e r h o l d (Cambridge: Cambridge University Press, 1993), 30.
2   Konstantin Rudnitsky, R u s s i a n a n d S o v i e t T h e a t e r (London: Thames & Hudson, 2000), 41.
3 Robert Leach, R e v o l u t i o n a r y T h e a t e r (New York: Routledge, 1994), 82.
4 Leach, R e v o l u t i o n a r y T h e a t e r, 83.
5 Claude Amey et al., Le Théâtre d'agit-prop de 1917 à 1932, vol. 1, L' U R S S – R e c h e r c h e s (Lausanne: La Cité – L'Age d'Homme, 1977), 55.
6 Devin Fore, "Introduction," O c t o b e r 118 (Fall 2006), 5.
7 Leach, R e v o l u t i o n a r y T h e a t e r, 170–72.
8 The article is by Harry Wilder, "Die 'Blauen Blusen' und wir," D a s A r b e i t e r t h e a t e r (1928), ms. underlining and marginalia in Harvard University, Houghton Library, Bertolt Brecht Archive 1440/14, reel 86; cited in Katherine Bliss Eaton, T h e T h e a t e r o f M e y e r h o l d a n d B r e c h t (Westport, CT: Greenwood Press, 1985), 13.
9 Heinz Bernard, "A Theatre for Lefty: USA in the 1930s," T h e a t r e Q u a r t e r l y 1, no. 4 (October–December 1971), 55.
10 Arthur Arent, "The Techniques of the Living Newspaper," T h e a t r e A r t s (November 1938); repr. in T h e a t r e Q u a r t e r l y 1, no. 4 (October–December 1971), 57.
11 S i n y a y a B l u z a [The Blue Blouse], no. 23/24 (1925), 10–14; quoted in Richard Stourac and Kathleen McCreery, T h e a t r e a s a W e a p o n : W o r k e r s ' T h e a t r e i n t h e S o v i e t U n i o n , G e r m a n y a n d B r i t a i n , 1 9 1 7 – 1 9 3 4 (New York: Routledge & Kegan Paul, 1986), 57.
12 Leach, R e v o l u t i o n a r y T h e a t r e, 127.

Redegesten aus den Ansprachen zur Lage der Nation, die Präsident Barack Obama 2012 und Präsident George H.W. Bush 1990 gehalten hatten; laut Laser war Bushs State-of-the-Union-Rede die erste, bei der im Fernsehen auch die gestikulierenden Hände gezeigt wurden. Während der Performance ist kein Ton zu hören, außer dem metronomartig klackenden Verschluss einer Kamera, der im Sekundentakt ausgelöst wird. Derweil muss das Publikum, das sich die beiden Performer und ihr Umfeld anschaut, die Aufmerksamkeit zwischen den beiden gegenüberliegenden Seiten des Raums aufteilen. Die Regelmäßigkeit des Taktschlags, die sich während der Performance ausbreitet, das undefinierte Kostüm der beiden professionellen Merce-Cunningham-Tänzer – all das verfremdet die politische Rede. Die Gesten, die eigentlich dazu gedacht sind, beim Publikum unterschwellig Empathie hervorzurufen, werden als offensichtlich wohl vorbereitete Darbietung kenntlich gemacht, die kunstvoll für das Fernsehpublikum durchchoreografiert wurde.

Der Titel der Arbeit bezieht sich auf François Delsarte, einen französischen Musiker und Lehrer des 19. Jahrhunderts, der alltägliche Muster von Reden und Gesten auf Podium und Bühne untersuchte. Bei seinem Modell meint „digital" die Finger der Hand (nach lat. *digitus*: Finger), deren verschiedene Positionen bestimmten emotionalen Zuständen entsprechen. Delsartes Theorie des Schauspielens versuchte die Körpergesten, die im Theater seiner Zeit allzu melodramatisch geworden waren, wieder stärker psychologisch zu motivieren. Später kamen Delsartes Ideen sowohl im Stummfilm als auch im modernen Tanz zur Anwendung, zwei Bereiche der darstellenden Künste, in denen der Körper als etwas Fragmentarisches und Mechanisches verstanden wurde (wie man beispielsweise in Chaplins Filmen sieht). So war auch Isadora Duncan, die 1921 nach Moskau ging, um dort eine Schule für modernen Tanz zu gründen, stark von den Arbeiten Delsartes beeinflusst.

Die Blaue Bluse setzte auf Delsartes Konzeption des Körpers, als die Truppe eine Form des theatralen Tanzes entwickelte, der auf „,industriellen' Bewegungen"[11] basierte. Es handelte sich um Tänze, bei denen die Darsteller die Bestandteile einer Maschine nachahmten, eine Strategie, die Figuren von psychologischer Innerlichkeit befreien sollte. Diese Form des Tanzes war von Nikolai Foregger entwickelt worden, der in den frühen 1920er Jahren aus dem Studio des TEREVSAT hervorgegangen war, um schließlich seine eigene Theaterwerkstatt, MastFor (MASTerskaja FOReggera), zu gründen, die mit ihren Theaterparodien (auch der Lebenden Zeitung), mit kabarettartigen Dramen und akrobatischen Aufführungen bald schon Anerkennung von Berühmtheiten wie Wladimir Majakowski fand. Foreggers originellster Beitrag war wohl der 1923 erstmals aufgeführte M a s c h i n e n t a n z. Seine Darsteller trugen schwarz-weiße Gymnastikanzüge und bildeten mit ihren Körpern Formationen, die Teile einer fantastischen Maschinerie nachahmten, mit Getrieben, Kolben und einem Transmissionsriemen. Die Bewegungen wurden zu strikt geometrischen Mustern systematisiert, die nicht mehr dazu dienten, Emotionen überzeugend zum Ausdruck zu bringen, wie noch bei Delsarte, die vielmehr versuchten, die individuellen Bewegungen des Körpers den universellen Funktionen der Maschine anzugleichen.[12]

Der Unterschied zwischen diesen Theaterexperimenten im Europa der Zwischenkriegszeit und Lasers Adaption ist grundlegender als die bloße Differenz des historischen Umfelds.

Während der revolutionäre Kontext bei Tretjakow und Meyerhold dem Glauben an die Wirksamkeit solcher Agitprop-Aktionen zuträglich war, zeigt sich das Publikum der heutigen Zeit, in der Laser arbeitet, gegenüber einem derartigen Idealismus wenig aufgeschlossen. Laser hat sich diesen Bedingungen angepasst, indem sie das pädagogische Potenzial der faktografischen Tradition nutzt. Die Zuschauer ihrer Performances lernen, die Rhetorik moderner Redner auseinanderzunehmen – wie ein bestimmtes Argument durch eine Folge von Gesten und emotionalen Taktiken an Legitimität gewinnt, um das Publikum für die Sache einzunehmen. Der Politiker oder die Politikerin setzt nicht mehr auf eine melodramatische Rhetorik, um Sympathie zu erzeugen, er oder sie tritt in einer Weise auf, die darüber hinwegtäuscht, dass es sich überhaupt um einen Auftritt handelt. Die Gesten sind auf subtile Unterschiede reduziert, wie hoch das Kinn gehalten und in welchem Winkel das Handgelenk gebeugt wird, wobei die Politiker versuchen, so natürlich wie möglich zu wirken, und dies in einem Umfeld, das heute durch die permanente Gegenwart von Kameras geprägt ist. Vermittels Humor, Ironie und Montage verhelfen Lasers Arbeiten den Zuschauern zu einer rhetorischen Kompetenz, die es ihnen ermöglicht, die körperliche Mechanik und die sprachlichen Muster von Reden zu analysieren, deren Botschaften sich zunehmend auf einen kleinsten gemeinsamen Nenner reduzieren. Die sowjetische Faktografie und die Lebende Zeitung sind als die ersten Fälle in Erinnerung, in denen die Medien zu Orten der Kunstproduktion wurden. Lasers jüngste Performances halten dieses Projekt nicht nur lebendig, sie rüsten ihre Taktiken für das digitale Zeitalter nach.

Anmerkungen

1 Robert Leach, Vsevolod Meyerhold (Cambridge: Cambridge University Press, 1993), S. 30.
2 Konstantin Rudnitsky, Russian and Soviet Theater (London: Thames & Hudson, 2000), S. 41.
3 Robert Leach, Revolutionary Theater (New York: Routledge, 1994), S. 82.
4 Leach, Revolutionary Theater, S. 83.
5 Claude Amey et al., Le Théâtre d'agit-prop de 1917 à 1932, Bd. 1: L'URSS – Recherches (Lausanne: La Cité – L'Age d'Homme, 1977), S. 55.
6 Devin Fore, „Introduction", in: October 118 (Herbst 2006), S. 5.
7 Leach, Revolutionary Theater, S. 170–172.
8 Der Artikel stammt von Harry Wilder: „Die ‚Blauen Blusen' und wir", in: Das Arbeitertheater (1928), mit handschriftlichen Unterstreichungen und Randnotizen, Harvard University, Houghton Library, Bertolt Brecht Archive 1440/14, reel 86, zit. nach: Katherine Bliss Eaton, The Theater of Meyerhold and Brecht (Westport, CT: Greenwood Press, 1985), S. 13.
9 Heinz Bernard, „A Theatre for Lefty: USA in the 1930s", in: Theatre Quarterly 1, Nr. 4 (Oktober–Dezember 1971), S. 55.
10 Arthur Arent, „The Techniques of the Living Newspaper", in: Theatre Arts (November 1938), Wiederabdruck in: Theatre Quarterly 1, Nr. 4 (Oktober–Dezember 1971) S. 57.
11 Sinyaya Bluza [Die Blaue Bluse], 1925, Nr. 23/24, S. 10–14, zitiert nach: Richard Stourac und Kathleen McCreery, Theatre as a Weapon: Workers' Theatre in the Soviet Union, Germany and Britain, 1917–1934 (New York: Routledge & Kegan Paul, 1986), S. 57.
12 Leach, Revolutionary Theater, S. 127.

Tom Williams
Street Scenes

At the opening of Liz Magic Laser's 2009 video c h a s e, an idiosyncratic restaging of Bertolt Brecht's M a n E q u a l s M a n (Mann ist Mann; 1926), a woman stands in an ATM vestibule and addresses both the machines and the patrons using them:

> Herr Bertolt Brecht maintains that man equals man
> – A view that has been around since time began.
> But then Herr Brecht points out how far one can
> Manoeuvre and manipulate that man
> Tonight you are going to see a man reassembled like a car
> Leaving all his individual components just as they are.
> [...]
> Herr Bertolt Brecht hopes you'll feel the ground on which
> you stand
> Slither between your toes like shifting sand.
> So that the case of Galy Gay the porter makes you aware
> Life on this earth is a hazardous affair.[1]

These portentous lines, spoken by the play's canteen proprietress the Widow Begbick (Cat Yezbak), originally appeared as an interlude in the middle of the play, but in Laser's version they become a prologue that summarizes, proleptically, Brecht's parable of reification and dehumanization.

The scenario the Widow describes – a person reconfigured like a machine – defines the central theme of M a n E q u a l s M a n. Set in colonial India, the play follows the exploits of a British battalion as its members vandalize a Tibetan pagoda and conspire to conceal their misdeed. Realizing that a wounded comrade would inevitably arouse suspicion, they abandon him and endeavor to find a replacement in a local Irish porter named Galy Gay. Doing so means convincing the porter that he is not himself but one of them, and through the course of the play they cajole, intimidate, and manipulate him in a sequence of episodes that anticipates midcentury notions of "brainwashing" and mind control. They compel him to assume the soldier's identity by giving him the soldier's bankbook, because, according

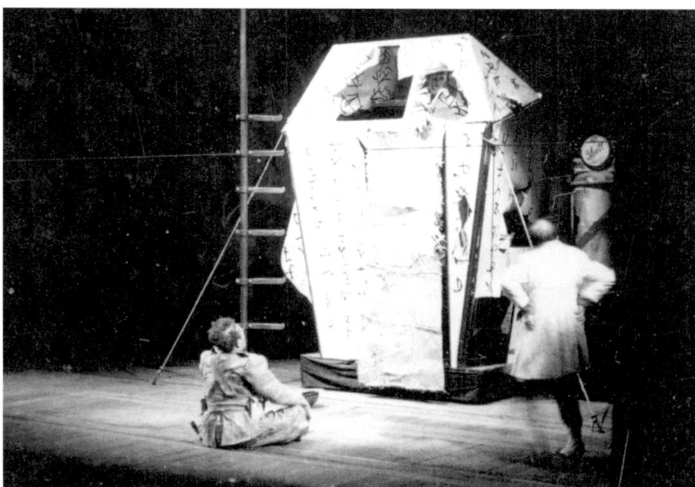

Bertolt Brecht's revival of M a n E q u a l s M a n, Staatstheater, Berlin, Germany, 1931. Featuring actor Peter Lorre / Bertolt Brechts Wiederaufnahme von M a n n i s t M a n n, Staatstheater, Berlin, Deutschland, 1931. Mit dem Schauspieler Peter Lorre

Tom Williams
Straßenszenen

Am Anfang von Liz Magic Lasers Video c h a s e (2009), einer eigenwilligen Neuinszenierung von Bertolt Brechts Stück M a n n i s t M a n n (1926), steht eine Frau bei den Geldautomaten einer Bank und spricht zu den Automaten und den Kunden, die sie nutzen:

> Herr Bertolt Brecht behauptet: Mann ist Mann.
> Und das ist etwas, was jeder behaupten kann.
> Aber Herr Bertolt Brecht beweist auch dann,
> Dass man mit einem Menschen beliebig viel machen kann.
> Hier wird heute abend ein Mensch wie ein Auto ummontiert
> Ohne dass er irgendetwas dabei verliert
> [...]
> Herr Bertolt Brecht hofft, Sie werden den Boden, auf dem
> Sie stehen
> Wie Schnee unter Ihren Füßen vergehen sehen
> Und werden schon merken bei dem Packer Galy Gay
> Dass das Leben auf Erden gefährlich sei.[1]

Diese bedeutungsschwangeren Worte, die bei Brecht von der Kantinenwirtin Witwe Begbick (Cat Yezbak) gesprochen werden, stammen aus einem „Zwischenspruch" in der Mitte des Stücks, doch in Lasers Version werden sie zum Prolog, der Brechts Parabel der Verdinglichung und Entmenschlichung vorwegnehmend zusammenfasst.

Das von der Witwe beschriebene Szenario – eine Person wird umgebaut wie eine Maschine – prägt das zentrale Thema von M a n n i s t M a n n. Das Stück spielt im Indien der Kolonialzeit und schildert die Geschehnisse in einem britischen Bataillon, dessen Mitglieder eine tibetische Pagode verwüsten und nachher einen Plan aushecken, wie sie ihre Untat vertuschen können. Als ihnen bewusst wird, dass ein bei der Aktion verwundeter Kamerad unweigerlich Verdacht erregen würde, lassen sie diesen zurück und versuchen, in dem irischstämmigen Packer Galy Gay einen Ersatzmann für ihn zu finden. Dazu müssen sie dem Packer einreden, dass er gar nicht er selbst ist, sondern einer von ihnen. Im Verlauf des Stücks erreichen sie ihr Ziel durch Überredung, Einschüchterung und Manipulation in einer Folge von Episoden, die vorwegnehmen, was man aus der Mitte des 20. Jahrhunderts als „Gehirnwäsche" und Bewusstseinskontrolle kennt. Sie nötigen ihn, die Identität des Soldaten anzunehmen, indem sie ihm dessen Sparbuch geben, denn nach der Logik der Zeit ist Identität eine Angelegenheit der ökonomischen und bürokratischen Berechnung, und so verwandeln sie ihn schließlich von einem einfachen Arbeiter in einen blutrünstigen Soldaten.

In Lasers Version war das Vorziehen des Zwischenspiels der Witwe zum Teil eine praktische Notwendigkeit. In ihrer Inszenierung setzt Laser Brechts Stück neu zusammen, wie dieser es mit seinem Protagonisten tut. Sie inszenierte nicht nur den Monolog der Witwe Begbick, sondern die gesamte Aufführung in mehreren Teilen vor Geldautomaten in verschiedenen New Yorker Bankfilialen. Laser filmte die einzelnen Darsteller, wie sie jeweils ihren Text den Maschinen und deren Nutzern darboten. Später montierte sie die Aufnahmen mehr oder weniger eng nach den Dialogen von Brechts Stück. Dem so entstandenen Video mit seinen notgedrungen harten Schnitten und Diskontinuitäten zu

to the logic of the day, identity is a matter of economic and bureaucratic calculus, and they ultimately transform him from a humble worker into a bloodthirsty soldier.

In Laser's version, the transposition of the Widow's interlude was partly a practical necessity. In staging this production Laser reassembles Brecht's play in the same way that the playwright reassembles his protagonist. She staged not only the Widow Begbick's speech, but the entire production in segments in ATM vestibules of banks throughout New York City. Laser filmed each actor delivering his or her lines to the machines and to their users, and she later assembled the footage according, more or less, to the dialogue of the original play. The resulting video, defined as it is by jarring jump cuts and discontinuity, is often nearly as challenging to follow as the performance must have been to the original audience of bank clients, and the Widow's rhyme makes the work more accessible by offering a prospectus of the action that follows.

Laser's turn to "the quizzical Stalinist," as Brecht has been called, will strike many as odd and anachronistic more than twenty years after the collapse of the Soviet Union.[2] Although Brecht's ideas had great currency during the 1970s and early 1980s, in recent years they have often been regarded as old-fashioned and tainted by authoritarianism. Revivals of his work have often aspired to, in Owen Hatherley's words, "take the Brechtian out of Brecht" – that is, to dispense with the ideology and preserve his purely artistic accomplishments.[3] Others, writing from the left, have followed Theodor Adorno's indictment of Brecht's "infantile simplification" of authoritarian politics (specifically in the allegory of Fascism A r t u r o U i). "[C]aricature," wrote Adorno, "loses its force and becomes silly by its own criterion."[4]

Laser's *détournement* of Brecht's parable initially seems to corroborate Adorno's critique. As a comment on contemporary automation and depersonalization as well as the vagaries of financial capitalism advanced by New York banks, the play's message seems broad and hyperbolic. It seems to caricature the operations and ambiance of global capitalism. As Laser has made clear, however, and as her sustained engagement with Brecht demonstrates, with c h a s e, she takes the playwright's critical project more seriously than do either his liberal proponents or his left-wing detractors. Her subsequent work, moreover, repeatedly returns to M a n E q u a l s M a n's themes of indoctrination and control, as she follows his ambitions to make theater an instrument of politics.

Many aspects of c h a s e demonstrate this sympathy for Brecht's enterprise. Indeed, even in the "non-places" of ATM vestibules, the staging – and certainly the opening sequence – recalls one of the playwright's own accounts of his so-called "epic theater." In a brief essay entitled "The Street Scene," written in the 1950s, Brecht described this theater in vernacular form. Epic theater, he argued, occurs on street corners all the time. It is evident in "an eyewitness demonstrating to a collection of people how a traffic accident took place."[5] Such situations dispense with traditional theater's commitment to illusion and catharsis. The performer never embodies the role like a method actor; there is no mimesis. "The bystanders may not have observed what happened," Brecht claimed, "or they may simply not agree with [the person reenacting the event], may 'see things a different way;' the point is that the demonstrator acts the

folgen, ist oft fast ebenso schwierig, wie es für die Bankkunden gewesen sein muss. Die vorangestellten Verse der Witwe machen das Werk verständlicher, weil sie einen Ausblick auf die folgende Handlung geben.

Vielen mag es sonderbar und anachronistisch vorkommen, dass Laser sich mehr als 20 Jahre nach dem Zusammenbruch der Sowjetunion ausgerechnet Bertolt Brecht zuwendet, den man einen „spöttischen Stalinisten" („quizzical Stalinist") genannt hat.[2] In den 1970er und den frühen 1980er Jahren hatten Brechts Ideen Konjunktur, doch in letzter Zeit galten sie meist als altmodisch und von autoritären Vorstellungen durchdrungen. Versuche, sein Werk wiederzubeleben, waren, wie Owen Hatherley es ausdrückt, oft bemüht, „Brecht das Brechtsche zu nehmen" – sich also der Ideologie zu entledigen und seine rein künstlerischen Errungenschaften zu bewahren.[3] Andere, die linke Positionen vertreten, haben sich Theodor Adornos Verdikt über Brechts „infantilistische Abkürzung" autoritärer Politik (vor allem in der Faschismus-Allegorie D e r a u f h a l t s a m e A u f s t i e g d e s A r t u r o U i) zu eigen gemacht. „[D]ie Karikatur", schrieb Adorno, werde „kraftlos, nach eigenen Maßstäben albern."[4]

Lasers *Détournement* von Brechts Parabel scheint zunächst Adornos Kritik zu bestätigen. Als Kommentar zur Automatisierung und Unpersönlichkeit unserer Zeit sowie zu den Kapricen des von den New Yorker Banken betriebenen Finanzkapitalismus wirkt die Botschaft des Stücks wie ein überzeichneter Rundumschlag. Man meint, es karikiere die Operationen und die Allgegenwart des globalen Kapitalismus. Laser hat aber deutlich gemacht, und ihre nachhaltige Beschäftigung mit Brecht bestätigt dies, dass sie mit c h a s e das kritische Anliegen des Dramatikers ernster nimmt als seine liberalen Befürworter oder seine linken Kritiker. So hat sie in späteren Arbeiten wiederholt die in M a n n i s t M a n n angesprochenen Themen Indoktrination und Kontrolle aufgegriffen, und sie folgt Brecht in dem Bestreben, das Theater zu einem Instrument der politischen Arbeit zu machen.

Viele Aspekte in c h a s e lassen eine gewisse Sympathie für Brechts Unterfangen erkennen. So erinnert die Inszenierung an den „Unorten" der Bankautomatenräume – und sicherlich die Eröffnungssequenz – an Brechts Ausführungen zu seiner Konzeption des „epischen Theaters". In einem kurzen Aufsatz D i e S t r a ß e n s z e n e aus den 1950er Jahren beschreibt Brecht diese Form eines alltäglichen Theaters. Episches Theater, meint Brecht, findet an jeder Straßenecke statt. Es zeigt sich in Situationen wie dieser: „Der Augenzeuge eines Verkehrsunfalls demonstriert einer Menschenansammlung, wie das Unglück passierte."[5] Solche Situationen kommen ohne das Bemühen des traditionellen Theaters um Illusion und Katharsis aus. Der Darsteller verkörpert die Rolle niemals wie ein professioneller Schauspieler, es findet keine Mimesis statt. „Die Umstehenden können den Vorgang nicht gesehen haben", fährt Brecht fort, „oder nur nicht seiner Meinung sein, ihn ,anders sehen' – die Hauptsache ist, daß der Demonstrierende das Verhalten des Fahrers oder des Überfahrenen oder beider in einer solchen Weise vormacht, daß die Umstehenden sich über den Unfall ein Urteil bilden können."[6] Dieser Modus des Schauspielens in der dritten Person ist einer von Brechts „Verfremdungseffekten", von denen er hoffte, dass sie das Publikum dazu bringen, sich kritisch mit den realen Bedingungen ihrer Existenz auseinanderzusetzen, und so politische Veränderungen einzuleiten.[7] Oder wie Walter Benjamin einen der Schlüsselbegriffe des epischen Theaters beschrieben

behavior of driver or victim or both in such a way that the bystanders are able to form an opinion about the accident."[6] This mode of acting in the third person is one of Brecht's "alienation effects" that, he hoped, would challenge the audience to engage critically with their real conditions of existence and provoke political change.[7] As Walter Benjamin described one of the key slogans of epic theater: "It can happen this way, but it can also happen quite a different way."[8] It compels its audience to consider alternatives to the present, both on stage and in the world.

There are undoubtedly other "street scenes," of course, and many of them have less radical histories. In Laser's piece, once the Widow Begbick concludes her soliloquy, an ATM user claps. When he announces: "You deserve applause for that," the whole situation suddenly seems less critically charged and begins to recall busking or street theater. At the same time, the Widow's testimonial, despite its verse form, and many of the sequences that follow, also evoke the "man on the street" interviews that became a staple of commercial television even as Brecht was developing his vernacular model for radical theater.

Both the "street scene" and the "man on the street" demonstrate the coincidence of theatricality and public address. Both point to a moment when dramaturgy becomes a central component of social and political participation, but one model is critical and the other is affirmative. One public is self-organized and spontaneous, while the other is manufactured. In the "man on the street" interview, the individual is called on as a figure of authenticity, and his testimony demonstrates a kind of political participation. As Laser has noted, the interview itself was an expression of the democratic transformations of the nineteenth century because it suggested equality between the politician and the reporter (something unthinkable in an era of monarchies). This kind of "street scene" further turned the tables by claiming the common person as a figure of political consequence.[9] Not only did this practice lend voices to people on the street, it made the reporter's microphone into a metonym for an egalitarian society. The "man on the street" interview becomes a central ritual of a democratic polity in an age of mass media. Its ascendency in the 1950s, a moment when a few commercial television channels attained a near-monopoly on the means of representation, points to a cynical concurrence of the concentrations of power and the dramaturgy of participation.

This contentious juxtaposition of manufactured consent with Brecht's political didacticism lies at the heart of P u b l i c R e l a t i o n s / Ö f f e n t l i c h k e i t s a r b e i t, and it pervades much of the work that Laser has made after c h a s e. For example, in 2012 CNN commissioned a video from her, and she used the opportunity to interrogate the mythologies of the "man on the street." For the resulting video, entitled P u s h P o l l, she organized a focus group and staged interviews with pedestrians on the streets of New York City. In a self-reflexive gesture, devised for the cable news context (successor to the media monopolies of the 1950s), she replicated the clichés of a nightly news broadcast. An anchorwoman (Liz Micek) poised before a bank of television monitors sets the stage before turning to focus group discussions and to reporters on the scene. Following conventions of news delivery, she directs us toward the "reality" of the streets and the micropublic of the roundtable discussion. In news broadcasts, this kind of deference to public opinion typically completes a circle – the news informs the public about what the public thinks of the news –

hat: „Es kann so kommen, aber es kann auch ganz anders kommen."[8] Es bringt das Publikum dazu, über Alternativen zum Vorhandenen nachzudenken, auf der Bühne wie in der Welt.

Es gibt zweifellos noch weitere „Straßenszenen", viele von ihnen mit weniger radikalen Geschichten. In Lasers Stück klatscht ein Kunde am Bankautomat, als die Witwe Begbick ihren Monolog beendet hat. Dann verkündet er: „Dafür haben Sie Applaus verdient." Die ganze Situation wirkt plötzlich weniger kritisch geladen, und man fühlt sich an Straßenmusiker oder ein Straßentheater erinnert. Zugleich lassen das Statement der Witwe, obwohl es in Versform vorgetragen wird, und viele der folgenden Szenen an Interviews mit dem „Mann von der Straße" denken, die gerade in einer Zeit zum festen Bestandteil im Repertoire des kommerziellen Fernsehens wurden, als Brecht sein Alltagsmodell des radikalen Theaters entwickelte.

Beide Formate, die „Straßenszene" und das Interview mit dem „Mann von der Straße", demonstrieren die Parallelen zwischen Theatralität und öffentlicher Ansprache. Beide verweisen auf den Moment, in dem die Dramaturgie zum wesentlichen Bestandteil gesellschaftlicher und politischer Teilhabe wird; nur ist das eine Modell kritisch, das andere affirmativ. Im einen Fall ist das Publikum selbstorganisiert und spontan, im anderen wird es zurechtgemacht. Beim Interview mit dem „Mann von der Straße", steht der Einzelne für Authentizität, seine Äußerung ist an sich schon Ausweis einer bestimmten Form der politischen Teilhabe. Das Interview selbst war, wie Laser anmerkt, im 19. Jahrhundert Ausdruck demokratischen Wandels, denn es vermittelte den Eindruck der Gleichheit zwischen Politiker und Reporter (was in der Zeit der Monarchien undenkbar gewesen wäre). Diese Art der „Straßenszene" schreibt die Entwicklung fort, indem sie gewöhnliche Menschen zu politisch bedeutsamen Personen erklärt.[9] Damit bekommt der Mensch auf der Straße nicht nur eine Stimme, das Mikrofon des Reporters wird zum Sinnbild für eine egalitäre Gesellschaft. Im Zeitalter der Massenmedien wird das Interview mit Menschen auf der Straße zum wichtigen Ritual der politischen Kultur demokratischer Gesellschaften. Der Umstand, dass das Format des Straßeninterviews in den 1950er Jahren aufkam, als einige wenige kommerzielle Fernsehsender ein fast vollständiges Monopol über die Mittel der medialen Repräsentation erlangten, ist Ausdruck einer zynischen Kopplung von Machtkonzentration auf der einen und einer Dramaturgie der Teilhabe auf der anderen Seite.

Dieses spannungsvolle Nebeneinander von künstlich erzeugter Zustimmung und Brechts politischer Didaktik macht auch den Kern der Arbeit P u b l i c R e l a t i o n s / Ö f f e n t l i c h k e i t s a r b e i t aus, und es zieht sich durch einen Großteil der nach c h a s e entstandenen Werke Lasers. So nutzte sie, als ihr der Sender CNN 2012 den Auftrag zu einer Videoarbeit erteilte, die Gelegenheit, die Mythologien des Straßeninterviews zu hinterfragen. Für dieses Video, P u s h P o l l, stellte sie eine Fokusgruppe zusammen und inszenierte Interviews mit Passanten in den Straßen New Yorks. In einem auf den Kontext der Nachrichtensendungen von Kabelsendern (den Nachfolgern der Medienmonopole der 1950er Jahre) abgestimmten Akt der Selbstreflexion, reproduzierte sie die klischeehaften Formen einer abendlichen Nachrichtensendung. Den Rahmen gibt eine Nachrichtensprecherin (Liz Micek), die selbstsicher vor einer Batterie von Fernsehmonitoren sitzt, dazwischen wird zur Diskussion in der Fokusgruppe und zu Reportern vor Ort geschaltet. Ganz im Stil konventioneller

but in Laser's conception this circle becomes entirely hermetic.
Here, the news addresses the conventions of the news. In a
sequence of increasingly absurd interactions, reporters on the
street poll passersby about the influence of polls and their role
in shaping the public responses they purport to reflect. The
reporters hold hands with their interview subjects and ask them
to turn the cameras off.

Earlier the same year, in Laser's video In Camera, this
absurd dynamic between an anchor, a reporter, and the "man on
the street" assumed the form of an existential nightmare.[10] In
this work, she returned to the history of modernist theater that
she previously explored with chase, but in this case she staged
Jean-Paul Sartre's unsettling depiction of hell in Huis clos
(No Exit) through the conventions of television news. Laser's
version substitutes the far-flung locales of the television studio,
the street, and a living room for the Second Empire décor of
Sartre's original set design for hell. Through her interpretation,
Sartre's famous declaration (or that of his character Joseph
Garcin) that "Hell is other people" became a metaphor for the
closed circuit between the anchor, the reporter on the scene,
and the "real" person giving testimony, and as in so much of her
work, this neurotic, emotionally fraught symposium became
a model of a dysfunctional public discourse.

Along these lines, I Feel Your Pain (2011) addressed
the politics of emotions through a complex combination of
agitprop performances (based on Soviet-era "Living Newspapers"
of the 1920s and '30s) and the choreographed spectacle of
contemporary political discourse. In this piece, Laser made the
public catharses of politicians such as Bill Clinton, Sarah Palin,
and John Boehner the content of a performance that she
orchestrated in a commercial movie theater. Actors performed
sequences derived from political interviews and speeches while
sitting within the rows of seats rather than in front of the
audience, and a clown mimed to a voice-over pieced together
from instructional manuals for pick-up artists and books on
public persuasion. Three cameramen videotaped the performances
while Laser edited and projected the video live onto the movie
screen. The audience members were confronted with their own
images and those of the actors in their midst.

Even a work such as Flight (2011), where Laser similarly
staged a performance in the midst of the crowd, shares some of
these concerns. In this piece, she adapted foot chases on stairs
from the history of cinema, beginning with the famous Odessa
Steps sequence from The Battleship Potemkin and moving
on to scenes from The Shining, Vertigo, and other more
recent films such as Final Destination IV. In both incarnations
of Flight (one at MoMA PS1 and the other in Times Square),
staircases served as both the theater and the stage. The performers darted and tumbled through the crowd, and their actions
made real the visceral, but fictive, experience of action and horror
movies as they are typically consumed in theaters and in homes.
"We psychologically rehearse for traumatic events by watching
movies; by enacting panic we anticipate its cause," Laser wrote
of this performance.[11] Whether or not such films are actually
propaedeutics for real-world terror, the performance makes manifest
the oft-noted coincidence of entertainment and disasters, and
particularly in the context of an increasingly militarized Times
Square, it implicates this entertainment in the contemporary
politics of fear.

Nachrichtensendungen präsentiert uns die Moderatorin die
„Wirklichkeit" auf den Straßen und in der Mikro-Öffentlichkeit
am Runden Tisch. Mit der Einbeziehung der öffentlichen
Meinung schließt sich in solchen Sendungen normalerweise ein
Zirkel – die Nachrichten informieren die Öffentlichkeit darüber,
was die Öffentlichkeit über die Nachrichten denkt –, doch bei
Laser wird dieser Zirkel zu einer vollständig hermetischen Aktion.
Die Nachrichten beschäftigen sich mit den Konventionen des
Nachrichtenmachens. In einer Folge von zunehmend abstrusen
Interaktionen befragen Reporter Passanten zum Einfluss von Meinungsumfragen und ihrer Rolle bei der Erzeugung von Reak-
tionen der Öffentlichkeit, die sie eigentlich nur wiedergeben
sollen. Die Reporter geben den Befragten während des Interviews
die Hand und bitten sie, die Kamera auszuschalten.

Das etwas früher im selben Jahr entstandene Video In
Camera, ein absurdes Wechselspiel zwischen einem Nachrichtensprecher, einer Reporterin und Passanten auf der Straße, entwickelt sich zu einem existenziellen Albtraum.[10] In dieser Arbeit
wendet sich Laser wieder der Geschichte des modernen Theaters
zu, die sie bereits mit chase erkundet hatte. Dieses Mal inszeniert
sie Jean-Paul Sartres beunruhigende Darstellung der Hölle in
Huis clos (Geschlossene Gesellschaft) nach den Konventionen
der Fernsehnachrichten. In Lasers Version treten die weit-
läufigen Spielorte eines Fernsehstudios, der Straße und eines
Wohnzimmers an die Stelle des Salons im Stil des Second
Empire, den Sartre als Höllen-Kulisse vorgesehen hatte. Sartres
berühmte Aussage „Die Hölle, das sind die anderen" (im Stück
geäußert von Joseph Garcin) wird in Lasers Interpretation zur
Metapher für die zirkuläre Beziehung zwischen dem Moderator,
der Reporterin auf der Straße und der „wirklichen", ihre
Statements abgebenden Person. Und wie bei so vielen anderen
ihrer Arbeiten wird diese neurotische, emotional aufgeladene
Zusammenkunft zum Modell eines dysfunktionalen öffentlichen
Diskurses.

Diesem Strang folgt auch die Videoarbeit I Feel Your Pain
(2011), bei der in einer komplexen Kombination von Agitprop-
Performances (nach dem Muster der sowjetischen „Lebenden
Zeitung" der 1920er und 30er Jahre) die Politik der Emotionalität und das durchchoreografierte Schauspiel der aktuellen
politischen Debatten thematisiert werden. Laser machte in
diesem Stück die öffentliche Läuterung von Politikern wie Bill
Clinton, Sarah Palin oder John Boehner zum Gegenstand einer
Performance, die in einem kommerziellen Kino stattfand. Die
Schauspieler spielen Sequenzen aus Interviews und Reden nach,
sitzen dabei aber nicht vor den Zuschauern, sondern selbst in
den Sitzreihen des Zuschauerraums, während ein Clown zu einer
Stimme aus dem Off gestikuliert, die Passagen aus Ratgebern
für angehende Verführer und Büchern über überzeugendes
öffentliches Auftreten vorträgt. Drei Kameraleute dokumen-
tierten die Performances auf Video, Laser selbst schnitt die
Aufnahmen und projizierte sie live auf die Leinwand des Kinos.
Die Zuschauer sahen also sich selbst *und* die Darsteller, die im
Publikum agierten.

Selbst bei einer Arbeit wie Flight (2011), bei der Laser auf
ähnliche Weise eine Performance in der Menschenmenge
inszenierte, spielten solche Anliegen eine Rolle. Hier setzte die
Künstlerin Verfolgungsszenen auf Treppen aus der Filmge-
schichte um, angefangen mit der berühmten Szene auf der Treppe
in Odessa aus Panzerkreuzer Potemkin bis hin zu Szenen

In Flight, as in so much of Laser's work, Brecht's strategies of defamiliarization address a popular culture and mass media that have become instruments for manufacturing consent. Her whole enterprise often appears to embrace a distinctive brand of political and social paranoia that is endemic to contemporary societies of control. When the news seems like propaganda, when public discourse becomes private sentiment, and when entertainment looks like terror, the media begins to appear more like a tool of manipulation than a means of disseminating information, and in this context, coded meanings and "subliminal messages" always haunt the pretense of rational debate.

This brand of the "hermeneutics of suspicion" is particularly evident in performances such as The Digital Face (2012) and Stand Behind Me (2013), which also address the themes of political manipulation in I Feel Your Pain and Public Relations / Öffentlichkeitsarbeit. The former two works take on the theater of politics by focusing, almost exclusively, on the oratorical gestures of politicians. For The Digital Face, Laser cataloged the gestures of State of the Union addresses by George H.W. Bush and Barack Obama and choreographed them in an elaborate pantomime. In the completed work (staged at MoMA PS1, among other venues), two dancers (Alan Good and Cori Kresge) faced each other while standing on individual pedestals. Like mimes, they each performed a silent ballet of hand gestures derived from an address by one of the two presidents. By eliminating the words of public figures, Laser calls attention to the latent messages of their gestures rather than the manifest claims of their speeches, and she suggests a shared commitment among politicians across the ideological spectrum to particular styles of presentation and persuasion.

Stand Behind Me, at the Lisson Gallery in London, was a complex elaboration upon The Digital Face. In this piece, a single performer (the dancer Ariel Freedman) stood with her back to the audience as she performed a sequence of gestures borrowed from a number of recent political speeches by public figures such as Barack Obama, Benjamin Netanyahu, and Angela Merkel. As in I Feel Your Pain, Laser filmed the performance, in this case from the front, and projected the footage on the wall opposite the performer, so that as she proceeded through the litany of movements, she faced her own image and that of the audience behind her. In a scenario reminiscent of Dan Graham's iconic Performer/Audience/Mirror (1975), members of the audience confronted both themselves and the performer as they watched her from behind.[12] In Graham's performance, the audience faced a mirror, rather than a projection, and he stood before them and described what he was seeing. While his piece addressed the complex phenomenological dynamic between the objectivity of the mirror and the subjectivity of the performer, Laser's performance addresses the constitution of political belonging. Through the projection, a gallery audience is interpellated as the public for the performer's gestures and for the words of the politicians that scroll down her teleprompter. This specific group becomes something more than itself – more, that is, than a disorganized, aggregate mass of individuals – through its proximity to the politician. The piece positions this audience as a public (or even as *the* public) and implicates its members in the political community figured by the address. Such images are, like the "man on the street," central to the iconography of a democratic society; by placing the politician in the midst of the people, the gallery

aus The Shining, Vertigo und anderen jüngeren Filmen wie Final Destination 4. In beiden Realisierungen von Flight (die eine im MoMA PS1, die andere auf dem Times Square) dienten die Treppen zugleich als Zuschauerraum und als Bühne. Die Darsteller sausten und stolperten durch die Menge, ihre Aktionen verliehen der aufwühlenden aber fiktiven Erfahrung von Action- und Horrorfilmen, die sonst im Kino oder zu Hause konsumiert werden, eine gewisse Wirklichkeit. „Wenn wir Filme schauen, proben wir psychologisch für traumatische Ereignisse; indem wir Panik nachspielen, nehmen wir ihre Ursache vorweg", schreibt Laser über diese Performance.[11] Ob solche Filme nun tatsächlich ein Propädeutikum für lebensweltlichen Horror sind oder nicht, die Performance macht jedenfalls die häufig festgestellte Koinzidenz von Unterhaltung und Katastrophe offenkundig, und gerade im Kontext eines zunehmend militarisierten Times Square bringt es Unterhaltung mit der aktuellen Politik der Angst in Verbindung.

In Flight sind – wie in vielen anderen ihrer Arbeiten – Brechts Strategien der Verfremdung auf die Populärkultur und die Massenmedien gerichtet, die bewusst instrumentalisiert werden, um Zustimmung zu erzeugen. Ihr gesamtes Unterfangen scheint sich um eine ganz bestimmte Art der politischen und gesellschaftlichen Paranoia zu drehen, die in den heutigen, umfassend überwachten Gesellschaften weit verbreitet ist. Wenn die Nachrichten wie Propaganda wirken, wenn der öffentliche Diskurs Züge privater Empfindungen annimmt, wenn schließlich Unterhaltung wie Terror anmutet, beginnen die Medien wie ein Werkzeug zur Manipulation der Massen zu wirken, nicht mehr wie ein Mittel zur Verbreitung von Informationen, und in diesem Zusammenhang wird die vermeintlich rationale Debatte unaufhörlich von kodierten Bedeutungen und „unterschwelligen Botschaften" heimgesucht.

Diese Form einer „Hermeneutik des Misstrauens" kommt besonders offensichtlich bei Performances wie The Digital Face (2012) oder Stand Behind Me (2013) zum Tragen, die ebenfalls die in I Feel Your Pain und Public Relations / Öffentlichkeitsarbeit angesprochenen Themen der politischen Manipulation angehen. Die beiden erstgenannten Arbeiten beschäftigen sich mit dem Theaterhaften in der Politik, in dem sie sich fast ausschließlich auf die Redegesten von Politikern konzentrieren. Für The Digital Face hat Laser die Gesten der Reden zur Lage der Nation von George H.W. Bush und Barack Obama katalogisiert und sie choreografisch zu einer aufwendigen Pantomime verarbeitet. Im fertigen Werk (das unter anderem im MoMA PS 1 aufgeführt wurde) standen sich zwei Tänzer (Alan Good und Cori Kresge) auf zwei getrennten Podesten gegenüber. Wie Pantomimen vollführten sie ein stummes Ballett von Handgesten, die aus den Ansprachen jeweils eines Präsidenten abgeleitet waren. Indem Laser den gesprochenen Text der Persönlichkeiten des öffentlichen Lebens weglässt, lenkt sie die Aufmerksamkeit auf die latenten Botschaften ihrer Gesten und weg von dem, was in den Reden offen proklamiert wird. Und sie erweckt den Eindruck, dass Politiker aus unterschiedlichen Lagern des ideologischen Spektrums alle einem bestimmten Stil des Vortrags und der Überzeugung anhängen.

Die Performance Stand Behind Me in der Londoner Lisson Gallery war eine komplexe Ausarbeitung von The Digital Face. In diesem Stück stand eine einzelne Darstellerin (die Tänzerin Ariel Freedman) mit dem Rücken zum Publikum

audience becomes the demos of democracy and this image signifies their assent. In Laser's treatment, these operations become the critical content of the work.

The figure of the public, as it becomes visible in S t a n d B e h i n d M e, is a notion that underlies Laser's themes of political manipulation and her strategy of defamiliarization, and it is at the very center of P u b l i c R e l a t i o n s / Ö f f e n t l i c h k e i t s a r b e i t. In this piece, as in so much of her work, she attempts to challenge the manufactured publicity behind the concept of the "man on the street" and to raise the possibility of a critical public sphere. Here, this possibility hinges on the dynamic interchange between three distinct locales of democratic participation: the news bureau, the street, and the café. Of these archetypal sites, the latter is novel in Laser's work, and its inclusion marks an attempt to introduce a third term into the dynamic of pieces like P u s h P o l l. In historical accounts of the public sphere, especially that of Jürgen Habermas's T h e S t r u c t u r a l T r a n s f o r m a t i o n o f t h e P u b l i c S p h e r e, the café was one of the crucial spaces of public discourse and debate. As a public sphere, it was that space that stood between the private spheres of the home and work and the institutions of formal politics, and it was through the contentious debates that often unfolded in these spaces that an informed public first emerged to pursue its political aspirations. In Laser's treatment, the café and its occupants mediate between the newsroom and the streets.[13] They represent that critically minded citizenry that stands apart from the logorrhea of the sidewalks. Laser's script presents a conversation between a journalist on the scene and the "kleine Mann" (little man) in the café (Florian Kleine). The "kleine Mann" is a stand-in for the "man on the street." Even as the reporter (Elisabeth Weydt) interacts with pedestrians in Münster, her scripted lines are often directed toward her viewer, the "kleine Mann." Through these exchanges, he becomes that idealized figure (or caricature) of the broader public and the public will.

The dialogue that develops between them is fraught and contentious. The reporter often seems bemused and insipidly literal while he is haughty and pedantic. "[S]he prefers to cozy up with the politicians and managers and we're left here to fend for ourselves," he proclaims. "You could be rough on them if you wanted to," he says to her before turning to others in the café and declaring, "But the fact is that she's not, so now we've gotta be rough on her." His comments throughout their exchange are hectoring and frequently amount to harassment.

At key moments, he responds to her jejune questions and newsroom slogans with innuendo and suggestion. Laser's point of departure for I F e e l Y o u r P a i n was the talk-show host Glenn Beck's bedroom demeanor as he interviewed Sarah Palin, but in this case, such flirtations take on a more adversarial tone. When Weydt surveys the crowds about their opinions on contemporary journalism, the "kleine Mann" replies, sneeringly, "If all journalists look like you, I think journalism's in great shape."

Such innuendo, of course, makes a mockery of all pretenses of disinterested inquiry. For all their misogynist disdain, his comments reiterate a conventional critique of the contemporary media's commodification and trivialization of public life. At the same time, they also replicate an exclusionary logic at work throughout much of the history of the public sphere. If the liberal model of public discourse assumes a free exchange of ideas, participation has frequently been the privilege of a very small

und vollführte dabei eine Folge von Gesten, die aktuellen politischen Reden von Persönlichkeiten wie Barack Obama, Benjamin Netanjahu oder Angela Merkel entlehnt waren. Wie bei I F e e l Y o u r P a i n filmte Laser die Performance, in diesem Fall aus frontaler Position, und projizierte die Aufnahmen auf die der Darstellerin gegenüberliegenden Wand, sodass diese, während sie die Litanei der Bewegungen absolvierte, die Bilder von sich selbst und vom Publikum hinter ihr vor Augen hatte. In einem Szenario, das an Dan Grahams legendäre Performance P e r f o r m e r / A u d i e n c e / M i r r o r (1975) erinnert, standen die Zuschauer sich selbst und der Darstellerin gegenüber, die sie zugleich von hinten sahen.[12] In Grahams Performance befand sich das Publikum vor einem Spiegel, nicht vor einer Projektion. Der Künstler stand vor den Zuschauern und beschrieb, was er sah. Während sein Stück die komplexe phänomenologische Dynamik zwischen der Objektivität des Spiegels und der Subjektivität des Performers thematisiert, ist es bei Lasers Performance die Struktur politischer Bindung. Durch die Projektion werden die Besucher der Galerie unweigerlich zum Publikum für die Gesten der Darstellerin und die Worte der Politiker, die über den Teleprompter laufen. Diese spezifische Gruppe wird durch ihre Nähe zum Politiker zu etwas, das mehr ist als sie selbst – also mehr als eine unorganisierte Ansammlung von Individuen. Die Arbeit versetzt das Publikum in die Rolle einer Öffentlichkeit (oder gar *der* Öffentlichkeit) und bindet seine Mitglieder ein in die politische Gemeinschaft, die durch die Ansprache evoziert wird. Solche Bilder sind, wie der „Mann von der Straße", zentrale Komponenten der Ikonografie einer demokratischen Gesellschaft. Wenn hier der Politiker mitten unter die Leute gesetzt wird, verwandelt sich das Publikum der Galerie zum Demos der Demokratie, und dieses Bild steht für ihre Zustimmung. Durch Lasers Intervention werden diese Operationen zum entscheidenden Inhalt der Arbeit.

Die Figur des Publikums, wie sie in S t a n d B e h i n d M e anschaulich wird, ist eine Vorstellung, die der Thematik der politischen Manipulation bei Laser und ihrer Verfremdungsstrategie zugrunde liegt, und sie macht den Kern von P u b l i c R e l a t i o n s / Ö f f e n t l i c h k e i t s a r b e i t aus. Wie in vielen ihrer Arbeiten versucht sie hier, die bewusst herbeigeführte und konstruierte Publicity zu hinterfragen, auf der das Konzept des „kleinen Manns von der Straße" basiert, und dabei die Möglichkeit einer kritischen Öffentlichkeit aufrecht zu erhalten. Diese Möglichkeit hängt hier an dem dynamischen Austausch zwischen drei unterschiedlichen Orten der demokratischem Teilhabe: der Nachrichtenredaktion, der Straße und dem Café. Der letztgenannte dieser archetypischen Orte ist neu in Lasers Werk, und seine Einbeziehung ist Ausdruck des Bestrebens, in der Dynamik von Stücken wie P u s h P o l l ein drittes Element hinzuzufügen. In Darstellungen zur Geschichte der Öffentlichkeit, besonders in S t r u k t u r w a n d e l d e r Ö f f e n t l i c h k e i t von Jürgen Habermas, wird das Kaffeehaus als einer der entscheidenden Orte des öffentlichen Diskurses und der Debatte beschrieben. Als ein öffentlicher Ort stand es zwischen der privaten Sphäre von Heim und Arbeitsstätte auf der einen und der Sphäre der förmlichen Politik auf der anderen Seite. Und erst durch die heftigen Debatten, die sich an solchen Orten oft entspannen, entstand eine informierte Öffentlichkeit, die den Anspruch hatte, politische Bestrebungen zu verfolgen. Bei Laser vermitteln das Café und seine Gäste zwischen dem Nachrichtenstudio und der

minority. Not only has it been denied to those outside bourgeois society, it has frequently been denied to women within it. Indeed, scholars have often pointed to the democratization of the bourgeois public sphere as a factor in its historical decline, as politicians responded less and less to reasoned debate and kowtowed increasingly to "the pressure of the street."[14] While many have pointed to the ways in which counter-public spheres have emerged to challenge this enduring elitism, Laser is preoccupied with the hegemonic institutions of the news media as sites of ideological contestation. The tension between the reporter's banality and the man's supercilious contempt exacerbates the deficiencies in the discursive models represented by both the newsroom and the café.

For Public Relations / Öffentlichkeitsarbeit, Laser has placed her audience in the anchor chairs of a mock-newsroom: they sit between a projection of the reporter on the opposite wall and a flat-screen monitor depicting the "little man" behind them. This maneuver places the viewer at the intersection between the reporter and the critical public on the scene. The crucial opposition in this piece is between two competing models of the public sphere, each emblematic of radically different eras: the café scene and the mass media. The viewers in the newsroom are confronted with the café as a nostalgic scene of participation and debate, but one that stands, however problematically, as a model for public discourse in a democratic age. In this scenario, the two models intermingle and interrogate each other, and each suggests the limits of the other. The café is discursive and participatory while the newsroom is autocratic, but face-to-face café discussions hardly seem viable as a democratic model in an era of broadcast and online media. While neither of these situations offers a model for genuine public discourse today, Laser's work points to the limits of each and begins to assess the current conditions of the public sphere.

As in Brecht's "street scene," the members of the audience are compelled to form their own opinions. For him, this scenario represented an alternative to the complacency and passivity of the typical theater audience and a means of changing consciousness and provoking political engagement, but Laser adopts this technique in confronting the theater and the increasing theatricality of politics and public life. It is here that Brecht's vision of the critical audience coincides with the aspirations for a critical public sphere. The conditions of the eighteenth-century public had long been eroded by the operations of capitalism, and it was only through a radical didacticism that such a critical perspective might be possible. Laser's work conjectures a place for artistic practice (and certainly for her own work) in realizing those aspirations. In an era marked by cynicism in politics and public life and by increasingly savage forms of capitalist enterprise, perhaps it is through aesthetic engagement, once again, that the critical public sphere embodied for many in eighteenth-century cafés and envisioned by Brecht in his "street scene" could ultimately emerge. At the very least, Laser raises this possibility and proposes an alternative to pessimism and paranoia alike.

Notes
1 Bertolt Brecht, Man Equals Man and The Elephant Calf, ed. John Willett and Ralph Manheim, trans. Gerhard Nellhaus (New York: Arcadia Publishing, 2000; originally published 1979), 38.

Straße.[13] Sie stehen für kritisch eingestellte Staatsbürger, die sich bewusst aus dem Geplauder auf dem Bürgersteig herausnehmen. Lasers Drehbuch präsentiert die Unterhaltung zwischen einer Journalistin im Außeneinsatz und dem „kleinen Mann" im Café (Florian Kleine), der an die Stelle des „Manns von der Straße" tritt. Auch wenn die Reporterin (Elisabeth Weydt) mit Passanten in Münster interagiert, scheint sie ihren vorformulierten Text an ihren Zuschauer zu richten, an den „kleinen Mann". Durch diesen Wortwechsel wird er zur idealtypischen Figur (oder Karikatur) für das breite Publikum und die öffentliche Meinung.

Der Dialog zwischen den beiden ist angespannt und kontrovers. Die Journalistin wirkt oft etwas irritiert und bis zur Fadheit platt, er überheblich und pedantisch. „Sieht fast so aus, als würde sie mit den Politikern und den Wirtschaftsbossen unter einer Decke stecken, und wir müssen uns alleine durchschlagen", meint er, und: „Sie könnten die hart rannehmen, wenn Sie wollten." Dann wendet er sich den anderen Gästen im Café zu und erklärt: „Sie macht es aber nicht. Und deswegen müssen wir jetzt eben mal sie hart rannehmen." Seine Kommentare sind durchweg herrisch und oft geradezu übergriffig.

An entscheidenden Stellen reagiert er auf ihre drögen Fragen und Reportersprüche mit anzüglichen Bemerkungen und Anmachen. Bei I Feel Your Pain beginnt Laser mit den mit Schlafzimmerblick vorgetragenen Vertraulichkeiten von Talkshow-Moderator Glenn Beck in seinem Interview mit Sarah Palin, doch hier ist das Flirten im Ton deutlich aggressiver. Als Weydt die Leute befragt, was sie vom heutigen Journalismus halten, antwortet der „kleine Mann" schnippisch: „Wenn alle Journalisten so aussehen wie Sie, dann macht der Journalismus doch eine ziemlich gute Figur, finde ich."

Solche Anzüglichkeiten ziehen natürlich den Anspruch, unvoreingenommen zu recherchieren, ins Lächerliche. Bei all ihrer frauenfeindlichen Verächtlichkeit greifen diese Bemerkungen doch auch die verbreitete Kritik auf, die Medien kommerzialisierten und trivialisierten das öffentliche Leben. Zugleich reproduzieren sie die ausgrenzenden Strukturen, die in der Geschichte der Öffentlichkeit lange Zeit wirksam waren. Auch wenn die liberale Vorstellung von Öffentlichkeit von einem freien Gedankenaustausch ausgeht, war die Teilhabe an der öffentlichen Auseinandersetzung doch oft das Privileg einer sehr kleinen Minderheit. Sie wurde nicht nur all denen verweigert, die außerhalb der bürgerlichen Gesellschaft standen, sondern häufig auch den Frauen, die Teil dieser Gesellschaft waren. Tatsächlich hat die Forschung die Demokratisierung der bürgerlichen Öffentlichkeit schon mehrfach als einen Faktor ihres Niedergangs benannt, da Politiker immer weniger auf eine vernünftig geführte Debatte reagierten und sich stattdessen vermehrt dem „Druck der Straße" beugten.[14] Während viele darauf abheben, wie Bereiche einer Gegenöffentlichkeit entstanden, um den sich hartnäckig haltenden elitären Strukturen etwas entgegenzusetzen, geht es Laser um die beherrschenden Institutionen der Nachrichtenmedien als Orte der ideologischen Auseinandersetzung. Die Spannung zwischen der Banalität der Reporterin und der anmaßenden Verächtlichkeit des Mannes lässt die Unzulänglichkeiten der Diskursmodelle, für die das Nachrichtenstudio und das Café stehen, umso deutlicher in Erscheinung treten.

Für Public Relations / Öffentlichkeitsarbeit versetzte Laser die Ausstellungsbesucher in den Sitz des Moderators im Nachrichtenstudio: Die Zuschauer saßen zwischen einer

2   Retort, "An Exchange on Afflicted Powers: Capital and Spectacle in a New Age of War," October 115 (Winter 2006), 4.
3   Owen Hatherley, Militant Modernism (Washington, DC: Zero Books, 2008), 98.
4   Theodor W. Adorno, "Extorted Reconciliation: On Georg Lukásc' Realism in Our Time", Notes to Literature, vol. 2, ed. Rolf Tiedemann, trans. Shierry Weber Nicholsen (New York: Columbia University Press, 1991), 222.
5   Bertolt Brecht, "The Street Scene," Brecht on Theater: The Development of an Aesthetic, ed. and trans. John Willett (New York: Hill and Wang, 1964), 121.
6   Ibid.
7   For a discussion of "third-person acting," see Fredric Jameson, Brecht and Method (New York: Verso, 1998), 51–58.
8   Walter Benjamin, "What Is Epic Theater?", Understanding Brecht, trans. Anna Bostock (New York: Verso, 1998), 8.
9   Liz Magic Laser, "The Interview," Art in America 100, no. 3 (March 2012), 62–63.
10   The title alludes to a 1964 production of the play for BBC television starring Harold Pinter.
11   Liz Magic Laser, "500 Words," Artforum.com, May 2, 2011, accessed April 19, 2014, http://www.artforum.com/words/id=28170.
12   For Graham's description of this piece, see his "Performance/Audience/Mirror," Rock My Religion: Writings and Art Projects, 1965–1990, ed. Brian Wallis (Cambridge, MA: MIT Press, 1993), 114–15.
13   Jürgen Habermas, The Structural Transformation of the Public Sphere: An Inquiry into a Category of Bourgeois Society, trans. Thomas Burger with Frederick Lawrence (Cambridge, MA: MIT Press, 1991).
14   Ibid., 132.

Projektion mit der Reporterin an der gegenüberliegenden Wand und einem Flachbildschirm hinter ihnen, auf dem der „kleine Mann" zu sehen war. Damit befand sich der Betrachter an der Schnittstelle von Reporterin und kritischer Öffentlichkeit. Die entscheidende Gegenüberstellung geschieht in diesem Stück zwischen zwei konkurrierenden Modellen der Öffentlichkeit, die jeweils sinnbildlich für radikal unterschiedliche Epochen stehen: die Kaffeehausszene und die Massenmedien. Die Zuschauer im Nachrichtenstudio werden mit dem Café als nostalgischem Szenario von Teilhabe und Debatte konfrontiert, das gleichwohl für ein – wenn auch problematisches – Modell des öffentlichen Diskurses in einem demokratischen Zeitalter steht. In dieser Konstellation vermischen sich die beiden Modelle, sie hinterfragen sich gegenseitig, und das eine macht die Begrenztheit des anderen deutlich. Das Café ist diskursiv und partizipatorisch, das Nachrichtenstudio autokratisch. Und doch erscheint im Zeitalter des Fernsehens und der Onlinemedien die persönliche Diskussion im Café kaum als ein praktikables Modell für den demokratischen Austausch. Keine der gezeigten Situationen taugt heute als Modell für einen echten öffentlichen Diskurs, und so weist Laser auf beider Grenzen hin und gibt damit eine Einschätzung über die aktuellen Bedingungen von Öffentlichkeit.

Wie in Brechts „Straßenszenen" sehen sich die Zuschauer auch hier gezwungen, sich eine eigene Meinung zu bilden. Für Brecht bot dieses Szenario eine Alternative zur Selbstzufriedenheit und Passivität des typischen Theaterpublikums und ein Mittel, das sich einsetzen lässt, um einen Bewusstseinswandel herbeizuführen und politisches Engagement zu provozieren. Laser aber übernimmt diese Technik, indem sie das Theater mit der zunehmenden Theatralik von Politik und öffentlichem Leben konfrontiert. In diesem Punkt fällt Brechts Vorstellung eines kritischen Publikums mit dem Streben nach einer kritischen Öffentlichkeit zusammen. Die Bedingungen der Öffentlichkeit im 18. Jahrhundert wurden durch die Auswirkungen des Kapitalismus längst aufgerieben. Erst durch einen radikal didaktischen Ansatz könnte eine solche kritische Sichtweise wieder möglich werden.

Lasers Werk lässt erahnen, welche Stellung die künstlerische Praxis (und jedenfalls ihr eigenes Schaffen) bei der Verwirklichung dieser Bestrebungen einnehmen könnte. In einer Zeit, in der Politik und öffentliches Leben von Zynismus geprägt sind und in der der Kapitalismus immer ungezügeltere Formen annimmt, könnte eine kritische Öffentlichkeit, für deren Verkörperung man gemeinhin das Kaffeehaus des 18. Jahrhunderts hält und auf die Brecht in seiner „Straßenszene" abzielt, am Ende vielleicht gerade durch künstlerisches Engagement von neuem entstehen. Ganz am Ende deutet Laser denn auch diese Möglichkeit an und zeigt damit eine Alternative auf zu Pessimismus und Paranoia.

Anmerkungen

1   Bertolt Brecht, Man Equals Man and The Elephant Calf, hrsg. von John Willett und Ralph Manheim, Übersetzung von Gerhard Nellhaus (New York: Arcadia Publishing, 2000; zuerst 1979), S. 38.
2   Retort, „An Exchange on Afflicted Powers: Capital and Spectacle in a New Age of War", in: October 115 (Winter 2006), S. 4.
3   Owen Hatherley, Militant Modernism (Washington, DC: Zero Books, 2008), S. 98.

4   Theodor W. Adorno, „Erpreßte Versöhnung. Zu Georg Lukács: ‚Wider den mißverstandenen Realismus'", in: Noten zur Literatur, Bd. 2 (Frankfurt: Suhrkamp, 1961), S.160.

5   Bertolt Brecht, „The Street Scene", in: Brecht on Theater: The Development of an Aesthetic, hrsg. und übersetzt von John Willett (New York: Hill and Wang, 1964), S. 121. Deutscher Originaltext zitiert nach Theater und Drama: theoretische Konzepte von Corneille bis Dürrenmatt, hrsg. von Horst Turk (Tübingen: Narr, 1992), S. 161.

6   Ebenda.

7   Zu einer Diskussion über das „Spielen in der dritten Person" siehe Fredric Jameson, Brecht and Method (New York: Verso, 1998), S. 51–58.

8   Walter Benjamin, „What Is Epic Theater?", in: Understanding Brecht, Übersetzung von Anna Bostock (New York: Verso, 1998), S. 8. Deutscher Originaltext zitiert nach Walter Benjamin, „Was ist episches Theater?", in: Versuche über Brecht, hrsg. von Rolf Tiedemann (Frankfurt a.M.: Suhrkamp, 3. Auflage, 1971), S. 15.

9   Liz Magic Laser, „The Interview", in: Art in America, Bd. 100, Nr. 3 (März 2012), S. 62–63.

10   Der Titel spielt auf eine Produktion des Stücks mit Harold Pinter an, die 1964 für das Fernsehen der BBC entstand.

11   Liz Magic Laser, „500 Words", erschienen auf: Artforum.com, 2. Mai 2011, Zugriff am 19. April 2014, http://www.artforum.com/words/id=28170.

12   Eine Beschreibung Grahams zu seiner Arbeit findet sich in seinem Beitrag „Performance/Audience/Mirror", in: Rock My Religion: Writings and Art Projects, 1965–1990, hrsg. von Brian Wallis (Cambridge, MA: MIT Press, 1993), S. 114–15.

13   Jürgen Habermas, The Structural Transformation of the Public Sphere: An Inquiry into a Category of Bourgeois Society, Übersetzung von Thomas Burger und Frederick Lawrence (Cambridge, MA: MIT Press, 1991).

14   Ebenda, S. 132.

Afterword / Nachwort

Public Relations / Öffentlichkeitsarbeit, the title of the exhibition and video installation, as well as this book, aptly describes Liz Magic Laser's practice, which repurposes strategies used to shape public opinion.

Many of Laser's performances and videos achieve their effect by using visual and linguistic mechanisms from television news in order to reveal the efficacy of those mechanisms in spite of the public's supposedly critical consumption of mass media. Laser's work references a host of literary forerunners ranging from Bertolt Brecht, Jean-Paul Sartre, and Edmond Rostand to interviews and speeches by contemporary politicians. Laser not only borrows gestures and phrases from such sources, but also appropriates their dramaturgic techniques.

Her recent work examines how speech coaches and public relations strategists teach the phraseology and gestures that have proved most successful in the art of persuasion according to nuanced market research reports. The scarcely noticeable smile and measured nod of the news presenter facilitates our acceptance of the most ghastly news evening after evening. The reporter's or politician's persuasive body language subverts our better judgment, subliminally affirming that everything is going to be all right.

Studied body language and careful costuming have long augmented the rhetoric of our politicians and news presenters; it often seems that their function is to incite empathy or to distract and reassure the public. Laser focuses on these manipulative techniques in politics and media, which, due to their ubiquity, appear deceptively inconsequential. How is it possible under such conditions to form one's own independent opinion, or indeed, to influence so-called "public opinion"?

Laser has identified the traditional acting techniques at play in the representation of current events; this led to her engagement with the avant-garde theater movements of 1920s Germany and Russia. There, too, the fusion of theater and information was present – albeit motivated by a different agenda. The disseminators of the Soviet "Living Newspaper" were devoted to an educational mandate as information was mostly inaccessible to the masses, who were largely illiterate.

In Brecht's era, the emphasis was on challenging illusionistic theater in an attempt to create a politically mature audience: he believed that actors should no longer try to elicit an empathetic response from the audience, but, rather, should convey ideas in a way that encouraged the audience to adopt a critical point of view. Henceforth, a model of provoking independent thinking in the audience would supplant illusionism in the theater.

Producing informed critical viewers ought to be the intention of today's political and news agencies involved in the dissemination of information, but instead politicians, managers, and journalists are trained in the very performance techniques of illusionistic theater that Brecht once fought against. The German term "Öffentlichkeitsarbeit," which literally translates as "public work" (or less prosaically, "public relations"), suggests that the formation of a particular public goes hand in hand with active effort and engagement. Furthermore, it is not merely a public that is being actively produced, but also an opinion.

Laser's two-channel video installation Public Relations / Öffentlichkeitsarbeit, which was developed on site in Münster, presents a distilled dialogue between the news media, embodied by a reporter on the scene (Elisabeth Weydt), and

Public Relations / Öffentlichkeitsarbeit, der Titel von Ausstellung, Videoinstallation und diesem Buch, ist eine adäquate Chiffre für die künstlerische Praxis von Liz Magic Laser, spricht er doch die professionalisierten Strategien der Meinungsbildung an, die sich Laser zu eigen macht.

Viele von Lasers Performances und Videos erzielen ihre Wirkung durch bestimmte visuelle, sprachliche und dramaturgische Codes, die die Künstlerin nachahmt, um uns deren Wirkmacht und unseren eigenen, zuweilen naiv-blauäugigen Medienkonsum vorzuführen. Ihre Referenzen spannen einen Bogen von literarischen Vorlagen etwa von Bertolt Brecht, Jean-Paul Sartre oder Edmond Rostand bis hin zu Politikerinterviews und -reden unserer Zeit.

In ihrer jüngsten Arbeit untersucht sie, wie Sprechtrainer und PR-Strategen bestimmte Phrasen und Gesten lehren, die sich als besonders erfolgreich in der Kunst der Überzeugung erwiesen haben. Das kaum merkliche, bedächtige und mild lächelnde Kopfsenken der Nachrichtensprecherin lässt uns allabendlich auch die schrecklichsten Neuigkeiten meist unreflektiert akzeptieren, suggeriert uns ihre Körpersprache doch unterbewusst, dass alles gut wird.

Einstudierte Körpersprache, sorgfältig ausgewählte Kostümierung, Blicke und Gesten haben das rhetorische Repertoire unserer PolitikerInnen und NachrichtensprecherInnen längst erweitert. Mal sollen sie aufrühren, motivieren oder Empathie hervorrufen, ein anderes Mal eher ablenken und beruhigen. In Lasers Arbeiten geht es um genau diese manipulativen Kräfte in Politik und Medien, die bei rapide steigender Verbreitung und damit einhergehender Habituation für uns immer unsichtbarer werden. Wie ist unter diesen Umständen noch die Herausbildung einer eigenen oder der „öffentlichen Meinung" möglich?

Laser identifiziert in diesen Choreografien traditionelle Schauspiel- und Performancetechniken, was sie zu einer intensiven Auseinandersetzung mit dem Avantgarde-Theater der 1920er Jahre in Deutschland und Russland führte. Auch hier gab es schon eine Verquickung von Theater und Information – allerdings aus einem völlig anderen Impuls heraus, fühlten sich die Akteure des epischen Theaters und der sowjetischen „Lebenden Zeitung" doch einem Bildungsauftrag für die illiteraten Massen verpflichtet.

Zu Zeiten Brechts probte man vor allem auch die Abkehr vom illusionistischen Theater und versuchte, einen mündigen Zuschauer heranzuziehen: SchauspielerInnen sollten nicht länger in Rollen schlüpfen und auch keine Empathie beim Zuschauer hervorrufen – Inhalte sollten so transportiert werden, dass das Publikum einen eigenen, kritischen Standpunkt beziehen kann. Differenzierte Rezeption und Meinungsbildung sollten verklärte Illusion und das Abdriften in Traumwelten ablösen.

Dies sollte eigentlich auch die Intention unserer heutigen Informationsvermittlung sein, stattdessen werden Politiker, Manager und Journalisten in Performancetechniken des illusionistischen Theaters trainiert, das Brecht einst anfocht. Der Begriff „Öffentlichkeitsarbeit" besagt schon, dass Arbeit und aktives Handeln erforderlich sind, um eine bestimmte Öffentlichkeit zu bilden, d.h. weiter, dass Öffentlichkeit und damit Meinungen bewusst hergestellt werden.

Lasers Zweikanalvideo Public Relations / Öffentlichkeitsarbeit, das vor Ort in Münster entstanden ist, lässt uns teilhaben an einem Dialog zwischen den Medien und der

the public, represented by an actor in the role of the proverbial "little man" (Florian Kleine), who is deployed as the spontaneous mouthpiece of public opinion. In one video channel the everyman character derides a newscaster he is watching on TV from his seat in a café, which is actually a stage set installed in the Kunstverein itself. Laser's second video channel shows the reporter, Weydt, who is an actual freelance journalist at a local television station, interviewing people on the streets of Münster about their views on journalism. The script transitions between English and German; Laser wrote it in close collaboration with the writer Sofia Pontén and the protagonists of the video, as well as with the team at the Kunstverein. The dialogue is meant to be understood by speakers of both languages and simultaneously to reveal culturally specific differences between news media in the United States and Germany.

The two video channels face each other and are incorporated into a television studio installation that borrows elements from a bar, including props such as liquor bottles and a disco ball altered to look like a globe. Laser's hybrid newsroom-café theater set was used to film the video, and the television studio-bar served to display the video, while also placing the viewer in the news anchor's seat.

Laser's theater-set installations and script for Public Relations / Öffentlichkeitsarbeit grew out of her consideration of the places historically used for public discourse: the café and the bar. In the exhibition at the Westfälischer Kunstverein, the stage set of the café was open for use by gallery visitors. International newspapers and various magazines updated on a daily basis were available for them to read; coffee and water were provided free of charge. In a sense I saw this as the Kunstverein's contribution to encouraging a critical discourse among our audience.

Five other projects are presented alongside Public Relations / Öffentlichkeitsarbeit in this, Laser's first book: I Feel Your Pain, The Digital Face, In Camera, Stand Behind Me, and Absolute Event. Laser made all five works, which dissect the relationship between the media, the politician, and the public, between 2011 and 2013.

This book also endeavors to address the conditions and challenges of forming a differentiated public opinion by avoiding prescriptive interpretations of Laser's work. Moreover, it is an apparatus, which – very much in keeping with Brecht's journals and notion of epic theater – renounces the illusion of *one* truth and demands instead individual participation in the production of truths.

Kristina Scepanski

Öffentlichkeit, verkörpert durch eine Außenreporterin (Elisabeth Weydt) und den sprichwörtlichen „kleinen Mann von der Straße" (Florian Kleine), der so oft für spontane und vermeintlich objektive Meinungsbilder der allgemeinen Bevölkerung herangezogen wird, sich hier aber in einem Café, einem Bühnenbild im Kunstverein, aufhält und die Berichterstattung der Reporterin spöttisch kommentiert. Das zweite Video zeigt die Reporterin (die Darstellerin ist tatsächlich freie Mitarbeiterin eines lokalen Fernsehsenders), die an belebten Orten Münsters eine Passantenumfrage zur Bedeutung von Journalismus durchführt. Das Skript wechselt ständig zwischen englisch und deutsch sowie den beiden kulturspezifischen Konventionen und entstand in enger Zusammenarbeit zwischen Liz Magic Laser, der Autorin Sofia Pontén, den Protagonisten des Videos sowie dem Team des Kunstvereins.

Im Westfälischen Kunstverein standen sich die beiden Videos von Reporterin und „kleinem Mann" gegenüber und waren in eine zweite Kulisse, die eines Fernsehstudios, integriert, das durch verschiedene Requisiten zugleich an eine Bar erinnerte und eine zum Globus umgestaltete Discokugel enthielt. Die Zuschauer konnten vom Pult der NachrichtensprecherInnen aus die Videos anschauen.

Beide Bühnenbilder sowie das Skript für Public Relations / Öffentlichkeitsarbeit nehmen Bezug auf Orte, an denen der öffentliche Diskurs traditionell mehr oder weniger ungezwungen realisiert wird: das Cafe und die Bar. Im Kunstverein war das Bühnenbild des Cafés für die Besucher als solches benutzbar. Hier konnten sie internationale Tageszeitungen und verschiedene Magazine lesen, die täglich aktualisiert wurden; es gab kostenlos Kaffee und Wasser. Dies war unser Beitrag zur Formierung eines mündigen Publikums, das imstande ist, eine differenzierte, öffentliche Meinung auszubilden.

Neben Public Relations / Öffentlichkeitsarbeit werden in dieser Publikation, der ersten der Künstlerin, noch fünf weitere Projekte Lasers vorgestellt, die alle zwischen 2011 und 2013 entstanden sind und sich thematisch ebenfalls mit der Einflussnahme von Medien und Politik auf die Öffentlichkeit auseinandersetzen. Dazu zählen I Feel Your Pain, The Digital Face, In Camera, Stand Behind Me und Absolute Event.

Den Bedingungen und Anforderungen einer differenzierten Meinungsbildung versucht auch dieses Buch zu entsprechen, indem es eben nicht diese Lesart und jene Interpretation vorschreibt. Es versteht sich als Apparat, der zwar alle Elemente und Informationen enthält, jedoch – im Sinne des epischen Theaters oder auch des Brecht'schen Arbeitsjournals – auf den Illusionismus der *einen* Wahrheit verzichtet und stattdessen eine eigenständige Teilnahme an der Produktion einfordert.

Kristina Scepanski

Biography / Biografie

Liz Magic Laser (b. 1981, New York) is a video and performance artist based in New York. She earned a BA from Wesleyan University (2003) and an MFA from Columbia University (2008). She attended the Skowhegan School of Painting & Sculpture (2008) and the Whitney Museum Independent Study Program (2009). Most recently, her work was the subject of solo exhibitions at Paula Cooper Gallery, New York (2013) the Westfälischer Kunstverein, Münster, Germany (2013); DiverseWorks, Houston, Texas (2013); Various Small Fires, Los Angeles (2012); and Malmö Konsthall, Malmö, Sweden (2012). Her work has also been exhibited at Lisson Gallery, London (2013); the Moscow Museum of Modern Art (2012); the Performa 11 Biennial, New York (2011); The Pace Gallery, New York (2011); the Biennial of Graphic Arts, Ljubljana, Slovenia (2011); and MoMA PS 1, New York (2010). Laser is the recipient of grants from Alfried Krupp von Bohlen und Halbach Foundation (2013), the Southern Exposure Off-Site Graue Award (2013), New York Foundation for the Arts Fellowship (2012), and the Franklin Furnace Fund for Performance Art (2010). She was the 2013 Armory Show Commissioned Artist and has been in residency at Recess, New York (2014), the Marie Walsh Sharpe Foundation Space Program, New York (2012), Forever & Today, Inc.'s Studio On The Street artist-in-residence program, New York (2012), Smack Mellon, Brooklyn (2011), and the Lower Manhattan Cultural Council, New York (2009). / **Liz Magic Laser** (geb. 1981 in New York) arbeitet als Video- und Performance-Künstlerin in New York. BA an der Wesleyan University (2003) und MFA an der Columbia University (2008); Studium an der Skowhegan School of Painting & Sculpture (2008) und Teilnahme am Whitney Museum Independent Study Program (2009). Ihre Arbeiten waren jüngst zu sehen in Einzelausstellungen in der Paula Cooper Gallery, New York, (2003) und im Westfälischen Kunstverein, Münster (2013), bei DiverseWorks, Houston, Texas, (2013), Various Small Fires, Los Angeles, (2012) und in der Malmö Konsthall in Schweden (2012). Ihr Werk war zudem vertreten in der Lisson Gallery, London, (2013), im Moskauer Museum der Modernen Künste (2012), auf der Performa 11 Biennal, New York, (2011), in der Pace Gallery, New York, (2011), auf der Biennale der Grafischen Künste im slowenischen Ljubljana (2011) und im MoMA PS 1, New York, (2010). Laser ist mit dem Katalogpreis der Alfried Krupp von Bohlen und Halbach-Stiftung ausgezeichnet worden (2013), war Stipendiatin des Southern Exposure Off-Site Graue Award (2013), der New York Foundation for the Arts Fellowship (2012) und des Franklin Furnace Fund for Performance Art (2010). 2013 war sie „Commissioned Artist" der Armory Show; Aufenthaltsstipendien bei Recess, New York, (2014), dem Pace Program der Marie Walsh Sharpe Foundation, New York, (2012), dem Studio On The Street Artist-in-Residence Program von Forever & Today, Inc., New York, (2012), bei Smack Mellon, Brooklyn, (2011) und dem Lower Manhattan Cultural Council, New York, (2009).

Contributors / Autoren

Sofia Pontén is a writer and novelist based in Brooklyn, originally from Sweden. She has closely collaborated with Liz Magic Laser on scripts for several projects, starting with In Camera in 2012. Pontén also runs the astrology blog S c o r p i o R i s i n g for Sweden's largest teen magazine V e c k o R e v y n. / **Sofia Pontén**, stammt aus Schweden und lebt als Publizistin und Romanautorin in Brooklyn. Sie hat 2012 für In Camera und in verschiedenen nachfolgenden Projekten bei der Skripterstellung eng mit Liz Magic Laser zusammengearbeitet. Sofia Pontén betreibt für das größte schwedische Teenager-Magazin V e c k o R e v y n das Astrologie-Blog S c o r p i o R i s i n g.

Jordan Troeller is a graduate of the University of California, Berkeley, and the Whitney Independent Study Program. She is currently a Ph.D. candidate in the Department of the History of Art and Architecture at Harvard University, where she is supported by a Jacob K. Javits Fellowship in the Humanities. Her dissertation examines site-specific art in Weimar Germany by artists associated with the Bauhaus. She has contributed essays on photography and contemporary art to A r t J o u r n a l, P r e f i x P h o t o, and exhibitions in the US and in Germany. / **Jordan Troeller** hat an der University of California, Berkeley, und am Whitney Independent Study Program studiert. Zurzeit ist sie im Rahmen eines Jacob K. Javits Fellowship in the Humanities Doktorandin am Department of the History of Art and Architecture an der Harvard University. Ihre Dissertation beschäftigt sich mit ortsspezifischer Kunst von Bauhauskünstlern in der Weimarer Republik. Sie hat Aufsätze zur Fotografie und zeitgenössischen Kunst in A r t J o u r n a l und P r e f i x P h o t o sowie in amerikanischen und deutschen Ausstellungskatalogen publiziert.

Tom Williams is assistant professor of art history at Watkins College of Art, Design & Film in Nashville, Tennessee. He is a graduate of Stony Brook University and the Whitney Museum Independent Study Program, and he has taught at the School of Visual Arts, the Museum of Modern Art, and Vanderbilt University. His writings have appeared in A r t i n A m e r i c a, G r e y R o o m, and other publications. He has also been active recently in co-organizing a series of exhibitions featuring artistic collaborations with prisoners on Death Row in Tennessee. / **Tom Williams** lehrt als Assistant Professor of Art History am Watkins College of Art, Design & Film in Nashville, Tennessee. Er hat an der Stony Brook University und am Whitney Museum Independent Study Program studiert und an der School of Visual Arts, am Museum of Modern Art und an der Vanderbilt University unterrichtet. Beiträge von Tom Williams erschienen unter anderem in A r t i n A m e r i c a und G r e y R o o m. Er war jüngst an der Organisation einer Ausstellungsreihe beteiligt, die der künstlerischen Zusammenarbeit mit Insassen der Todeszellen in Tennessee gewidmet war.

Kristina Scepanski is an art historian and curator, graduated from the University of Cologne. She has worked for the European Kunsthalle in Cologne, a discursive platform without a physical location, and the Kunstverein für die Rheinlande und Westfalen in Düsseldorf. In 2011/2012, she was Helena Rubinstein Fellow in the Curatorial Program at the Whitney Independent Study Program. Since 2013 she is the artistic director of Westfälischer Kunstverein in Münster where she is aiming to create forums to engage an audience with discussions of today's political and social realities through the cultural and artistic repercussions these structures create. / **Kristina Scepanski** ist Kunsthistorikerin und Kuratorin. Nach ihrem Studium an der Universität zu Köln war sie unter anderem für die European Kunsthalle, einer diskursiven Plattform ohne festen Ort, sowie für den Kunstverein für die Rheinlande und Westfalen in Düsseldorf tätig. 2011/12 absolvierte sie in New York das Whitney Independent Study Program als Helena Rubinstein Curatorial Fellow und übernahm 2013 die künstlerische Leitung des Westfälischen Kunstvereins in Münster. Diesen versucht sie vor allem als Forum für freie Diskussionen über gegenwärtige politische und soziale Realitäten bereit zu stellen, die aus deren Widerhall in künstlerischer und kultureller Produktion angestoßen werden können.

This book has been published on the occasion of Liz Magic Laser's solo exhibition Public Relations / Öffentlichkeitsarbeit, at the Westfälischer Kunstverein in Münster, from July 13 to September 22, 2013. / Dieser Katalog erscheint anlässlich Liz Magic Lasers Einzelausstellung Public Relations / Öffentlichkeitsarbeit im Westfälischen Kunstverein, Münster, 13. Juli bis 22. September 2013.

Credits / Bildnachweise

122: From / Aus: Richard Stourac and Kathleen McCreery, Theatre as a Weapon: Workers' Theatre in the Soviet Union, Germany and Britain, 1917–1934 (New York: Routledge & Kegan Paul, 1986), 78. 129: Copyright Akademie der Künste, Berlin, Bertolt Brecht Archive, theater documentation 2057/166, Photo: unknown / Bertolt-Brecht-Archiv, Theaterdokumentation 2057/166, Foto: unbekannt

Acknowledgements / Dank

The artist and the team at Westfälischer Kunstverein would like to thank / Die Künstlerin und das Team des Westfälischen Kunstvereins danken herzlich Becca Albee, Nils von Berg, Winfried Bettmer, Anna Bitter, Jan Enste, Rita Feldmann, Michael Frühling, RoseLee Goldberg, Till Julian Huss, Sanya Kantarovsky, Christian Kiehl, Florian Kleine, Ken Laser, Holger Lüsch, Wendy Osserman, Gunar Peters, Jan-Dirk Poggemann, Sofia Pontén, Gregor Quack, Wolfgang Schälte, Ludger Schnieder, Raphael Smarzoch, Dan Solbach, Michael Spengler, Sven Stratmann, Renate Terstiege, Elisabeth Weydt, and / und Meinhard Zanger.

Special thanks to / Besonderer Dank gilt: Performa, Malmö Konsthall, Lisson Gallery and / und Paula Cooper Gallery for supporting the works featured in this book / für die Unterstützung der hier vorgestellten Arbeiten.

We are very grateful to the Alfried Krupp von Bohlen und Halbach-Stiftung for supporting Liz Magic Laser with their program Catalogs for Young Artists and enabling her to realize her catalog and exhibition project. / Die Alfried Krupp von Bohlen und Halbach-Stiftung hat Liz Magic Laser im Rahmen ihres Förderprogramms Kataloge für junge Künstler ausgezeichnet und damit das Katalog- und Ausstellungsvorhaben ermöglicht.

 Alfried Krupp von Bohlen und Halbach-Stiftung

Additionally, the exhibition and catalog are kindly supported by the Kunststiftung NRW / Die Ausstellung und der Katalog wurden darüber hinaus von der Kunststiftung NRW unterstützt.

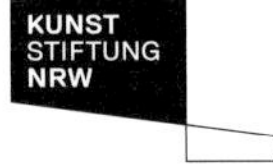

Colophon / Impressum

Publication / Publikation

Published by / Veröffentlicht von
Westfälischer Kunstverein, Sternberg Press
Editor / Herausgeber
Kristina Scepanski
With contributions by / Mit Beiträgen von
Jordan Troeller, Tom Williams, Kristina Scepanski
Concept, Design / Konzept, Gestaltung
Benedikt Reichenbach
Editing / Redaktion
Jenni Henke, Liz Magic Laser, Benedikt Reichenbach, Kristina Scepanski
Translations / Übersetzungen
Tim Connell, Michael Müller, Jenni Henke
Copy Editing / Lektorat
Kristin M. Jones, Michael Müller, Jenni Henke
Lithography / Lithografie
Max Color
Print / Druck
Ruksaldruck, Berlin

Team Westfälischer Kunstverein Münster

Director / Direktorin
Kristina Scepanski
Curatorial Assistant / Kuratorische Assistenz
Jenni Henke, Anna Sabrina Schmid (bis / until Sept 2013)
Assistant to the director and board / Assistent Direktion und Vorstand
Tono Dreßen
Interns / Mitarbeit
Tim Höltje, Anne Neier

ISBN 978-3-95679-069-0

Westfälischer Kunstverein

Westfälischer Kunstverein
Rothenburg 30
48143 Münster
www.westfaelischer-kunstverein.de

Sternberg Press

Sternberg Press
Caroline Schneider
Karl-Marx-Allee 78
10243 Berlin
www.sternberg-press.com